Managing foreign exchange risk

Managing foreign exchange risk

Essays commissioned in honor of the centenary of the Wharton School, University of Pennsylvania

Edited by RICHARD J. HERRING

The Wharton School, University of Pennsylvania

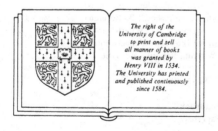

The right of the
University of Cambridge
to print and sell
all manner of books
was granted by
Henry VIII in 1534.
The University has printed
and published continuously
since 1584.

CAMBRIDGE UNIVERSITY PRESS

Cambridge
London   New York   New Rochelle
Melbourne   Sydney

CAMBRIDGE UNIVERSITY PRESS
Cambridge, New York, Melbourne, Madrid, Cape Town, Singapore,
São Paulo, Delhi, Dubai, Tokyo

Cambridge University Press
The Edinburgh Building, Cambridge CB2 8RU, UK

Published in the United States of America by Cambridge University Press, New York

www.cambridge.org
Information on this title: www.cambridge.org/9780521311205

First published 1983
Reprinted 1984
First paperback edition 1986

A catalogue record for this publication is available from the British Library

Library of Congress Cataloguing in Publication data

Main entry under title:

Managing foreign exchange risk.

Based on essays and perspectives presented at a
conference entitled "Managing international risk," held
in Philadelphia, Oct. 26–27, 1981, sponsored jointly
by the Global Interdependence Center, the Group of
Thirty, and the Wharton School, University of
Pennsylvania.

Includes bibliographical references.

Contents: Macroeconomic determinants of real exchange
risk / William H. Branson – Perspectives: on exchange-
rate analysis and foreign exchange risk / Marina v. N.
Whitman – Modeling exchange rate fluctuations and
international disturbances / Lawrence R. Klein – [etc.]
1. Foreign exchange problem – Congresses.   2. Foreign
exchange administration – Congresses.   3. Wharton School.
I. Herring, Richard.   II. Global Interdependence Center.
III. Group of Thirty.   IV. Wharton School.   V. Title:
Foreign exchange risk.
HG205   1981a   658.1′55   82–21999

ISBN 978-0-521-25079-5 Hardback
ISBN 978-0-521-31120-5 Paperback

Transferred to digital printing 2009

Contents

Contents

Contributors

JOHN F. O. BILSON is Associate Professor of International Economics at the University of Chicago's Graduate School of Business, and Research Associate at the National Bureau of Economic Research. He has served as a National Fellow at the Hoover Institution, economist in the research department of the International Monetary Fund, and assistant professor at Northwestern University. He has written widely on exchange rate determination and forecasting.

WILLIAM H. BRANSON is Professor of Economics and International Affairs at Princeton University. He is Director of the Research Program in International Studies and Research Associate at the National Bureau of Economic Research and is coeditor of the *Journal of International Economics*. He has been a visiting professor at the Institute for International Economic Studies, Stockholm University, and the Institute for Advanced Studies in Vienna. He served as Deputy Director of the OECD "Interfutures Project" in Paris and has been a consultant to several national and international agencies.

RICHARD J. HERRING is Associate Professor of Finance at the Wharton School of the University of Pennsylvania. He has been an International Affairs Fellow at the Council on Foreign Relations, an IBM Postdoctoral Fellow, and a consultant to several firms and government agencies. He has written on interest rate determination, capital flows, and public policy toward international banking.

YUJI IJIRI is Robert M. Trueblood Professor of Accounting and Economics at Carnegie–Mellon University's Graduate School of Industrial Administration. During 1982–3 he was president of the American Accounting Association. He has been a consultant to the American Institute of CPAs, Financial Accounting Standards Board, Ford Foundation, and Gulf Oil Corporation. He has written extensively on the theory of accounting measurement.

PETER B. KENEN is Walker Professor of Economics and International Finance at Princeton University. He has taught at Columbia Univer-

ix

sity, where he served as Chairman of the Department of Economics and Provost of the University, at the Hebrew University in Jerusalem, at the Stockholm School of Economics, and at the University of California at Berkeley. At Princeton he serves as Director of the International Finance Section. He has been a consultant to several U.S. government and international agencies.

LAWRENCE R. KLEIN, winner of the 1980 Nobel Prize in Economics, is Benjamin Franklin Professor of Economics and Finance at the Wharton School of the University of Pennsylvania. He is the founder of Wharton Econometric Forecasting Associates, Inc. Dr. Klein has received honorary degrees from Bonn University, University of Michigan, University of Vienna, Free University of Brussels, University of Paris–X, and the Autonomous University of Madrid.

HENK A. KLEIN HANEVELD is a Vice-President in the London office of Morgan Guaranty Trust, where he manages multicurrency fixed-income portfolios and is responsible for developing global diversification strategies for portfolios of short-term assets, bonds, and equities that are managed for clients of the bank. Mr. Klein Haneveld was awarded cum laude master's degrees in economics (University of Groningen) and industrial administration (Carnegie–Mellon University). He is a chartered financial analyst.

HAIM LEVY is Professor of Finance at the Jerusalem School of Business Administration of the Hebrew University. He has served as the Dean of the School of Business and has been a visiting professor at the Universities of Pennsylvania, Florida, Illinois, and California at Berkeley. He is the editor of *Research and Finance* and associate editor of the *Journal of Finance*. He has written more than 100 articles and books on investment analysis and statistics.

EUGENE H. ROTBERG is Vice-President and Treasurer of the World Bank. He is responsible for the borrowing of resources from governments and from capital markets throughout the world to finance the World Bank's lending program. His responsibility also includes the management and investment of the World Bank's holdings in various currencies throughout the world. He has served as Chief Counsel of the Office of Policy Research at the U.S. Securities and Exchange Commission and was a recipient of the U.S. government's Distinguished Service Award.

MARSHALL SARNAT is Professor of Finance at the Jerusalem School of Business Administration of the Hebrew University. He is currently President-Elect of the European Finance Association and coeditor of the *Journal of Banking and Finance*. He has served as visiting professor at New York University, the University of Toronto, UCLA, and the University of California at Berkeley. He has written extensively on financial economics, investment analysis, and capital markets.

HARRY TAYLOR is President of Manufacturers Hanover Corporation. He is Director of Manufacturers Hanover Export Finance, Ltd.; a director of Bank Mendes Gans, N.V.; Manufacturers Hanover Ltd., London; and Manufacturers Hanover Asia, Ltd., Hong Kong. He is also Vice-Chairman of Manufacturers Hanover Banque Nordique, Paris, and Manufacturers Hanover Property Services, Ltd., London, and is Chairman of the U.S.–Korea Economic Council.

MARINA v. N. WHITMAN is Vice-President and Chief Economist of the General Motors Corporation. She has served as a member of the Price Commission and the Council of Economic Advisers and was for many years Distinguished Public Service Professor of Economics at the University of Pittsburgh. She has written widely on policy issues and international finance, including a 1979 book entitled *Reflections of Interdependence: Issues for Economic Theory and U.S. Policy.*

Acknowledgments

Earlier versions of these essays and perspectives were presented at a conference entitled "Managing International Risk," held in Philadelphia on October 26 and 27, 1981. The conference focused on three of the risks that distinguish international from purely domestic transactions: (1) foreign exchange risk – the risk that an unanticipated change in the exchange rate will affect the profitability of a transaction or a stream of transactions; (2) country risk – the risk that a sovereign power will interfere with the repatriation of profits, interest payments, principal payments, or the control of foreign assets; and (3) the risk of a breakdown in the rules and practices that govern international trade and investment flows. The essays and perspectives that deal with the latter two risks are collected in a companion volume (see R. J. Herring, editor, *Managing International Risk*, Cambridge University Press, 1983). The conference was sponsored jointly by the Global Interdependence Center, the Group of Thirty, and the Wharton School, University of Pennsylvania. This joint venture arose from complementary interests and coincidental plans.

In forming the Wharton Center for International Management Studies during 1980, the Wharton School began by taking an inventory of international research in progress at the School. The survey disclosed that in almost every academic department researchers were attempting to deal with some aspect of international risk and uncertainty. But despite the common concern with international risk, there was regrettably little interchange or cross-fertilization among disciplines. The celebration of the centenary of the Wharton School presented an opportunity to help remedy this deficiency with an international conference that would bring an interdisciplinary perspective to the problem of managing international risk. Meanwhile, in developing plans for their third international conference, the Global Interdependence Center and the Group of Thirty found that their constituents were also concerned about how to assess and manage international risk. In order to avoid duplication of effort and to take advantage of a wider range of resources, the leaders of the three organizations – Donald C. Carroll, Dean of the Wharton School; Frederick Heldring, President of the Global Interdependence Center; and Johannes Witteveen, Chairman of the Group of Thirty – decided to join forces in sponsoring the conference.

As editor, my greatest debt is to the authors, who managed to meet deadlines despite the pressure of busy schedules. I am also grateful for help from Jerry Wind, Karen Freedman, and Anne Hearn at the Wharton School, from Michael Granito at Morgan Guaranty Trust Company, and from Reine Dempsey, Anne Grace, and Brewster Grace at the Global Interdependence Center. JoLynn Horvath skillfully typed draft upon draft of material for the conference and this volume.

The Global Interdependence Center and the Wharton School gratefully acknowledge financial assistance for this undertaking from BankAmerica Foundation, Delaware Steel Company, Inc., Exxon Education Foundation, First National Bank in St. Louis, Hunt Manufacturing Company, International Business Machines Corporation, INA Foundation, Pfizer Inc., Rorer Group, Inc., SmithKline Corporation, and Xerox Corporation.

Introduction and overview

RICHARD J. HERRING

Of all the dramatic events during the turbulent decade of the seventies, perhaps none has had such important consequences for economic policy and the conduct of international business as the collapse of the Bretton Woods system of fixed exchange rates. The resulting greater flexibility of exchange rates has had a pervasive impact on the world economy. As Lawrence Klein relates anecdotally in his contribution to this volume, even Nobel laureates have been troubled by unanticipated changes in exchange rates.

Most of the major currencies were stable relative to the dollar during the sixties; systematic government intervention in the foreign exchange markets kept fluctuations within a narrow band that was plus or minus 1 percent of the par value of each currency expressed in dollars.[1] In contrast, during the seventies there were substantial movements in the dollar value of all major currencies within a range bounded by the Swiss franc, which appreciated by nearly 200 percent with respect to the dollar, and the Italian lira, which depreciated by more than 40 percent relative to the dollar. Exchange rate movements were not only large; they were also erratic. Figure 0.1 provides a compact summary of exchange rate developments over the decade.

The exchange rate developments depicted in Figure 0.1 had an important impact on all economic sectors and posed new challenges for policy makers, managers, accountants, and economists. Government policy makers found it necessary to consider the consequences of domestic policy actions on the exchange rate (rather than reserve flows) and the impact of the exchange rate on domestic policy goals such as the attainment of price stability and full employment. (In addition, some governments became acutely aware of the impact of exchange rate changes on the value of international reserves.) Corporate decision makers found that, in the absence of an active hedging strategy, capital gains and losses from exchange rate fluctuations could overwhelm operating results during any given quarter. In addition, experience showed that movements in the real exchange

---

[1] Until 1969, only the German mark, the Dutch guilder, and the British pound required par value adjustments.

1

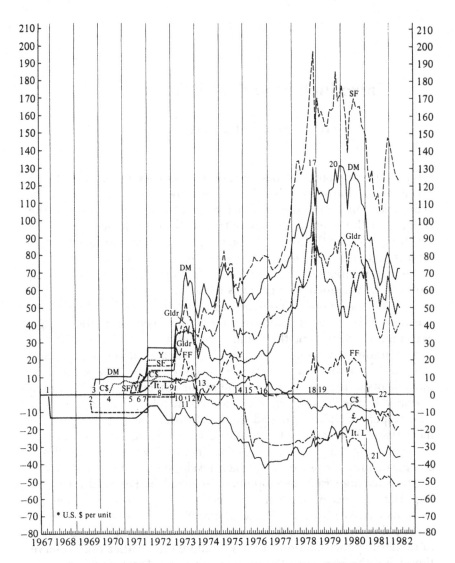

Figure 0.1. Exhange rates of major currencies against the dollar (percentage deviations with respect to dollar parities of October 1967 end-of-month figures). **1.** £ devalued (Nov. 18, 1967). **2.** French franc devalued (Aug. 10, 1969). **3.** DM floated (Sept. 30, 1969) and revalued (Oct. 26, 1969). **4.** Canadian dollar floated (June 1, 1970). **5.** DM and Dutch guilder floated. Swiss franc devalued (May 9, 1971). **6.** Dollar–gold convertibility suspended (Aug. 15, 1971). Major currencies de facto floated. **7.** Smithsonian realignment: dollar formally devalued (Dec. 18, 1971). **8.** £ floated (June 23, 1972). **9.** Swiss franc floated (Jan. 23, 1973). Dollar devalued. Yen and Italian lira floated (Feb. 13, 1973). **10.** Markets closed (March 2, 1973). DM revalued. Joint float (March 19, 1973). **11.** DM revalued (June 29, 1973). **12.** Dutch guilder revalued (Sept. 17, 1973). **13.** French franc left the joint float (Jan. 19, 1974). **14.** French franc returned to the joint float (July 10, 1975). **15.**

rate – the nominal exchange rate adjusted for relative price movements at home and abroad – could sharply alter the competitiveness of alternative production locations. The magnitude and frequency of exchange rate adjustments caused accountants to reassess their standards for treating exchange rates in the consolidation of financial statements of foreign subsidiaries with those of the parent corporation. And economists were faced with the challenge of explaining (and demands for predicting) the behavior of exchange rates.

Unfortunately, the prevailing theories about exchange rate determination from the sixties proved inadequate to explain exchange rate developments during the seventies, much less to predict such developments. The popular view of exchange rate determination, prominently featured in most textbooks from the era, focused on trade flows. The foreign exchange value of the dollar, for example, was viewed as equilibrating the demand for imports by residents of the United States with the demand for U.S. exports by foreign residents. The question of exchange rate stability turned on the issue of the price responsiveness of supplies and demands for internationally traded goods: The more sensitive quantity adjustments were to changes in prices, the smaller the exchange rate adjustments that would be required to equilibrate the exchange market in the face of any given disturbance.

The difficulty with this explanation is that, on close inspection, it has very little to say about what influences the exchange rate in the short run. Although empirical studies tended to confirm that over the long run trade flows are sufficiently price responsive to establish at least some minimum degree of stability in the foreign exchange rate, they also indicated that the quantity adjustments took a very long time, perhaps as long as three to five years. Moreover, the evidence showed that in the short run trade flows are likely to respond perversely to a change in the exchange rate; instead of immediately reducing a trade deficit, a depreciation of the exchange rate is likely to exacerbate the deficit at least until enough time has elapsed for sufficient quantity adjustments to occur.

In addition to this theory emphasizing the price responsiveness of trade flows was perhaps the oldest, and certainly the most durable,

Figure 0.1. *(Cont.)*

French franc left the joint float (March 15, 1976). **16.** DM revalued (mid-Oct. 1976). **17.** DM revalued (mid-Oct. 1978). **18.** Dollar support package (Nov. 1, 1978). **19.** EMS introduced (mid-March 1979). **20.** First EMS realignment: DM revalued (late Sept. 1979). **21.** EMS realignment: lira devalued (March 1981). **22.** EMS realignment: DM and Dutch guilder revalued. French franc and lira devalued (Oct. 1981).

explanation of exchange rate developments – the doctrine of purchasing power parity. In fact, the relationship makes an appearance in almost all of the contributions in this volume. Although none of the authors would argue that purchasing power parity is a complete explanation of exchange rate movements, it remains a convenient point of reference.

The term "purchasing power parity" dates from Gustav Cassel's work in 1918, but the idea can be traced to Ricardo and Thornton,[2] more than a century earlier. The basic idea has been very little altered or clarified since that time. The precise mechanism by which the exchange rate equalizes purchasing power parity in different countries and, indeed, the measures of purchasing power that are equalized are still a matter of controversy.[3]

Perhaps the simplest explanation of the purchasing power parity relationship relies on the intuitively appealing "law of one price" to argue that the exchange rate equates the price of internationally traded goods in all countries. For example, consider the German mark price of the dollar (DM/$). Arbitrage in traded goods would insure that the German mark price of the dollar would equal the ratio of the mark price of the traded good (P_G^T) to the dollar price of the traded good (P_{US}^T): DM/$ $= P_G^T/P_{US}^T$. If the purchasing powers of the mark and the dollar are not equated in this sense, then (neglecting transactions costs) an enterprising trader could buy goods in the country where they are relatively cheap and make a profit selling the goods in the country where they are relatively expensive. The resulting purchases and sales of foreign currency will cause the exchange rate to adjust until it equalizes the prices of internationally traded goods expressed in either currency.[4]

---

[2] Indeed, Einzig claims that the notion can be found in the writings of Spanish authors in the sixteenth century. See Paul Einzig, *The History of Foreign Exchange*, 2nd ed. (London: Macmillan, 1970, p. 264).

[3] For recent assessments of the doctrine of purchasing power parity, see Jacob Frenkel, "The Collapse of Purchasing Power Parities During the 1970's," *European Economic Review* 16 (May 1981): 145–65; or Louka Katseli-Papaefstratiou, "The Re-emergence of the Purchasing Power Parity Doctrine in the 1970's," *Special Papers in International Economics No. 13*, Princeton University (1979).

[4] Although traditionally price changes are viewed as causing exchange rate changes, it is clear that causation also runs in the opposite direction. During the seventies, many governments with depreciating currencies learned the painful lesson that exchange rate changes also cause price changes.

This arbitrage condition can be related to the general price level in each country by noting that the prices of internationally traded goods may be stated as some proportion (k_i) of the price level (P_i) : $P_G^T = k_G x P_G$, $P_{US}^T = k_{US} x P_{US}$, and so DM/\$ = $(P_G/P_{US}) \times (k_G/k_{US})$. Neglecting second-order terms,[5] this relationship can be restated in the more familiar percentage change form:

$$\%\Delta(DM/\$) = (\%\Delta P_G - \%\Delta P_{US}) + (\%\Delta k_G - \%\Delta k_{US})$$

So long as there is effective arbitrage in internationally traded goods and so long as the internal price structures in each country remain unchanged – that is, the k_i terms remain constant – percentage changes in the German mark price of the dollar will equal the differences in the rate of inflation between Germany and the United States. Although the relationship holds up well in the short run for highly inflationary economies and for most economies over longer spans of time when the cumulative impact of inflation tends to dominate other factors, short-run movements in the major currencies exhibit marked departures from the purchasing power parity relationship.

There are several reasons why the relationship between inflation differentials and exchange rate changes should not be expected to hold continuously. Real disturbances that change internal price structures (causing the k_i to change), such as shifts in demand, productivity gains in the manufacturing sector, or the discovery of exploitable natural resources, may dominate the impact of generalized inflation. Tariffs, transport costs, restrictions on cross shipping, product differentiation, and inertia in buying habits may give rise to violations of the law of one price.[6] And financial flows may completely overwhelm trade-related supplies and demands for foreign exchange in any given time period.

But if purchasing power parity does not anchor the exchange rate movements to the path determined by relative price movements at

---

[5] Although customary, it is clearly unwise to neglect the second-order terms, i.e., $\%\Delta k_G \%\Delta P_G - \%\Delta k_{US} \%\Delta P_{US} - \%\Delta(DM/\$)(\%\Delta k_{US} + \%\Delta P_{US} + \%\Delta k_{US} \%\Delta P_{US})$, when dealing with large changes in the variables.

[6] See Peter Isard, "How Far Can We Push the 'Law of One Price,'" *American Economic Review* (December 1977): 942–8, for evidence that we cannot realistically push the "law" very far at all. See also Irving Kravis and Robert Lipsey, "Price Behavior in Light of Balance of Payments Theories," *Journal of International Economics* (May 1978): 281–99, and J. David Richardson, "Some Empirical Evidence on Commodity Arbitrage and the Law of One Price," *Journal of International Economics* (May 1978): 341–51.

home and abroad, then exchange rate movements introduce a new dimension of risk in international transactions. Decision makers must contend not only with movements in domestic and foreign prices, but also with movements in the exchange rate that may alter the relationship of domestic to foreign prices. This foreign exchange risk is the subject of this volume.

This book begins with a chapter by William Branson that synthesizes much of what has been learned about short-term exchange rate fluctuations during the seventies and presents new empirical evidence on the determinants of exchange rates. Lawrence Klein writes about the problem of analyzing exchange rate fluctuations and other international disturbances in a large econometric model. Haim Levy and Marshall Sarnat investigate the gains from diversifying asset portfolios internationally in an environment of fluctuating exchange rates. John Bilson develops a portfolio approach for managing foreign exchange positions and evaluating the worth of exchange rate forecasting services. Yuji Ijiri reviews the history of foreign exchange accounting and analyzes the new standards for dealing with exchange rate fluctuations adopted by the Financial Accounting Standards Board. These chapters are accompanied by perspectives written by a distinguished panel of experts, most of whom are practitioners rather than academic researchers. Their views provide a practical emphasis on the concerns addressed by the academic writers and identify some of the key challenges in managing international risk. What follows is a selective summary highlighting some of the issues raised by each of the contributors.

William H. Branson presents a framework for analyzing the factors that give rise to real exchange risk (or unanticipated movements in real exchange rates). Real exchange rates – nominal exchange rates adjusted for relative price movements at home and abroad – are the focus of analysis because they determine international competitiveness. In an earlier era, when divergences in national rates of inflation were relatively unimportant, the distinction between real and nominal exchange rates could be safely ignored, but during the last decade the distinction has become crucial.

If purchasing power parity were a complete explanation of exchange rate movements, then real exchange rates would remain constant (even though nominal exchange rates and foreign and domestic price levels might change), and there would be no real exchange risk. Recent experience, however, has indicated that exchange rates have exhibited abrupt and irregular movements like those usually associated with stock and bond prices, rather than moving smoothly along the path determined by relative national price levels. Branson presents formal evidence showing that the purchasing power parity relationship has not held in the medium term.

Over the last decade, theorizing about what determines exchange rates has undergone a transformation from which a new, consensus view has emerged. Some variant of this view underlies most contemporary academic research and the economic analysis of international organizations such as the Bank for International Settlements, the International Monetary Fund, and the Organization for Economic Cooperation and Development. In the consensus view, exchange rates are determined in the short run by conditions in the financial markets and in the long run by the factors that influence the balance of payments on current account.

Branson develops a model that integrates these factors – monetary conditions, relative prices, and the current account – to explain movements in nominal exchange rates; as a consequence, monetary conditions and the current account are cast in the role of proximate determinants of real exchange risk.

In the short run, Branson regards the exchange rate as determined by the requirements of asset-market equilibrium, that is, by the condition that the exchange rate (and other asset prices) adjust so that existing stocks of money, domestic assets, and foreign assets are willingly held. At this stage, the exchange rate may be characterized as an asset price. This short-run value of the nominal exchange rate may not, however, be consistent with long-term equilibrium. In combination with income, relative prices, and other factors, the short-run value of the exchange rate may give rise to a current-account imbalance. In order to finance the current-account imbalance (which reflects an imbalance between national spending and national output), supplies and demands for foreign assets will change, causing adjustments in the exchange rate. The current-account imbalance also will change national wealth and thereby, aggregate demand for goods and services, causing additional adjustments in the exchange rate. These exchange rate adjustments will alter the international competitiveness of goods and services at home and abroad until balance is restored to the current account. In the long term, the exchange rate may be characterized as the relative price of national outputs. In the absence of permanent changes in tastes, technology, or endowment of natural resources, the long-term equilibrium exchange rate will correspond to the purchasing power parity relationship.

In order to highlight the role of expectations in determining the time path of exchange rate adjustments, Branson works through his model using two different assumptions regarding the formulation of expectations. First, for simplicity of exposition, he employs the assumption that the exchange rate is expected to remain at the current level. Then he introduces the assumption of rational expectations (or, strictly speaking, perfect foresight), which holds that future changes in the equilibrium exchange rate are fully anticipated. This latter assumption leads to a telescoping of adjustments. Since market participants look ahead to the ultimate consequences of a disturbance, the exchange rate moves as soon as the disturbance is perceived. New information or innovations in monetary conditions, relative prices, or the current account will lead to immediate exchange rate adjustments. For example, an unanticipated increase in the current-account balance leads to an expectation of an appreciation in the nominal and real exchange rates in order to move the current account back to equilibrium by reducing net exports. The expectation itself will cause an immediate, discontinuous appreciation in both the nominal and real exchange rates.

Unanticipated changes in both monetary and real variables are likely to cause jumps in the real exchange rate. If such disturbances are repetitive and random, they will generate random movements in real exchange rates. Thus, even though purchasing power parity does not determine short-term exchange rate variations, it may nonetheless serve as a long-term center of gravity for the exchange rate. Branson emphasizes, however, that if sustained structural shifts occur, such as the economic resurgence of Europe and Japan following World War II, or the emergence of the newly industrialized countries in the seventies, permanent departures from purchasing power parity should be expected.

Branson concludes with some empirical evidence regarding the consensus view. It is extraordinarily difficult to implement the theory empirically because of the central importance of expectations. Anticipated values of explanatory variables may be of crucial importance in determining the level of the exchange rate. Observed values of these variables, on the other hand, may be misleading or irrelevant. In consequence, the traditional practice of regressing the exchange rate on observed values of relative prices, the current account, and monetary factors is clearly inadequate. A change in the money supply, for example, may have no impact on the exchange rate if it was fully anticipated in the previous period, but new information about future developments may affect the exchange rate. Only unanticipated movements in the explanatory variables will cause unanticipated movements in the exchange rate. Thus the challenge to the econometrician is to develop proxies for unanticipated movements in each of the variables.

Branson meets this challenge by attempting to extract all information about future movements of each variable from past movements of the variables. The differences between these predictions and the observed values are interpreted as the innovations or unanticipated movements. Correlations between innovations in the exchange rate and innovations in each of the explanatory variables are then examined to see whether they correspond to the theoretical predictions. Branson employs quarterly data for Germany, Japan, the United Kingdom, and the United States from 1973 through 1980 in his empirical analysis. His results for the current account are strongly supportive of the theory: Unanticipated current-account surpluses are associated with unanticipated appreciations in the exchange rate. His results regarding monetary factors are mixed. He argues that they require further investigation regarding the role of exchange rate movements in determining changes in monetary policy. Branson's results regarding relative price levels are consistent with the theory but are also consistent with the reverse channel of causation that unanticipated exchange rate changes cause unanticipated changes in relative prices. In a broad sense, however, the time series characteristics of the data seem to correspond to the implications of the consensus model. The foreign exchange markets appear to move closer to equilibrium in response to news about the key factors that determine equilibrium exchange rates.

Unfortunately, Branson's model is of little help in forecasting exchange rates. Indeed, a fundamental implication of the model is that most sharp fluctuations in the exchange rate are due to unanticipated movements in real and monetary factors. But it does provide a useful framework for understanding exchange rate movements and why real exchange rate risk must be regarded as an unpleasant fact of life.

Marina v. N. Whitman presents three different perspectives on exchange rate analysis. She considers Branson's consensus view from the vantage points of her former positions as academic researcher and government policy maker, as well as from her current position as corporate decision maker.

With regard to academic research, she notes that the consensus view incorporates a much wider range of explanatory variables than earlier theories of exchange rate determination. Branson's model takes into account not only monetary factors, such as relative rates of inflation or relative growth rates in money supplies, but also real variables, such as income and the current-account balance, and financial variables, such as expected returns and relative risks. (She notes that Branson, however, treats the latter only implicitly.) Whitman observes that the consensus view presents a much more comprehensive explanation of what determines the time path of exchange rate adjustments, taking into account not only portfolio balance considerations that determine financial equilibrium but also income flow relationships that determine macroeconomic equilibrium. Moreover, expectations regarding future developments are given a central role in spelling out the mechanisms through which exchange rate adjustments occur. Whitman expresses the view, however, that much more work still needs to be done in incorporating expectations. She is also dissatisfied with the "knife-edged" stability properties of the saddle-point solution to the long-term equilibrium value of the exchange rate in Branson's model (and other similar models).

Whitman observes that an upshot of the consensus view is that economists have changed their explanation of the sources of exchange rate instability. Formerly, many economists placed emphasis on low elasticities of demand for imports or an insufficiency of stabilizing speculation due to a learning process in the transition to more flexible exchange rates. In the new view, however, jumps in exchange rates must be regarded as an inherent feature of any period in which market participants are surprised by financial, economic, and political developments. Since exchange rates must be regarded as asset prices, it follows that they will be subject to sharp readjustments in response to news that seems to have implications for future asset values.

For policy makers, the consensus view has some discouraging implications. Although some earlier proponents of flexible exchange rates had argued that flexible exchange rates would insulate economies from foreign disturbances, the consensus view implies that both monetary and real disturbances abroad may continue to affect domestic output and prices. As a practical matter neither do flexible exchange rates permit policy makers to focus monetary and fiscal policy exclusively on domestic policy targets such as unemployment and inflation without regard for the external consequences of policy actions. Changes in monetary and fiscal policy will cause exchange rate adjustments that will have feedback effects on inflation and unemployment. Flexible exchange rates do not provide a refuge from the international interdependence that is a pervasive feature of economic life.

The consensus view indicates that concerns over the social costs of exchange rate volatility may be well-founded; it provides support for the pro-position that exchange rates tend to overshoot their equilibrium levels. The consensus view does not, however, offer support for exchange market intervention. It makes clear that purchasing power parity is not necessarily an accurate guide to the equilibrium exchange rate (or appropriate intervention target) without offering any substitute guide. Moreover, the lesson of the consensus view for how best to achieve exchange rate stability is very difficult to implement. Since unanticipated developments lead to abrupt readjustments in the exchange rate, policy makers can contribute to exchange rate stability directly by avoiding surprises and pursuing predictable policies. Moreover, since exchange rate adjustments depend on economic conditions both at home and abroad, there is a presumptive case for coordinating macroeconomic policies internationally to minimize unanticipated differences.

Whitman identifies three kinds of exchange risk that confront corporate decision makers. The first is short-term risk due to unanticipated changes in the nominal exchange rate that occur over a period before selling prices have had to adjust. These risks can be readily hedged in the forward exchange market when appropriate forward facilities are available. The second kind is translation risk associated with the impact of changes in nominal exchange rates on the valuation of balance sheets. (See Ijiri's contribution to this volume for a discussion of this problem.) These risks can be minimized by balancing assets and liabilities in each currency or through forward exchange transactions. The third kind of risk is real exchange risk or unanticipated changes in real exchange rates that cause changes in the competitiveness of production locations. Real exchange risk is especially perplexing because it cannot be hedged through offsetting financial transactions. Corporate decision makers therefore place considerable importance on attempting to forecast real exchange rates in planning the location of production facilities. But the consensus view, with its emphasis on expectations and the importance of unsystematic factors in determining exchange rate movements, has discouraging implications for the success of forecasting efforts. Nonetheless, Whitman asserts that the jury is still out on whether exchange rate markets are fully efficient or whether forecasts can beat the market.

Lawrence Klein suggests that an appropriate measure of exchange risk is the divergence between exchange rate predictions and subsequent realized values. (Since exchange rates are so much more volatile than prices, this is a good proxy for real exchange risk as well.) He believes that exchange risk can be reduced to some extent through improvements in our ability to predict exchange rate movements; but, as a veteran forecaster, he is keenly aware of the limited scope for such improvements, especially with respect to forecasting exchange rates. He asserts that exchange rate projections are inherently much more difficult than projections of other economic variables such as consumer prices, real activity, or trade flows that are less sensitive to expectations of future political and economic events. He argues that in dealing with risky events, the primary usefulness of econometric modeling is less for forecasting the incidence of such events than for understanding the economic consequences of such events once they occur and for analyzing policy responses.

In order to illustrate the challenge of dealing with risky events in the context of a large econometric model, Klein reviews attempts to cope with three of the most significant disturbances to the world economy during the seventies in Project LINK, an international research effort aimed at modeling the world economy by linking structural econometric models of major countries and various groups of countries. Klein describes the uses of the LINK system to understand the impact of grain shortages, oil supply interruptions, and the fluctuations of exchange rates that have occurred since the dismantling of the Bretton Woods adjustable peg system that governed exchange rates during most of the period since World War II. He presents simulation results indicating the impact on the world economy of a sustained increase in the price of oil, of a severe cutback in oil supplies, and of a harvest failure. These simulations demonstrate that even the indirect impacts of a disturbance can have important economywide repercussions.

Klein reports that attempts to explain exchange rate movements within Project LINK focus on the same variables that play a leading role in Branson's consensus view of exchange rate determination: relative inflation rates, relative interest rates, relative growth rates, and international payments imbalances. He interprets the evidence developed in Project LINK as supporting the view that exchange rate movements are determined largely by the purchasing power parity relationship in the medium to long term, with short-term departures from purchasing power parity determined by interest rate movements and balance-of-payments disturbances. Klein describes the three-pronged approach to modeling exchange rate fluctuations in Project LINK. The first approach relies on annual data that are pooled and normalized across countries to yield estimates of exchange rate adjustments that can be easily incorporated in the rest of the LINK system. Although this approach has proven itself useful and has the advantages of simplicity and efficiency in the use of the meager supply of annual observations in the post–Bretton Woods era, these benefits are purchased at the cost of assuming that all behavioral relationships are the same across all countries.

The second approach allows for behavioral variations across countries and yields estimates at shorter intervals by making individual estimates of exchange rate behavior for each country for which sufficient quarterly data are available. Exchange rate movements are explained directly as a function of relative price, interest rate, and current-account data that are generated in the rest of the LINK system. Although this is a departure from the structural approach to econometric modeling that characterizes most sectors in the LINK system, Klein contends that it may yield more accurate forecasts, particularly since the underlying demand and supply relationships are difficult to specify and estimate.

Klein emphasizes, however, that work must also proceed along a third approach of explaining the exchange market in structural terms, with attention to individual components of the supply and demand for foreign exchange. He places particular importance on financial flows and the importance of developing more elaborate financial sectors in each of the national models that will have better-articulated international financial linkages. He argues that only this kind of approach can yield a better understanding of what determines foreign exchange risk.

Klein identifies the main obstacles to further improvements in modeling exchange rate fluctuations as inadequate data and information about intervention in the foreign exchange markets by official monetary institutions, a component of the supply and demand for foreign exchange that may have had important consequences in some instances. In one sense the data problem is mitigated by the passage of time: As time passes the pool of observations on behavior in the post–Bretton Woods era increases and so does the scope for making strong statistical inferences about relationships between exchange rates and other variables. But unfortunately, the problem is not just the quantity of data, but also the quality and kind of data. More sophisticated modeling will require observations on some variables at much shorter intervals – monthly or even weekly in some cases – and a much more detailed description of the currency denomination of financial flows than is currently available. Without appropriate data collection systems in place, valuable evidence is lost with the passage of time.

Peter Kenen provides a perspective on the usefulness of simulations for coping with international risks. He observes that the essence of the technique is to use the information embodied in an econometric model to judge how the economy is likely to respond to very large and unpleasant shocks. The technique makes it possible to simulate an event that lies outside previous experience, one which with luck and careful planning may never occur.

Kenen argues, however, that because of the learning process that occurs after a shock, such simulations are likely to be much more valuable after we have experienced at least one instance of the disturbance. Economic agents learn from the experience and undertake measures to protect themselves that will alter the impact on the economy of subsequent shocks. Moreover, econometricians learn from such disturbances and often revise not only the parameters, but also the structures of their models in order to incorporate such phenomena more completely. Kenen emphasizes his point by asking how much any model could have told us in 1973 about the consequences of the fourfold increase in oil prices.

Kenen also expresses dissatisfaction with the usual assumption that behavioral responses to very large disturbances will be proportional to responses to relatively minor disturbances. To continue the previous illustration, in effect, he questions whether it is sensible to assume that the response to a 400 percent increase in oil prices is simply forty times the response to a 10 percent increase. This is inherently an awkward problem to resolve empirically because the very nature of the approach is to make use of information about economic behavior observed under ordinary circumstances in order to project what behavior may be under unusual circumstances.

Kenen observes that the sorts of simulations Klein presents – the impact on the world economy of an oil price increase, of an oil supply shortfall, and of a harvest failure – are much more useful for formulating public policy than for making private decisions. He notes that decision makers in the private sector must not only consider the impact of the shock on the world economy, but, equally important, must also evaluate the policy responses to the shock. Since Kenen is keenly aware of the difficulties in predicting the behavior of policy makers, he advocates performing simulations under a variety of assumptions regarding policy responses. Such simulations would provide policy makers with insights regarding the consequences of their actions (or inactions) and private decision makers with a range of outcomes to consider.

Kenen endorses the general approach to modeling exchange rates that Klein describes. But he urges that researchers shift their emphasis from short-term forecasting to testing alternative hypotheses regarding exchange rate determination in the medium to long term. He argues that it is no more sensible to attempt to forecast exchange rates in the short run than to try to forecast bond prices or stock prices from week to week or from month to month.

Haim Levy and Marshall Sarnat emphasize that currency fluctuations offer opportunities as well as risks. For example, they show that from July 1971 through December 1973, investors in the United States could have earned higher returns by holding even non–interest-bearing bank deposits denominated in Belgian francs, French francs, German marks, Italian lire, Japanese yen, Dutch guilders, or Swiss francs than by holding the diversified portfolio of domestic stocks represented by the Standard and Poors' Common Stock Index. Considering currencies as individual, mutually exclusive investment opportunities, however, is a departure from their principle theme, namely, the gains from international portfolio diversification across currencies.

Levy and Sarnat make a systematic examination of the scope for reducing risk through international portfolio diversification. They point out that the potential for profitable diversification depends on the degree of correlation of asset prices denominated in different currencies, or more fundamentally, on the extent of integration among national financial markets. If national financial markets are as perfectly integrated as, say, the regional stock exchanges in the United States, there may be negligible gains from international portfolio diversification. They also stress that the gains from diversification will depend on the home currency of the investor. The investor's home currency is the standard against which nominal exchange rate gains and losses are measured, and the array of assets denominated in that currency determine the scope for domestic portfolio diversification. Of course, if national financial markets are completely integrated in one world market and if exchange rate movements are completely determined by the purchasing power parity relationship, the real return on any portfolio will be the same for each investor regardless of home currency.

Levy and Sarnat present computations of the nominal and inflation-adjusted (real) returns on an array of non–interest-bearing bank deposits, short-term debt instruments, and equities denominated in different currencies. The returns on each asset and their correlations with the returns on other assets are used to form optimal portfolios for investors residing in several different countries. The returns and correlations of returns are used to identify portfolios that are efficient in the sense that, given the variability of the portfolio, no higher return can be achieved by altering the composition of the portfolio. From the set of efficient portfolios, the optimal portfolio is determined by use of the separation theorem developed by James Tobin, John Lintner, and William Sharpe. The separation theorem makes possible enormous economies in computation. It implies that, without knowing the investors' preferences between less risk and higher return, it is possible to identify the composition of the optimal portfolio of risky assets from among the set of efficient portfolios so long as the investor can borrow and lend at some riskless rate of interest. As a proxy for the nominally riskless rate of interest in each country, Levy and Sarnat use the rate on short-term government debt.[7] In order to emphasize the importance of greater exchange rate flexibility, Levy and Sarnat compare optimal portfolios based on data generated during the sixties, when the Bretton Woods exchange rate arrangements were in effect, with optimal portfolios based on data from the seventies, when exchange rates became much more flexible.

In order to emphasize the role of exchange rate fluctuations in international portfolio diversification, Levy and Sarnat first examine portfolios of non–interest-bearing bank deposits denominated in various foreign currencies. All returns in these portfolios are due to exchange rate fluctuations. Next they investigate the more realistic case of international investment in interest-bearing deposits denominated in various currencies. Finally, Levy and Sarnat examine portfolios of common stocks, and their focus shifts from nominal exchange risks to real exchange risks. Inflation-adjusted returns are emphasized since there is a presumption that investors hold common stocks (and thereby expose themselves to the risk of changes in nominal asset values) primarily out of a desire to maintain the purchasing power of their assets. Levy and Sarnat compute optimal

---

[7] Although it is plausible that investors can lend at such a rate, their ability to borrow at that rate is more doubtful. At the price of some additional complexity, higher borrowing rates could be specified in the analysis.

portfolios from the perspective of investors residing in the United States, Germany, Israel, Italy, Canada, France, Belgium, Japan, and the United Kingdom. They proceed by measuring the nominal rate of return on common stocks in each local currency, then adjusting the nominal return expressed in the local currency by the change in the exchange rate relative to the investor's home currency, and finally, by adjusting this nominal return expressed in the investor's home currency by the rate of inflation.[8] The result is an inflation-adjusted rate of return.

Their examination of correlations among inflation-adjusted rates of return across national markets indicates that correlations tended to be higher during the seventies than during the sixties. This is consistent with (though by no means proof of) a greater degree of integration among national equity markets during the seventies.

Levy and Sarnat present two measures of the gains from international diversification. First, holding risk constant at the level achieved with an optimally diversified domestic portfolio, they show the amounts by which investors could have increased returns through international diversification. They find that without increasing risk, investors in the United States could have increased quarterly real returns by nearly 25 percent during the period 1960–9 and nearly 21-fold during the period 1970–9. Second, holding the return constant at the level that would have been achieved in an optimally diversified domestic portfolio, they show how much risk could have been reduced (as measured by the reduction in the standard deviation in quarterly real returns) through optimal international diversification. Without sacrificing any return, U.S. investors could have reduced risk by nearly 30 percent during the period 1960–9, but by only about 14 percent during the period 1970–9. The higher correlations of real returns among national security markets during the latter period reduced the scope for risk reduction through international portfolio diversification.

Levy and Sarnat make a strong case for the gains from international portfolio diversification, but as they note, their empirical results are subject to several qualifications. First, their computations are based

---

[8] The use of the home currency price deflator, like the home currency assumption itself, assumes that the investor is exclusively concerned with maintaining purchasing power over domestic goods. If the investor has more cosmopolitan consumption preferences, then a more complicated price index and a more sophisticated notion of home currency are necessary.

on ex post data even though investment decisions must be made on the basis of ex ante expectations. This raises the question of how useful past correlations are in predicting future outcomes. The striking differences between their results for the sixties and the seventies suggest that there can be substantial changes in the variance–covariance structure over time. In addition, the empirical results do not take into account taxes, transactions costs, and capital controls that may have an important negative impact on realized investment returns.

Henk Klein Haneveld brings to the topic of international diversification the perspective of an active manager of internationally diversified portfolios of assets. He reinforces the emphasis of Levy and Sarnat on inflation-adjusted rates of return, noting that not only individual investors but also institutional investors have increasingly come to formulate their investment objectives in real rates of return. He also endorses their emphasis on the investor's home currency.

He observes that Levy and Sarnat have omitted an important category of assets from their analysis of possibilities for international diversification – bonds denominated in different currencies. Since the total value of bonds traded in various national and international markets is more than twice the value of common stocks, he argues that this omission is of practical relevance. Klein Haneveld reports, however, that his own studies of the prospects for profitable international diversification of bond portfolios are broadly consistent with the results that Levy and Sarnat present for equities and short-term money market investments. He urges that investors consider a still broader range of assets, but notes that data problems preclude the formal statistical analysis of real estate and other assets. Klein Haneveld emphasizes that the principle of diversification should be applied not just to particular categories of assets across national markets, but also to diversification across categories of assets in national markets.

Klein Haneveld observes that the chief practical difficulty in using the statistical technique employed by Levy and Sarnat as a guide to investment is that correlations among returns from different markets are unstable over time. He urges that much more research be focused on trying to understand the behavioral relationships that generate observed asset returns. He speculates that such factors as geographical proximity of national markets or similarities in national industrial or economic structures or likenesses in national financial policies such as exchange market intervention policies may offer insights into correlations in returns across national markets and why such correlations vary over time. He argues that it is not surprising that such correlations are unstable over time, since the performance of individual markets is influenced by both global and local factors – national and international – financial, economic, and policy developments that are often unanticipated. When local factors predominate, correlations will be low; when external factors are dominant, correlations are likely to be higher, but even then differences in economic structures or variations in policy responses may lead to very different impacts on asset prices.

Despite the instability of correlations in asset returns over time, Klein Haneveld asserts that computations based on the historical structure of correlations play a useful role in formulating investment strategies when modified by judgments regarding shifts in correlations among returns. He concludes that even when taxes, transactions costs, capital controls, and other frictions are taken into account, experience validates the central theme that Levy and Sarnat emphasize. Internationally diversified portfolios can offer investors stabler returns in comparison to domestic portfolios yielding the same return, and internationally diversified portfolios can offer investors higher returns than comparably risky domestic portfolios.

The proposition that foreign exchange markets are efficient, that is, that exchange rates fully reflect all available information so that investors cannot earn extraordinary profits by exploiting available information, has been an active area of research during the seventies. The proposition holds important implications for the efficiency of the allocation of resources under the flexible exchange rate system, the rationale for and effectiveness of official intervention in the foreign exchange markets, and the usefulness of attempts to forecast fluctuations in exchange rates. The proposition has proven to be very difficult to refute or confirm, however, because researchers have found it hard to develop a persuasive representation of speculators' expectations of the future spot rate and also because observed divergences between the forward rate and speculators' expectations of the future spot rate might simply be normal compensation for the risk of speculating in foreign exchange. Nonetheless, many economists would have agreed with John Bilson's assertion in 1977[9] that the evidence seemed to confirm not just market efficiency, but also

[9] See John F. O. Bilson, "Comment," in Rudiger Dornbusch and Jacob A. Frenkel, eds., *International economic policy, theory and evidence* (Baltimore: Johns Hopkins University Press, 1979, 267–9).

the much stronger proposition of forecasting efficiency – that forward exchange rates were equal to the best available forecast of the future spot rate. But if forward exchange rates really were the best available predictors of future spot rates, how was one to explain the proliferation of exchange rate forecasting services, a veritable growth industry during the seventies? Given the respect proponents of efficient markets hold for the investment decisions of profit-oriented speculators, the observation that many speculators pay substantial sums for presumably worthless forecasts is troublesome. As evaluation of the performance of the forecasting services proceeded, moreover, it became clear that some services had some systematic ability to predict exchange rate movements better than forward exchange rates.

Bilson moves beyond the question of whether it is possible to forecast exchange rate movements more effectively than the forward market to present a technique for computing how much a particular forecasting service is worth to a foreign exchange manager and how to combine any number of different forecasts into a composite forecast. He shows how to use the information in the composite forecast to construct efficient foreign exchange positions allocated across currencies and maturities.

Bilson agrees with the consensus view that exchange rate movements are dominated by unanticipated events and are therefore largely unpredictable; but he emphasizes that even though it may not be possible to predict the exchange rate levels accurately, it is possible to predict correlations in exchange rate movements among currencies and across forward maturities of any one currency. These correlations enable him to construct portfolios of foreign currency positions.

Bilson illustrates his approach with three different forecasts: one from a long-standing econometric forecasting service and two others, "Efficient Market Modeling" and "Random Walk Consulting," that are based on interpretations of market rates and are therefore virtually costless to acquire. Efficient Market Modeling interprets the forward rate as the forecast of the corresponding future spot[10] rate, and Random Walk Consulting identifies the current exchange rate at each maturity as the forecast for the exchange rate at that maturity in the future.[11] Bilson performs the traditional right side of the

---

[10] This is the optimal forecast if the efficient market hypothesis holds.

[11] This approach to forecasting is consistent with Branson's model if real and monetary shocks are random and repetitive.

market test to see whether the econometric forecasting service and the Random Walk Consulting service provide forecasts that are closer to the future spot rate than the forward rate (or Efficient Market Modeling service), but he emphasizes that such results are of no help in assessing the value of a particular forecasting approach or in forming a composite forecast. Moreover, the contest among alternative forecasts conveys no information that can guide the diversification of foreign exchange exposure across currencies or across forward rate maturities.

He contrasts this traditional emphasis on the comparative accuracy of forecasting approaches with a portfolio approach that combines each of the forecasts into a composite forecast. The estimated weights of the individual forecasts in the composite forecast provide a measure of the incremental value of each forecasting service. If more than one of the forecasts enters the composite with a nonzero weight, the forecast will be superior to any of the component forecasts. But most important, the composite forecasts provide information for constructing portfolios of foreign exchange positions. The composite forecasts yield two crucial inputs: (1) The difference between the composite forecast and the forward rate provides a measure of the expected profit for each position; and (2) the forecast errors show how well each composite forecast predicts each exchange rate and how errors in forecasting individual rates are correlated. Errors in forecasting different maturities of a particular currency tend to be highly correlated. An unanticipated movement in the dollar price of the pound, for example, is almost certain to be reflected in a similar movement in the price of the pound for delivery in three months. To a lesser extent, forecast errors for different currencies also tend to be correlated, reflecting common responses to external events, similarities in economic structure, or exchange market intervention arrangements such as the European Monetary System. From these two inputs, Bilson constructs an efficient portfolio that minimizes risk (as proxied by the variance of profits) for the expected level of profit. This computation determines the composition of the portfolio of exposures. Greater levels of expected profit (and risk) can be obtained by increasing exposures proportionately and lower levels, by scaling down exposures.

Bilson develops a summary statistic to represent the speculative opportunities confronting foreign exchange managers: the standardized profit. The standardized profit from a portfolio of foreign exchange exposures is the expected profit divided by the standard deviation of profits for that portfolio.

Bilson's evidence suggests that even when transactions costs are taken into account, market opportunities may offer a standardized profit as high as 1. This suggests that if an investment manager adopts a scale of foreign exchange exposures that would yield an expected profit of $1 million, there is a 95 percent chance that the actual outcome will fall between a loss of $1 million and a profit of $3 million. Although the prospect for profit is not certain for any one set of positions, if the forecast errors cancel over time the investment manager can expect to earn an average profit of $1 million during each period.[12]

Given the standardized profits available in the market opportunities, the actual size of the foreign exchange exposures adopted will depend on the manager's attitude toward risk and the corporation's ability to sustain losses in the short run in pursuit of a strategy that is expected to be profitable over the long run. The actual portfolio of exposures may also depend on corporate (or possibly regulatory) constraints on position taking, such as a requirement that every position must be between zero and 100 percent of the exposure that naturally arises from corporate activities.

Once the portfolio of exposures is determined, the value of any particular forecasting service can be compiled in a very straightforward manner. The speculative strategy can be simulated over past data with and without a particular forecast service in the composite forecast. If the difference in average profits exceeds the cost of the forecasting service, it would have been worthwhile to purchase the service. And if future performance is like the past the service should be retained. But that raises an important qualification to Bilson's empirical results. His results, like those of Levy and Sarnat, show the profits a portfolio strategy could have earned in the past. Unfortunately, there is no guarantee that similar portfolio performance can be attained in the future.

Bilson's evidence nonetheless suggests that relative to a passive approach to foreign exchange management, there may be some merit to an active approach in which the manager intentionally speculates or assumes open positions in foreign exchange. There are clear benefits to a passive strategy in which all anticipated net foreign

[12] These results are a refutation of the forecasting efficiency hypothesis; clearly it is possible to do better than the forward exchange rate in forecasting future exchange rate developments. But these results do not necessarily refute the efficient markets hypothesis. The profits that Bilson shows could have been made may be simply the normal compensation for the risks inherent in speculation in foreign exchange.

currency cash flows are exchanged for domestic currency cash flows in the forward market and all foreign exchange positions are thereby closed or hedged. The income statement is insulated from gains and losses from foreign exchange transactions. The informational and administrative costs of managing open foreign exchange positions are avoided. Moreover, if the forward rate is an unbiased forecast of the future spot exchange rate – that is, if it overestimates the future spot rate about as often and by about as much as it underestimates it – then even if the forward rate is not an especially accurate forecast of the future spot exchange rate, a passive strategy will not entail additional costs relative to a do-nothing strategy of converting all net foreign currency cash flows in the spot market as they occur.[13] Thus, the fundamental rationale for an active strategy must be the expectation of profits. Bilson shows that, if the future is like the past, an active strategy using the portfolio approach can yield substantial profits.

Even though accounting balance sheets capture only a fraction of the impact of an exchange rate change on corporate profitability, balance sheet exposures (or translation exposures) have often been the central focus of managerial concern. The treatment of balance sheet items denominated in foreign currencies is one of the most controversial topics in accounting, and the practical importance of the controversy has intensified with the increased volatility of exchange rates. The controversy reflects fundamental dilemmas as to which exchange rate to use in translating the assets and liabilities of a foreign subsidiary into the domestic currency and how (and whether) to recognize in reported income the capital gains and losses that may arise in the translation process. Yuji Ijiri reviews the history of foreign exchange accounting culminating in the new Statement 52 of the Financial Accounting Standards Board (FASB) and shows why the controversies are unlikely to be resolved to everyone's complete satisfaction.

FASB Statement 8, the standard that prevailed before FASB Statement 52, resolved the which-exchange-rate dilemma by requiring that all monetary items on the foreign balance sheet – cash or a claim to, or against, a fixed amount of cash – be translated at the current exchange rate (i.e., the rate prevailing on the reporting date)

---

[13] This statement is subject to the qualification that transactions costs are generally substantially higher for forward transactions than for spot transactions.

and that all nonmonetary items – inventories, plant and equipment, and other long-term investments – be translated at the historical exchange rate that prevailed when the items were acquired or at the current rate if they are valued on the balance sheet at current market prices. (This is known as the temporal approach.) The dilemma of what to do with the resulting translation gains and losses was resolved by recognizing all translation gains and losses in current income. Every transaction was treated as if it had been carried out by corporate headquarters. The consequence of this approach was that exchange rate volatility gave rise to volatility in translation gains and losses and thus to volatility in reported income, unless the corporation systematically hedged its exposure to translation gains and losses. After the adoption of Statement 8, several major international corporations reported translation gains and losses that were much larger than income from current operations. In order to avoid reporting such variations in income, many corporations responded to the standards by making use of the forward market much more extensively and by altering their financial strategies in an effort to insulate their income statements from translation gains and losses.

Some academic observers question why corporate managers attach such importance to stabilizing accounting measures of income. Ijiri rationalizes the emphasis on accounting measures of income, even when they may differ from true economic income, by noting that, in complex situations where there is considerable uncertainty, the accounting measure of income is often regarded as if it were true economic income. Moreover, he observes that in many instances, accounting income has important contractual and legal consequences because of profit-sharing plans, taxes, cost-plus contracts, and loan covenants.

Widespread dissatisfaction with the income volatility that resulted from the application of Statement 8 in an environment of fluctuating exchange rates led to the adoption of a new approach. FASB Statement 52 resolves the which-exchange-rate dilemma more simply by requiring that all assets and liabilities be translated at the current rate, thus preserving the relationship among various items in the foreign balance sheet. The dilemma of what to do with the resulting translation gains and losses is resolved in an entirely different way. The concept of a functional currency is introduced to determine which translation gains and losses are recognized in current income and which are relegated to an adjustment to shareholder's equity in the balance sheet. The functional currency for a foreign subsidiary is usually the local currency, but if the primary currency of that subsidiary's operations is some other currency or if there is substantial inflation in local currency prices, other choices are possible. The balance sheet of the foreign subsidiary is first stated in the functional currency using generally accepted U.S. accounting principles so that translation gains and losses between the functional currency and foreign currencies, as well as all transactions gains and losses, are taken into the income statement as under FASB 8. Then the balance sheet stated in the functional currency is translated into dollars. All translation gains and losses between the functional currency and the dollar are accumulated in a translation adjustment account to be netted against the shareholder's equity. This approach attempts not only to insulate reported income from translation gains and losses, but also to preserve the integrity of the balance sheet of the foreign enterprise. A consequence is that a transaction may affect net income if it is undertaken by the headquarters corporation, but not if it is undertaken by the subsidiary. For example, suppose a U.S. corporation prices a contract in pounds sterling and the pound depreciates relative to the dollar at the reporting date, but before the transaction is completed. The loss on the account receivable will be reflected in the income statement. If, instead, the British subsidiary of the U.S. corporation performs the same transaction and uses the pound as its functional currency, the exchange loss on the account receivable relative to the dollar will appear only as an adjustment to the shareholder's equity of the U.S. corporation.

Ijiri has misgivings about the functional currency approach. He questions the value of attempting to measure the performance of a foreign subsidiary relative to its own environment. Ijiri draws an analogy between monitoring the performance of subsidiaries located in different countries and monitoring the progress of sailors climbing the masts of different ships. He observes that although there may be some intrinsic interest in how high each sailor climbs on each mast, if the fundamental concern is with the survival of the sailor, attention should be focused on the progress each sailor has made relative to the water level. Similarly, if the ultimate objective of foreign investment is to earn some target rate of return in dollars, it may be much less important to preserve foreign balance sheet relationships than to obtain an accurate evaluation of the foreign balance sheet and income in dollars. Ijiri is also concerned that the discretion afforded corporations in selecting functional currencies may make it very difficult to compare the performance of corporations even when they have very similar foreign operations.

Ijiri develops an analytical framework – a network model of foreign exchange transactions – to illuminate some of the controversies in foreign exchange accounting. His model analyzes changes in the value of real and financial assets over time and across currencies. He demonstrates the implications of the international Fisher relationship, that is, the proposition that interest rates on assets denominated in different currencies differ by an amount precisely equal to the expected changes in exchange rates, and of purchasing power parity for the relationship among prices, interest rates, and exchange rates. He observes that a fundamental problem in developing a totally satisfactory approach to foreign exchange accounting is that actual exchange rate adjustments frequently depart from the international Fisher relationship and purchasing power parity.

Ijiri's network model reveals one potential difficulty in the translation approach taken in Statement 52. The use of the current exchange rate for translation of nonmonetary items valued at historical cost in the functional currency is inconsistent with the implication of purchasing power parity that exchange rates adjust to offset inflation differentials between countries. If, for example, the functional currency prices are rising while dollar prices are steady, the dollar will tend to appreciate relative to the functional currency. Indeed, if purchasing power parity holds precisely, the value of the dollar will appreciate by exactly the rate of inflation in the functional currency. Under these circumstances, translation at the current rate will show a decline in the dollar value of the foreign asset even though, if the asset is price adjusted at the general inflation rate in the functional currency, the dollar value actually remains constant. This example is also evidence in support of Ijiri's broader theme, namely, that the FASB Statement 52 solution to the problem of foreign exchange accounting is incomplete until it is accompanied by systematic inflation accounting at home and abroad. He regards the comprehensive incorporation of price-level adjustments as the most important challenge facing the accounting profession.

Eugene Rotberg describes the World Bank's approach to managing foreign exchange risk and liquidity. He advocates an active approach to financial management, emphasizing that managers should evaluate performance in terms of opportunity costs rather than by conventional accounting measures. In particular, he argues that concern over translation exposure should not deter financial managers from borrowing in foreign currencies if the full expected cost (including both interest and expected exchange rate changes) is lower. He also contends that concern over reporting realized losses in asset values should not deter financial managers from making portfolio shifts that yield higher expected returns or avert further losses. In his view, an important function of top management is to shield financial managers from pressure to consider the accounting consequences of their actions so that they can focus on the goal of achieving the highest returns consistent with corporate constraints on risk exposure.

Rotberg argues that dollar-based institutions should consider borrowing opportunities denominated in foreign currencies as well as those denominated in dollars. He notes that the staff at the World Bank is continually alert to market opportunities that seem to violate the international Fisher relationship. For example, he considers a recent choice between borrowing for fifteen years in Swiss francs at 8 percent or in U.S. dollars at 17 percent. The interest differential suggests that the borrower will break even if the dollar depreciates by 9 percent per year relative to the Swiss franc. Compounded over the fifteen-year term of the borrowing, that would imply a 364 percent depreciation of the dollar relative to the Swiss franc or a movement in the exchange rate from about 48 cents per Swiss franc to about $1.75 per Swiss franc. Such a change in the exchange rate is possible, but if financial managers think that the depreciation of the dollar is likely to be much smaller, they should borrow in Swiss francs. Rotberg notes that accounting conventions discourage this kind of comparison, however. Financial managers who borrow dollars at 17 percent for a U.S. corporation will never have to report an exchange loss, whereas if they borrow Swiss francs at 8 percent, they may be subjected to criticism for exposing the corporation to translation losses on the outstanding debt even though such losses may be much less than the savings from borrowing at the lower Swiss interest rate.

Of course, the success of an active strategy of financial management is dependent on the quality of the forecasting inputs. Rotberg advocates using information from a wide variety of sources that reflect many different approaches to forecasting, but he also places considerable emphasis on establishing the appropriate climate for making speculative decisions. He insists that predictions of interest rates and exchange rates must be accompanied by probabilities that the predictions are correct. Rotberg also stresses that the performance of financial managers should not be measured simply by their contribution to reported net income, but by a variety of standards. He insists that one such measure should be the opportunity cost of the financial strategy adopted, determined from the superior vantage point of hindsight. He argues that the opportunity cost of a strategy should be computed as the return that could have been earned if the financial manager had chosen what proved to be the highest yielding option each week. Against this exacting standard, even a strategy that yielded a very high return may be regarded as an error if the ideal strategy would have yielded an even higher return. In addition, he argues that performance should be compared to a variety of mechanical financial strategies such as buy and hold, randomly selected portfolios, and portfolios with perfectly balanced maturities.

Harry Taylor asserts that the basic function of accounting should be to communicate effectively. From this perspective, he charges that FASB Statement 8 was a complete failure. He emphasizes that, under the accounting approach in Statement 8, translation gains could mask a deterioration of basic profitability and managerial incompetence, whereas translation losses could obfuscate even superior operating results. Although he acknowledges that sophisticated analysts could disentangle translation gains and losses from more fundamental developments in the net income statement, he echoes Ijiri's assertion that the accounting definition of net income is important nonetheless. Taylor argues that the importance of accounting definitions of income derives from the fact that public perceptions of corporate perform-ance are based primarily on reports of net income in the news media, which seldom trouble to disentangle transitory phenomena such as translation gains or losses from basic operating results. Because the accounting approach in Statement 52 will reduce the volatility of reported income by taking most of the translation gains and losses out of the net income statement and putting them into an adjustment item in the capital account in the balance sheet, he welcomes the change. Yet at the same time, Taylor expresses concern that the new approach may insulate corporate managers too thoroughly from the consequences of bad investment decisions in high-inflation countries. Net income statements will not reveal whether local currency oper-ating results are sufficiently high to compensate for depreciation in the functional currency against the dollar.

Turning from the problem of accounting for exchange rate variability to managing exchange rate variability, Taylor endorses, with minor qualifications, Bilson's argument for an active approach to foreign exchange management, but he argues that a broader range of strategies should be considered. He emphasizes that there are many alternatives to using the forward market for hedging or for assuming speculative positions.

One obvious approach is to combine net foreign currency flows from all subsidiaries, but Taylor observes that many international corporations have not centralized their treasury operations. He argues that centralization of the foreign exchange management function can yield significant gains since net foreign currency receipts in one subsidiary can often be used to hedge net foreign currency payments in another subsidiary or, if desired, to build a speculative position in a foreign currency without incurring the transactions costs involved in forward market operations. There are, however, significant internal transactions costs in developing a sophisticated computer system that will permit centralized control of cash flows. He argues that, as technological advances reduce costs, the centralized approach to foreign exchange management is likely to be more common.

Taylor notes that corporate financing strategies can be easily adapted to implement foreign exchange management objectives as well. Echoing Rotberg's emphasis on departures from the international Fisher relationship, he points out that the corporation can borrow in currencies in which the interest rate differential relative to that in the home currency seems inadequate to compensate for the expected depreciation against the home currency, or it can invest when the interest differential seems to more than compensate for any likely depreciation of the foreign currency against the home currency. He also emphasizes that leads and lags in payments often provide a flexible means of developing short-term positions in foreign currencies either to hedge exposures arising from other activities or to build a speculative position. Long-term positions, he notes, can often be hedged through back-to-back loans or currency swaps with some other market participant who wants to hedge an opposite position or who wants to build a long-term speculative position. Finally, Taylor predicts that as interest rate futures markets develop, they will increasingly become important vehicles for executing foreign exchange management strategies.

Taylor concludes on a cautious note. Although he favors an active approach to managing foreign exchange risk, he is acutely aware that many exchange rate adjustments are unanticipated and, at our present state of knowledge, unpredictable. Thus, he warns that the case for an active approach to managing foreign exchange risk is not yet proven.

These essays reflect many of the advances in economics, finance, and accounting over the last decade that have enhanced our understanding of exchange risk and our ability to deal with it effectively. Yet despite this progress, it is clear that much remains to be done. And so, perhaps it is useful to conclude this overview by reiterating some of the important issues for further research that have been emphasized by the contributors to this volume.

With regard to our understanding of the factors that generate foreign exchange risk, there are important questions about the stability of a system of flexible exchange rates. Although the consensus view presents a compelling case for the central role of expectations in determining the timing of exchange rate adjustments, the assumption of rational expectations is not a totally persuasive characterization of short-run behavior. It would be useful to have a firmer understanding of how expectations are actually formulated and whether there is some scope for government policies to influence expectations. Modeling government policy responses is a crucial challenge for empirical work since the effects of a policy depend critically on whether the policy change is temporary or permanent, anticipated or unanticipated. These distinctions are especially important in testing the implications of the consensus view for the impact of monetary factors on the exchange rate. They are also important in designing simulations of the response of the world economy to various international disturbances.

With regard to accounting for exchange rate variations, the new standards in FASB 52 stop short of a fully consistent solution to the problem. Translation at current exchange rates is potentially misleading until price adjustments are systematically incorporated in financial statements. And the functional currency, multi-environment approach is undercut when all translations are made into the home currency. The logic of the multi-environment approach seems to require the adoption of a composite reporting currency that reflects the multiple currency environments in which the corporation functions.

With regard to the management of foreign exchange risk, the portfolio approach seems to show promise of generating profits that can justify an active approach to foreign exchange management. But the usefulness of the approach depends critically on the stability of correlations of exchange rates and asset returns over time. Much more work needs to be done on the behavioral relationships and structural factors that underlie these correlations. A better understanding of these underlying factors may enable us to predict how the correlations will shift over time. There are also important questions about how to evaluate and motivate financial managers:

Which kinds of incentives and standards are useful, and which are counterproductive? And finally, the long-standing question of the efficiency of the foreign exchange market remains unresolved: Are the returns to an active strategy of foreign exchange management adequate compensation for the risks?

CHAPTER 1

Macroeconomic determinants of real exchange risk

WILLIAM H. BRANSON

1. Introduction and summary

In 1973, the international monetary system began a period of continuous movement of exchange rates among major currencies. Rather than moving smoothly following the paths of relative national price levels, exchange rates have exhibited the volatile movements that are generally associated with asset market prices. This has been amply documented by Jacob Frenkel (1981a, b). Sharp movements of the exchange rate relative to relative price levels are fluctuations in "real exchange rates." This term is defined here to mean the nominal exchange rate adjusted for relative price movements. Exchange rate risk results from movements in real exchange rates. If the nominal rate followed perfectly the path of relative national price levels, no exchange risk would exist. There would, of course, remain risk associated with movements in relative prices at the microlevel, but not from exchange rate movements per se. Since real exchange risk is the result of fluctuations in real exchange rates, this chapter will focus on the macroeconomic determinants of these fluctuations.

During the period since 1973, theory about the determinants of exchange rate movements has undergone a transformation. We began with alternative models in which rates moved to clear the current-account balance (the "elasticities" approach) or responded to movements in relative money stocks (the "monetary" approach). These have been integrated into a more general framework in which exchange rates are determined in the short run by conditions of asset-market equilibrium, in the same way as asset prices or interest rates, and in the long run by real conditions affecting the current account. This integrated theoretical view is expressed, for example, in Dornbusch (1980). In this view, monetary disturbances generally do not change the equilibrium real exchange rate, but real disturbances to the current account do. This theoretical view has been accepted widely enough that the Organization for Economic Cooperation and Development's (OECD) *Economic Outlook* (29 [July 1981]: 59) reports it as the conventional wisdom:

The main economic variables generally thought to explain exchange rates are monetary conditions (and especially interest rate differentials), current account developments, and relative price performance. But over recent months the influence of inflation differentials has been uncharacteristically small, or operated with considerable delay, the dominant role being played by monetary conditions and current account developments.

It is this movement in exchange rates relative to "inflation differentials" that causes real exchange risk.

Since the variables cited in the quote are generally thought to determine movements in exchange rate, one would expect new information about these variables to move exchange rates in the short run through its impact on expectations. Some initial evidence that "news" or "innovations" in the relevant variables move exchange rates is reported in Dornbusch (1980) and Frenkel (1981b). More evidence is presented in section 8.

This chapter presents a model that integrates money, relative prices, and the current-account balance as factors explaining movements in nominal (effective) exchange rates. Thus, money and the current account are the proximate determinants of changes in real (effective) rates and of exchange rate risk. In sections 2 through 4, we present the basic model with static expectations. It is an extension of Branson (1977) to include explicitly exogenous disturbances to the current account.[1] The result is gradual adjustment of the real exchange rate following a current-account disturbance. In section 5 we introduce (rational) expectations and see that the nominal (and real) rate should be expected to jump instantaneously in response to new information or innovations in money, the current account, and relative prices.

In sections 6 through 8 we study the quarterly data on effective exchange rates, relative prices, money, and the current account for four countries – the United States, the United Kingdom, Germany, and Japan – since 1973. Section 6 describes the time-series properties of the data. All are approximately first-order autocorrelations *except* all relative prices and Japan's effective exchange rate and current-account balance. These are second-order autocorrelations. We see in section 7 that purchasing power parity does not hold in the short

---

[1] Readers familiar with that model can easily skip sections 2 and 3 and begin with section 4.3.

run. This confirms evidence presented, for example, by Frenkel (1981a).

Finally, in section 8 we see the results of estimation of vector autoregressions (VARs) among the four variables for each country. The residuals from these equations are the innovations in the data, that is, the current movements not predicted by the past. The correlations among these innovations provide a test of the theory; we would expect a systematic relationship between innovations in money, current-account balance, relative prices, and the effective exchange rate. These correlations are shown in Tables 1.9 and 1.10; they are generally consistent with the theory.

Thus, the broad conclusion to be made from this chapter is that the theoretical consensus expressed by the OECD, which integrates money, the balance on current account, and relative prices, is consistent with movements in these variables since 1973. Real exchange rates adjust to real disturbances in the current account, and time-series innovations in the current account seem to signal the need for adjustment. Unanticipated movement in the real exchange rate is the source of exchange risk mentioned in the title of this chapter.

2.   The short-run asset-market model with static expectations

2.1.   Introduction

In sections 2 and 3, a representative model of exchange rate determination is developed that explicitly includes the three elements mentioned in the introduction. We begin by specifying the underlying economic structure with static expectations. In section 5, rational expectations concerning movements in the exchange rate are introduced.

The model is an extension of the asset-market model sketched in Branson (1975) and developed in full in Branson (1977, 1979a). There the focus was on the roles of relative prices and asset markets, mainly in the short run. Here the model is extended to study the effects of underlying "real" disturbances influencing the current-account balance, with price dynamics specified explicitly.

2.2.   Asset-market equilibrium in the short run

To make the analysis manageable, let us consider one country in a many-country world. We can aggregate the assets available in this country into a domestic money stock M, which is a nonearning asset, net holdings of domestically issued assets B, which are denominated in home currency, and net holdings of foreign-issued assets F, which are denominated in foreign exchange.[2] B (i.e., bonds) is essentially government debt held by the domestic private sector. F (foreign assets) is the net claims on foreigners held by the domestic private sector. The current account in the balance of payments gives the rate of accumulation of F over time. The rate of accumulation of B is new government debt issue sold to the private sector, and the rate of accumulation of M is given by home central bank (Federal Reserve) purchases of government debt.

The rate of return on F is given by $\bar{r}$, fixed in the world capital market, plus the expected rate of increase in the exchange rate, $\hat{e}$. The rate of return on B is the domestic interest rate r, to be determined in domestic financial markets. Total private-sector wealth, at any point in time, is given by $W = M + B + eF$, so here the exchange rate e, in home currency per unit of foreign exchange (e.g., \$0.50 per DM), translates the foreign exchange value of F into home currency.

The total supplies of the three assets, M, B, and F, to domestic holders are given at each point in time. Each can be accumulated only over time through foreign or domestic investment.[3] These interact with demands for the three assets in determining equilibrium values for the home interest rate r and exchange rate e. The demand for each asset depends on wealth, $W = M + B + eF$, and both rates of return, r and $\bar{r} + \hat{e}$. As wealth rises, demands for all three assets increase. The demands for B and F depend positively on their own rates of return and negatively on those of the other assets. The

[2] Since the analysis here applies to any single country in the international financial system, I use the terms "home" and "foreign" to denote the country being discussed and the rest of the system, respectively.

[3] Since F is home claims on foreigners less home liabilities to foreigners, an asset swap that exchanges a claim and a liability with a foreign asset holder is a transaction within F, changing claims and liabilities by the same amount. This transaction would leave F and B unchanged. The reason for using this particular aggregation will become clear when we later study dynamic adjustment. Basically, we want to define net foreign assets consistently with the balance of payments and national income and product accounts, which record the capital account balance as the change in U. S. private holdings of net foreign assets. The assumptions outlined make M and B nontraded assets. This implies that the total stocks of M, B, and F in domestic portfolios are given at any point in time.

demand for money depends negatively on both r and $\bar{r} + \hat{e}$; as either rises, asset holders attempt to shift from money into the asset whose return has gone up.

These asset-market equilibrium conditions are summarized in equations (1)–(4).

$$M = m(r, \bar{r} + \hat{e}) \cdot W \tag{1}$$

$$B = b(r, \bar{r} + \hat{e}) \cdot W \tag{2}$$

$$eF = f(r, \bar{r} + \hat{e}) \cdot W \tag{3}$$

$$W = M + B + eF \tag{4}$$

Equation (4) is the balance sheet constraint, which insures that $m + b + f = 1$. The three demand functions give the desired distribution of the domestic wealth portfolio W into the three assets. Specifying the asset demand functions as homogeneous in wealth eliminates the price level from the asset-market equilibrium conditions. Given the balance sheet constraint (4), and gross substitutability of the three assets, we have the constraints on partial derivatives of the distribution functions:

$$m_r + f_r = -b_r < 0; \qquad m_{\bar{r}} + b_{\bar{r}} = -f_{\bar{r}} < 0$$

Here a subscript denotes a partial derivative. The three market equilibrium conditions (1)–(3) contain two independent equations in e and r, given the balance sheet constraint. Any pair of (1)–(3), with W substituted from (4), can be used to determine short-run equilibrium values for e and r.

In this section we assume static expectations, that is, $\hat{e} = 0$. In section 5, we will see the important difference that expectations make for the dynamic path to the long-run equilibrium.

We can study short-run equilibrium determination of the exchange rate and the interest rate holding $\bar{r} + \hat{e}$ constant, using Figure 1.1. There we show the pairs of interest rate r and exchange rate e that alternatively hold the demand for money equal to its supply (MM), the demand for domestic assets equal to their supply (BB), and the demand for foreign assets equal to their supply (FF). To obtain the slopes of MM and BB, consider what happens as e rises. This increases the home currency value of wealth, W, increasing the demand for both M and B. As the demand for money rises, the equilibrium r that maintains demand for money equal to the fixed supply rises, giving the positive slope to MM. As the demand for domestic assets rises, this pulls up their price, depressing the equilibrium interest rate. This gives the negative slope to BB.

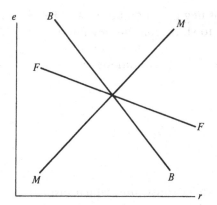

Figure 1.1.   Short-run equilibrium in asset markets

For the slope of *FF*, consider what happens as the home rate of return *r* rises. As the domestic *r* rises, the demand for foreign assets falls, and *e* falls as asset holders attempt to sell *F*. This gives *FF* a negative slope. Since a given increase in *r* reduces the demand for *F* by less than it increases the demand for *B*, a smaller drop in the exchange rate is required to restore equilibrium in the foreign asset market than would restore equilibrium in the domestic asset market. This makes *BB* steeper than *FF*.

Movements of equilibrium *r* and *e* can be analyzed by asking how the market-equilibrium curves of Figure 1.1 shift as monetary policy or the world rate $\bar{r} + \hat{e}$ or *F* shifts, for example. This analysis can be done by using any two of the three curves. Since the three assets sum to total wealth, if a given change in *e* and *r* restores equilibrium in two markets, it must in the third. Thus, since all three curves go through the same equilibrium *r, e* point (the one that yields equilibrium in all three markets simultaneously), we need to use only two to analyze changes in short-run equilibrium; the third will follow.

2.3.   Stability of short-run equilibrium

Before we move on to study the comparative statics of the system, we should establish that the equilibrium of Figure 1.1 is stable. If the markets begin the day with an *r, e* pair not at equilibrium, will they converge toward the equilibrium point in the course of trading? If not, analysis focusing on the equilibrium point is irrelevant.

In Figure 1.2 we focus on the *BB* and *FF* curves. This is because they control the short-run dynamics of *r* and *e* adjustment in the asset markets. If an initial *r, e* pair is not on the *BB* curve, the market for domestic assets *B* is out of equilibrium, and their excess demand

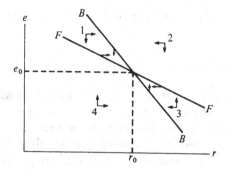

Figure 1.2. Short-run stability

or supply is moving r. If the market for foreign assets F is out of equilibrium, e will be moving.

At a point such as point 1 in Figure 1.2, which is above FF and left of BB, both markets are out of equilibrium. The interest rate is too low for equilibrium in the domestic asset market, given e. This means that asset holders are trying to sell domestic assets, pulling r rightward (increasing r) toward BB. In general, if an initial point is left of BB, r will be increasing, as at points 1 and 4; if it is right of BB, r will be decreasing, as at points 2 and 3. Along BB, r is not changing since the domestic asset market is in equilibrium.

Considering movement of the exchange rate, at point 1 the exchange rate is too high for equilibrium in the foreign asset market, given r. Thus, asset holders are attempting to sell F, moving e down toward FF. Similarly, at point 2, e is moving down toward FF. At points 3 and 4, e is rising since the rate is too low for equilibrium in the foreign asset market.

Thus, at points such as 1, 2, 3, and 4 in Figure 1.2 off both BB and FF, movement will be toward the equilibrium, as shown by the arrows at those points. If an initial point is on FF but not on BB, only r will be changing, and if it is on BB but not on FF, only e will be changing. Initial disequilibrium points such as 1 and 3 result in convergence directly toward equilibrium; initial points such as 2 or 4 move into either zone 1 or zone 3 and then converge.[4] So the short-run equilibrium r_0, e_0 point is stable, and we can proceed to

---

[4] To convince yourself of this, think of an initial point as an atomic particle moving in the e, r plane. The arrows of Figure 1.2 show the forces of motion of the particle. If it gets into zone 1 or 3, it cannot escape because on the BB and FF boundaries of those zones it is redirected to the interior. If it begins in zone 2 or 4 and hits an FF or BB boundary, it passes into the adjacent zone 1 or 3 and thus converges to r_0, e_0.

study the effects of exogenous changes in the asset stocks, M, B, and F.

2.4.   *Effects of asset accumulation*

2.4.1. Introduction: There are two basic types of change in asset stocks to analyze: (a) accumulation of one or more with the others unchanged, or (b) exchanges of two between the government or central bank and the private sector. Accumulation involves both wealth effects, as W increases, and substitution effects, as asset holders try to rebalance their portfolios. Exchanges are generally the result of open-market operations by the central bank, in which it buys (or sells) either domestic or foreign assets (B or F) in exchange for money (M). Open-market operations generate only substitution effects, since the initial swap holds wealth constant. In this subsection we will study the effects of accumulation on r and e; in the next we will look at monetary policy.

The stock of money or bonds can increase exogenously through an aggregate government deficit. The Treasury sells government debt, a major component of B, to the public or to the central bank to finance a deficit. The fraction of the new debt sold to the public appears as an increase in B, the fraction sold to the central bank is an increase in M. The stock of net foreign assets F is increased by a surplus or current account in the balance of payments. In a purely floating exchange rate system, official foreign exchange reserves never change since the central bank is not intervening in the foreign exchange market. Thus, the sum of the current and capital accounts must be zero, and the capital-account deficit is the current-account surplus. A capital-account deficit is an increase in holdings of net foreign assets F. This will be the key to the dynamic adjustment of the exchange rate, which will be discussed later in section 3.

2.4.2. Increase in M: The effects of an increase in the supply of money M through a money-financed budget deficit are clear. As the public's holdings of money increase, it attempts to rebalance portfolios by buying both F and B. With given supplies of these two assets, the increased demand pulls e up and pushes r down (as bond prices rise). These effects are illustrated in Figure 1.3. The increased demand for bonds reduces the interest rate that would maintain bond-market equilibrium at a given exchange rate e, shifting BB left. At the same time, the increased demand for foreign assets raises the value of the exchange rate that would maintain F-market equilibrium

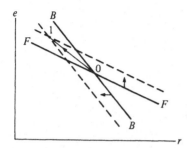

Figure 1.3. Increase in money, M

at a given r, shifting the FF curve up. The result is an increase in e and a drop in r, with the equilibrium point moving from point zero to point 1 in Figure 1.3.[5]

2.4.3. Increase in B: The effects of an increase in domestic assets B through a bond-financed government deficit are not as clear. The increase in bond supply will raise the interest rate r, as the supply increase exceeds the increase in demand through the wealth effect. But the effect on the exchange rate is ambiguous. The increase in wealth increases the demand for F, but the increase in the interest rate on domestic assets tends to reduce the demand. To the extent that domestic and foreign assets are viewed as better substitutes in portfolios than are domestic assets and money, the effect of the increase in B on the exchange rate will tend to be negative. This is because the shift of demand from F to B in response to the fall in r will be greater, the better substitutes the two are.

The effect of an increase in B is illustrated in Figure 1.4. The increase in B raises the r value that will clear the B market for a given e, shifting BB out. Through the wealth effect, it increases the e value that maintains F-market equilibrium given r, shifting FF up. The net result is movement from point zero to point 1 in Figure 1.4, with an increase in r but an unclear effect on e.

2.4.4. Increase in F: The initial effect of an increase in domestic holdings of net foreign assets F is to create excess supply in the

---

[5] The positively sloped MM curve through point zero also shifts left to pass through point 1. At any given exchange rate, the increase in money supply would require a decrease in the interest rate to maintain money-market equilibrium. The MM curves are not drawn into Figure 1.3 since they are unnecessary and would confuse the diagram.

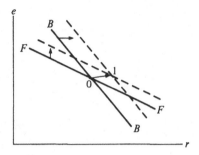

Figure 1.4.   Increase in domestic assets, B

foreign exchange market. Domestic portfolio balancers attempt to sell some of the increment in F in order to rebalance portfolios, and in doing so, push the exchange rate down. As the exchange rate falls, the home-currency value of total foreign assets is reduced. If the exchange rate falls by the same proportion that F increased, home-currency value of net foreign assets, eF, is restored to its original value. In this case wealth, $W = M + B + eF$, is unchanged, and the money and bond markets are undisturbed, so there is no change in the domestic interest rate r. Thus, an increase in F generates an opposite but equiproportionate reduction in e in this (overly) simple model, leaving the rest of the asset markets undisturbed. The movement would be illustrated by a vertical downward movement of the original equilibrium point in Figures 1.3 and 1.4, with MM, BB, and FF all shifting proportionately down. This negative reaction of e to accumulation of F is a crucial element of the dynamic process, which will be discussed later.

2.5.   Effects of monetary policy

2.5.1.   Introduction: In our framework, monetary policy is a purchase by the central bank of either domestic or foreign assets in exchange for money. Since money is taken to be a nontraded asset, the bank's instantaneous open-market operation has to be an exchange with a domestic asset holder.

Two features distinguish open-market swaps from asset accumulation, as described. First, the open-market operation is an instantaneous asset exchange at one point in time, whereas asset accumulation goes forward through time as a government deficit or current-account surplus cumulates. Strictly speaking, open-market swaps are

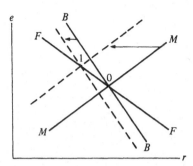

Figure 1.5. Open-market operations in *B*

part of the instantaneous equilibrium of the system, whereas accumulation is part of the dynamic adjustment. Second, accumulation involves an increase in wealth, and thus both wealth and substitution effects on *r* and *e*. Open-market operations hold initial wealth constant in an asset exchange, so they involve only substitution effects and give clear-cut results for both *r* and *e*.

2.5.2. Money and domestic assets: The usual open-market operation is a swap of money for domestic assets, with $\Delta B = -\Delta M$.[6] At the initial value of *e* and *r*, domestic asset holders find themselves with an excess supply of money and demand for bonds. As they attempt to buy bonds they push the rate of return *r* down. This redirects demand to foreign assets, pulling the exchange rate up. In the final equilibrium, *r* has decreased and *e* has increased.

The effect of an open-market swap of money for domestic assets is illustrated in Figure 1.5. With a swap between *B* and *M*, the *FF* market-equilibrium curve is unshifted, but at a given exchange rate the *r* value that would maintain equilibrium in the bond and money markets falls. Thus, *MM* and *BB* shift left along *FF*, giving movement from point zero to point 1 in Figure 1.5.

2.5.3. Money and foreign assets: The central bank could do open-market operations in foreign assets, buying foreign-denominated assets from domestic asset holders. The Federal Reserve does this as part of its exchange-market operations, although in quantities that

---

[6] In general, we will discuss expansionary open-market operations, in which $\Delta M > 0$. Results would be symmetrically opposite for contractionary open-market swaps where $\Delta M < 0$.

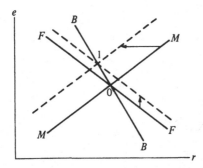

Figure 1.6.   Open-market operations in F

are infinitesimally small compared to usual open-market operations.[7] In this case the initial shifts come in the money and foreign-asset markets. With an excess supply of money, the interest rate that would maintain equilibrium in the money market falls, shifting MM left in Figure 1.6. With excess demand for foreign exchange, the value of e maintaining equilibrium in the F market rises, shifting FF up. The intersection of MM and FF shifts up along the BB curve of Figure 1.6 from point zero to point 1.

It is clear from Figures 1.5 and 1.6 that open-market operations in domestic assets have a greater effect on r and a smaller effect on e than do open-market operations in F. Thus, the split of the real effects of monetary policy between the sector producing traded goods (through e) and that producing interest-sensitive durable goods (through r) will depend on the mix of open-market operations between B and F.

2.6.   Summary on short-run equilibrium

The results of the open-market and accumulation experiments are summarized in Table 1.1.

The entries in Table 1.1 give the direction of change of the interest rate and the exchange rate following (a) an increase in any one of the asset stocks, holding the others constant, in the first three columns, and (b) an expansionary open-market operation, with M exchanged for B or for F, in the last two columns. One important implication

[7] For example, in 1975 the Federal Reserve bought $9.1 billion in U. S. government debt, and $0.3 billion in foreign assets, not all of which was purchased from domestic asset holders.

Table 1.1. *Effects of increases in asset stocks on short-run equilibrium interest rate (r) and exchange rate (e)*

Effects on	Effects of accumulation of stocks			Effects of open market operations	
	ΔM	ΔB	ΔF	$\Delta B = -\Delta M$	$e\Delta F = -\Delta M$
r	−	+	0	−	−
e	+	?	−	+	+

of Table 1.1 is that an increase in the domestic money stock M, either through a budget deficit or an open-market operation, directly raises the exchange rate e, without reference to the effect on the domestic price level. A second implication of Table 1.1 is that if the country is running a surplus on current account, so that net foreign assets F are increasing, this tends to reduce the exchange rate; a deficit in current account, with F falling, raises the exchange rate. This is the key to dynamic adjustment of the exchange rate as we move from short run to long run.

The short-run comparative statics of Table 1.1 yield an implicit reduced-form equation for the exchange rate:

$$e = e\,(F, M; B); \qquad e_F < 0; \qquad e_M > 0 \qquad (5)$$

This gives the *instantaneous* equilibrium value for e as a function of the supplies of the relevant assets. The partial derivatives e_M and e_F are comparative-static solutions de/dM and de/dF.[8] An increase in M raises instantaneous equilibrium e, and an increase in F reduces it. Inspection of the system (1)–(4) with $\hat{e} = 0$ (static expectations) shows that the elasticity of e with respect to F, $e_F \cdot F/e$, is -1. The variables e and F enter only multiplicatively.

[8] The precise equation for de from the comparative statics can be obtained by total differentiation of (1) and (2) with (4) written in for W and inversion to solve for de:

$$de = [F(bm_r - mb_r)]^{-1} \cdot \left\{ \begin{array}{l} - [b_r(1 - m) - m_r b]dM \\ + [b_r m - m_r b]edF \\ [b_r m + m_r(1 - b)]dB \end{array} \right\} \qquad (5')$$

e_F from (5) is the coefficient of dF in (5'), and e_M is the coefficient of dM. (See Branson [1979a], Appendix equation [A.11]. There b_F in the coefficient matrix should be b_r.)

3.   Dynamics and long-run equilibrium

3.1.   *The adjustment mechanism*

In the short run the exchange rate is determined by requirements of asset-market equilibrium, given existing stocks of money, domestic assets, and foreign assets. But this is not the end of the story. The value of the exchange rate at one point in time, $t(0)$, given income, the domestic price level, and other real variables, may yield a nonzero balance on current account. With flexible exchange rates and no central bank intervention in foreign exchange markets, the sum of the balances on capital account and current account is identically zero. Thus, a nonzero current-account balance implies an equally nonzero capital-account balance of the opposite sign. If the current account shows a surplus, the capital account is in deficit and the private sector is accumulating foreign assets; F is increasing. If the current account is in deficit, F is decreasing. As F changes, the exchange rate changes through the short-run mechanism of subsection 2.4. Thus, if the initial value of the exchange rate $e(0)$, yields a nonzero current-account balance, F is either increasing or decreasing, moving e from $e(0)$. The point of this section is to study the dynamic adjustment through the current account and to show the condition under which it leads to a stable long-run equilibrium value for e where the current-account balance is zero and the stock of net foreign assets is not changing.

In addition to the exchange rate dynamics, the price level presumably responds to changes in the domestic money stock, but with a lag. For price dynamics, we follow Dornbusch (1976) in assuming slow adjustment of the price level to monetary shocks. We also assume that in the long run, the price level changes proportionately to the money stock; the economy is homogeneous in monetary variables. Rather than specify the entire domestic economy, I will assume long-run homogeneity and gradual adjustment of the price level.[9]

The technical analysis of dynamic adjustment will be presented in this subsection. Then in subsections 4.2 and 4.3, we will describe the response of the system to monetary and real shocks.

The assumption on price dynamics is captured simply by

$$\frac{dp}{dt} \equiv \dot{p} = \lambda(m - m^*) \tag{6}$$

[9] Readers interested in the underlying model of the economy might consult Branson (1979b, ch. 7).

Here $m = M/p$, and m^* is the equilibrium value of real balances corresponding to long-run equilibrium output. Equation (6) says that if M is increased, raising m above m^*, the price level will rise to restore $m = m^*$.[10]

The other dynamic equation is provided by the balance-of-payments identity. With no central bank intervention, and thus zero change in reserves, the capital account and current account must sum to zero:

$$0 \equiv X + \bar{r}F - \dot{F}$$

Here X is net exports of goods, $\bar{r}F$ is income on net foreign assets, and $\dot{F} \equiv dF/dt$ is the rate of accumulation of net foreign assets, the rate of capital outflow. This gives us an expression for $\dot{F}$:

$$\dot{F} \equiv X + \bar{r}F$$

Net exports, in turn, depend on the real exchange rate e/p, and an exogenous shift factor z. The real exchange rate here is the relative price of foreign to home bundles of goods, $e\bar{p}/p$, with the foreign price level $\bar{p}$ set equal to unity. An assumption of purchasing power parity (PPP) would impose constancy on $e\bar{p}/p$, as e follows exactly the path of $p/\bar{p}$. This assumption has not held in the 1970s, but we will see that it may be a reasonable description of the average long-run path of e.[11]

The exogenous shift factor z represents real events, such as changes in tastes or technology, oil discoveries, and so on, that increase net exports (in foreign exchange terms) for a given value of e/p. Thus, we write

$$X = X(e/p, z); \qquad X_e > 0; \qquad X_z > 0$$

An increase in e/p is a real devaluation; $X_e > 0$ assumes the Marshall-Lerner condition holds in the short run.

With the reduced-form expression for e and the exports function both included, the dynamic equation for $\dot{F}$ is now

$$\dot{F} = X[e(F, M; B)/p, z] + \bar{r}F \tag{7}$$

The variable B is not of interest here. M and z are exogenous to the

---

[10] This is a formalization of the argument on price-level adjustment in Branson (1977, 1979a).

[11] See Katseli-Papaefstratiou (1979) and Frenkel (1981a) for the breakdown of PPP in the 1970s.

dynamic system given by (6) and (7). F and p are the slowly adjusting state variables, and e can jump in the short run in response to changes in F and M.

3.2.   Long-run equilibrium

The long-run equilibrium conditions are $\dot{p}$ and $\dot{F} = 0$ in equations (6) and (7). The implication for long-run movements in p have already been assumed. The price level moves proportionately to changes in M.

The effect of an increase in z is more interesting. From (7), an increase in z initially generates a current-account surplus, $\dot{F} > 0$. As F accumulates, e falls, as shown in the short-run comparative statics. This reduces X and $\dot{F}$. When X has fallen to its initial value, $\dot{F}$ is still positive, since F has increased. Therefore, e must fall further, until the reduction in X just outweighs the increase in $\bar{r}F$. Thus, because income on foreign assets is part of the current-account balance, the exchange rate must appreciate enough to offset the original increase in z *plus* the increase in investment income due to accumulation of F between equilibria.

3.3.   Dynamic stability

Equations (6) and (7) for $\dot{p}$ and $\dot{F}$ can be combined and linearized into the system:

$$
\begin{pmatrix} \dot{F} \\ \dot{p} \end{pmatrix} = \overset{\displaystyle S_M}{\begin{bmatrix} X_e e_F + \bar{r} & - X_e \\ 0 & - \lambda \end{bmatrix}} \begin{pmatrix} F - F_0 \\ p - p_0 \end{pmatrix} + \begin{bmatrix} X_z & X_e e_M \\ 0 & \lambda \end{bmatrix} \begin{pmatrix} z - z_0 \\ M - M_0 \end{pmatrix} \quad (8)
$$

A sufficient condition for stability is that $X_e e_F + \bar{r} < 0$. This is the "super Marshall-Lerner" condition in Branson (1977). X_e is positive and e_F is negative. Their product is the effect of F accumulation on X, through the normal Marshall-Lerner effect. This must be large enough to offset the effect of rising F on $\bar{r}F$ to ensure stability.

If this super Marshall-Lerner condition holds, this system moves toward its long-run equilibrium monotonically after a disturbance to M or z. This can be seen from the form of the stability matrix S_M in

(8). The roots of the system that govern its dynamics are simply the diagonal elements, both real and negative. This insures monotonic stability.[12]

Thus, the super Marshall-Lerner stability condition insures long-run stability. Reassured, we can move on to describe adjustment in reaction to monetary shocks on M or real shocks to z.

4. The effects of permanent disturbances

4.1. Introduction

The analysis of short-run comparative statics of section 2 and of the dynamic adjustment in section 3 can now be combined to study the effect of monetary or real disturbances. We will describe the characteristics of the model by analyzing the results of permanent single increases in M and in z, the exogenous real factor in the current account. This description will integrate the short-run comparative statics and dynamic adjustment to long-run equilibrium and set the stage for discussion of the rational expectations version of the model in section 5.

4.2. Monetary disturbance

Here we will follow the path of adjustment of the exchange rate following a one-time shift arising in the monetary sector. Such a disturbance could originate on the supply side, owing to a shift in monetary policy or the supply behavior of the banking system, or on the demand side, owing to a shift in the public's demand for money. A sudden decrease in the demand for money, at initial values for exchange rates and interest rates, should produce the same results as an increase in the supply of money, due to monetary policy, for example. In the following discussion, we will focus on the example of an increase in the money supply (expansionary open-market operation). The result would be equally applicable in the event of a reduction in money demand.

We begin with the effects on the domestic price path of a monetary shift. This is the underlying path about which the exchange rate is moving as the current account adjusts. Then we move on to study the impact and adjustment effects on the exchange rate, relative to the price path.

---

[12] I did not see this when I said in Branson (1977, 1979a) that adjustment is not necessarily monotonic.

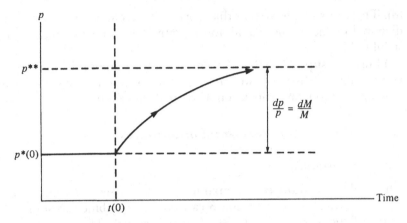

Figure 1.7.   Adjustment of the domestic price level

Following equation (6), the price level will rise in response to the excess level of real balances, moving to a new equilibrium where the price level has increased proportionately to the increase in the money supply. This is shown in Figure 1.7. The domestic price level begins at an initial equilibrium value $p^*(0)$, indexed to 1.0 at time $t(0)$. It rises to a new equilibrium value p^{**}, where $dp/p = dM/M$. This is the price path around which the exchange rate e adjusts.

Next we turn to the path of exchange rate adjustment. We begin with the system in full equilibrium, with the current-account balance zero, so that $X(e/p, z) = -\bar{r}F$, with given initial stocks of M, B, and F. We want to trace the path of the exchange rate following an initial increase in the money supply, through an open-market operation. To avoid the second-order complications that come from a reallocation of investment income on foreign assets between the private sector and the government if the open-market operation is done in the foreign exchange market, we will focus on the case where $\Delta B = -\Delta M$: an open-market operation in government debt. Again, the effects of a downward shift in the demand for money would be the same. The result of a contraction of supply or increase in demand would be symmetrically opposite.

The initial effect of the increase in the money stock is an upward jump in the exchange rate to maintain asset-market equilibrium. This is the increase shown in Table 1.1. Figure 1.8 shows the adjustment path of the exchange rate, superimposed on the price path of Figure 1.7. Initially, e^* and p^* are normalized to 1.0. The increase in the money stock pushes the exchange rate up to e_1

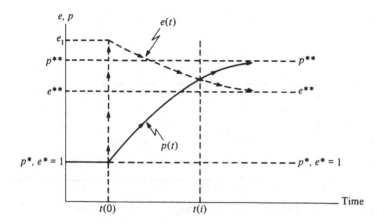

Figure 1.8. Adjustment of price level and exchange rate to an increase in M

instantaneously. The next step is to trace the dynamic adjustment path as net foreign assets accumulate.

At e_1 in Figure 1.8, the price ratio (e/p) has risen above the e^*/p^* value that gave $\dot{F} = 0$ at the original value of F at time $t(0)$. In the initial equilibrium at $t(0)$, the current-account balance was zero. After the increase in the money supply, with F still at $F(0)$, the price ratio rises to $e_1/p^*) > (e^*/p^*)$. Assuming the Marshall-Lerner condition holds, the movement on the price ratio increases net exports, so that the current account becomes positive at $t(0)$, and net foreign assets F begin to accumulate. As F increases, e falls and X falls, following the dynamic adjustment path discussed in section 3 and shown in Figure 1.8.

With F accumulating, at a decreasing rate since the current-account surplus is shrinking, the exchange rate follows the $e(t)$ path in Figure 1.8 converging toward the rising $p(t)$ path. At the point $t(i)$ where the paths cross, the price ratio e/p is the same as the original $e^*/p^* = 1$. This implies that at the crossing point $t(i)$ where $e(t) = p(t)$, net exports have fallen to their original value. But since F has accumulated in the interval between $t(0)$ and $t(i)$, the current-account balance is positive at $t(i)$ due to the increase in investment income from $\bar{r}F(0)$ to $\bar{r}F(i)$. Thus, at $t(i)$, where $e(i) = p(i)$, F is still accumulating and e must fall further. It falls until the price ratio e/p reaches the value where $X(e/p, z) = \bar{r}F$ once again. At that point the current-account balance is zero, and the adjustment process is completed. There has been an accumulation of foreign assets and a concomitant increase

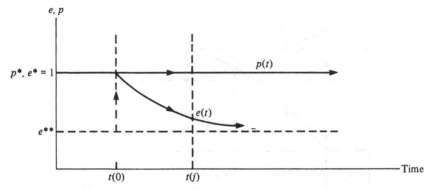

Figure 1.9.   Adjustment of the real exchange rate to an increase in z

in investment income, and the ratio e/p has decreased so that the net export deficit just offsets the investment income in the balance on current account. Given the long-run equilibrium value p^{**} in Figure 1.8, the exchange rate has settled at e^{**}, such that $e^{**}/p^{**} < e^{*}/p^{*}$.

4.3.   The effect of a real disturbance (in z)

Let us now consider the effect of an increase in the current-account balance due to exogenous real factors, represented by z in the net export function. Beginning from an initial equilibrium, the current-account balance suddenly increases, making $\dot{F}$ positive. Foreign assets accumulate, since the current-account surplus *is* net foreign investment. The accumulation of F drives e down; the real exchange rate appreciates. This in turn reduces the current-account surplus.

Movement of e around the original (and unchanged) equilibrium p^{*} is shown in Figure 1.9. The increase in z at time $t(0)$ makes $\dot{F}$ positive. This causes e to begin to fall (an appreciation). At some point $t(j)$, e has fallen enough to restore X to its initial value, but because F has accumulated, e must fall farther. It falls to the new value e^{**} where the current-account balance is again zero. The appreciation of the real exchange rate e/p must reduce X enough to offset the initial impulse from z *plus* the accumulation of F between equilibria.

4.4.   Conclusions from the theory with static expectations

The patterns of relationships between the key variables as the system is disturbed by random monetary and real shocks can be summarized easily. Since we are assuming static expectations, it does not matter whether disturbances are anticipated.

1. A permanent, one-time monetary shock will cause an initial jump in the nominal and real exchange rates, which is reversed as the accumulation dynamics take over. The long-run effect of any single shock is a movement in the real exchange rate e/p due to the change in the foreign asset position between equilibria. If monetary shocks are repetitive and random, this will produce random movement in the real exchange rate, related to F.

2. *Real* disturbances to the current account, represented by z, will cause a gradual adjustment of e relative to p, with static expectations. The adjustment must offset not only the initial effect on X from dz, but also the resulting accumulation of F. If real disturbances are repetitive and random, this will also generate random movement in the real exchange rate.

3. Current-account surpluses will generally be associated with an appreciating currency, and deficits with a depreciating currency, under either source of disturbance.

4. The PPP path $\bar{p}/p$ will be the long-run average around which the exchange rate e moves as the system is hit by random and repetitive monetary or real disturbances. The PPP path does *not* determine short-run movements in e, but may serve as a long-run anchor in the absence of "permanent" structural change.

5. Rational expectations and the current account

5.1. Introduction

In sections 2 through 4 we saw that with static expectations the nominal *and* real exchange rates adjust gradually to a current-account disturbance. The path of the exchange rate follows the accumulation path of net foreign assets. Technically, the exchange rate can be solved in short-run equilibrium as a function of the levels of the asset stocks. This was possible because the assumption of static expectations eliminates the term in expected change in the exchange rate $\hat{e}$ from the asset–demand functions.

When we move to the assumption of rational expectations, we restore the $\hat{e}$ term and obtain a separate equation for the path of the exchange rate. This will result in a model with two dynamic equations – for F and $\hat{e}$. The rational expectations assumption, here literally perfect foresight because the model is nonstochastic, imposes the condition that the *expected* change in the rate is the actual change.

The main characteristic of the rational expectations version of the model is that since the market looks ahead to the consequences of a current-account disturbance, the exchange rate jumps at the time when the change is perceived. Some of the gradual adjustment of e is pulled forward into a jump in the present with rational expectations.

In the next subsection we go through the technical aspects of solution of the rational expectations version of the model. Then, using the basic diagram in Figure 1.13, in subsection 5.3 we will discuss the implications of the model for the effects of current-account disturbances on the nominal and real exchange rates.

5.2.   Solution of the model

The model begins with the original equations for the financial sector plus the dynamic adjustment equation for $\dot{F}$. These are repeated here for convenient reference.

$$M = m(r, \bar{r} + \hat{e})\cdot W \tag{1}$$

$$B = b(r, \bar{r} + \hat{e})\cdot W \tag{2}$$

$$eF = f(r, \bar{r} + \hat{e})\cdot W \tag{3}$$

$$W = M + B + eF \tag{4}$$

$$\dot{F} = X(e/p, z) + \bar{r}F \tag{7}$$

The dynamics with separate equations for $\hat{e}$ and $\dot{F}$ are sufficiently complicated that in this section we will suspend the p equation and take p as exogenous. This will permit us to focus on the relationship between the current-account and the exchange rate (real and nominal).

Solution of the model proceeds as follows. First, the rational expectations assumption is that $\hat{e}$ is the rate of change of e. Then two equations of (1)–(3), with wealth substituted from (4), can be used to solve for r and $\hat{e}$ as functions of M, W, eF. The $\hat{e}$ and $\dot{F}$ equations then are two dynamic equations in e and F that can be solved for the movement in these two variables.

Divide equations (1) and (3) by W and differentiate totally, holding $\bar{r}$ constant:

$$d\left(\frac{M}{W}\right) = m_r dr + m_{\hat{e}} d\hat{e}$$

$$d\left(\frac{eF}{W}\right) = f_r dr + f_{\hat{e}} d\hat{e}$$

These can be solved in matrix form as:

$$\begin{pmatrix} dr \\ d\hat{e} \end{pmatrix} = \frac{1}{(f_r m_{\hat{e}} - m_r f_{\hat{e}})} \begin{bmatrix} m_{\hat{e}} & -f_{\hat{e}} \\ -m_r & f_r \end{bmatrix} \begin{pmatrix} d\left(\dfrac{eF}{W}\right) \\ d\left(\dfrac{M}{W}\right) \end{pmatrix}$$

The solution for $d\hat{e}$ is then

$$d\hat{e} = \frac{1}{(+)} \left[-m_r d\left(\frac{eF}{W}\right) + f_r d\left(\frac{M}{W}\right) \right]$$

The coefficients of eF/W and M/W are the partial derivatives of the $\hat{e}$ adjustment function.

$$\hat{e} = \phi\left(\frac{eF}{W}, \frac{M}{W}\right) \qquad \phi_1 > 0; \quad \phi_2 < 0 \qquad (9)$$

This is the dynamic equation to be solved along with (5) for $\dot{F}$ to obtain equilibrium e and F.

In the e, F space of Figure 1.10, the $\hat{e} = 0$ locus is a rectangular hyperbola. This can be seen by observing that in ϕ, eF enters multiplicatively (in W as well as the numerator eF), so changes in e and F that hold the product eF constant will hold $\hat{e}$ constant. Combinations of e and F off the locus move e away from it, as the arrows show. For example, since $\phi_1 > 0$, an increase in e or F from a point on the locus makes $\hat{e} > 0$.

The $\dot{F} = 0$ locus in Figure 1.11 gives e, F pairs from equation (7) that hold F constant. Total differentiation of (7) gives the slope

$$\frac{de}{dF}\bigg|_{\dot{F}=0} = \frac{-\tilde{r}}{X_e}$$

Combinations off the $\dot{F} = 0$ locus move F away from it. In (7) we see that an increase in F from a point on $\dot{F} = 0$ results in $\dot{F} > 0$.

The equilibrium is shown in Figure 1.12. With the $\dot{F} = 0$ locus flatter than $\hat{e} = 0$, the equilibrium is a "saddle point." There is one path into the equilibrium point, shown as the dotted line. Any initial e, F choice off that path will lead away from equilibrium, as indicated in the figure. A basic assumption in rational expectations models is that following a disturbance the market will pick the value for e that puts the system on the stable path to the equilibrium.

If the $\dot{F} = 0$ locus is steeper than $\hat{e} = 0$, the system is completely

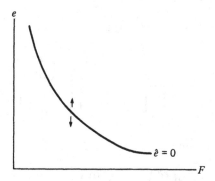

Figure 1.10. Locus where $\hat{e} = 0$

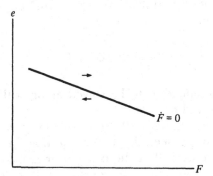

Figure 1.11. Locus where $\dot{F} = 0$

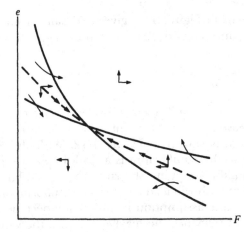

Figure 1.12. Equilibrium path for e, F

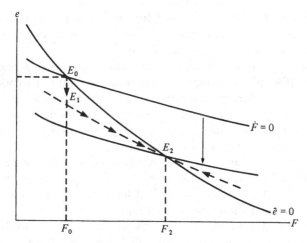

Figure 1.13.   Effect of current-account disturbance

unstable. The slope of $\dot{F} = 0$ is $-\bar{r}/X_e$, and since $\hat{e} = 0$ is a rectangular hyperbola, its slope is given by

$$\frac{de}{dF}\bigg|_{\hat{e}=0} = -\frac{e}{F}$$

Saddle-point equilibrium therefore requires

$$-\frac{e}{F} < -\frac{\bar{r}}{X_e}$$

Since along $\dot{F} = 0$, $\bar{r}F = X$, this condition for stability in the rational expectations version of the model is the ordinary Marshall-Lerner condition, $eX_e/X > 1$. If this condition holds, following a disturbance the exchange rate will initially move in the right direction.

Now consider the effect of a permanent increase in z, the real current-account disturbance in (5) for $\dot{F}$. In Figure 1.13 the rise in z shifts the $\dot{F} = 0$ locus down. Why? The rise in z requires an offsetting fall in e or F in equation (5) to hold $\dot{F} = 0$. The new long-run equilibrium is at point E_2, with a saddle path running to it as indicated by the dashed line. To put the system immediately on that path with initial F_0, the market appreciates the currency from E_0 to point E_1 in a jump. Then the e, F dynamics carry the system to E_2, with F accumulating and e appreciating further.

Referring back to the financial market equations (1)–(4), we see that the jump in e reduces eF, whereas the expectation of further appreciation, $\hat{e} < 0$, reduces demand for eF. Thus, the jump in e is needed to maintain market equilibrium with (rational) expectations of appreciation of e in the adjustment process.

In the new long-run equilibrium e has fallen relative to p enough to offset the effect of the exogenous disturbance z on net exports X *plus* the increase in foreign earnings $\bar{r}(F_2 - F_0)$. Thus the real disturbance to the current account causes an adjustment in the real exchange rate e/p that comes in an initial jump, then a continued gradual movement to long-view equilibrium.

The same figure can be used to analyze the effects of an (exogenous) change in the domestic price level p. A fall in p (relative to the foreign price level) will shift the $\dot{F} = 0$ locus down by stimulating net exports. This will then give a jump appreciation from E_0 to E_1, and further appreciation to E_2. Again, the value of the real exchange rate at E_2 is lower than it was at the initial equilibrium, in order to increase the trade deficit enough to offset the rise in investment income $\bar{r}(F_2 - F_0)$.

5.3.   Current-account disturbances and exchange rate fluctuations

The important implication of the rational expectations model is not the necessary precision with which the market chooses the saddle-point path. Rather, it is the result that disturbances with foreseeable implications for the exchange rate will cause the rate to jump when the disturbance appears. Thus, in addition to jumps when unanticipated changes in monetary policy appear, their rate will jump in reaction to real disturbances to the current-account balance.

This modifies the conclusion from section 4 concerning real disturbances and the exchange rate. An unanticipated increase in the current-account balance creates an expectation of appreciation of the nominal and real exchange rate to move the current account back to equilibrium. The expectation itself causes a jump appreciation of the nominal rate, which is also an appreciation of the real rate. After the jump, there is further movement to long-run equilibrium.

Thus, unanticipated changes in the current-account balance, as well as the money stock, are likely to generate jumps in the exchange rate. In the case of the current account, however, the jump is not reversed. If disturbances are random, we still expect the exchange rate to fluctuate around the PPP path. This would make the real exchange rate roughly follow a random walk. Jacob Frenkel (1981b) provides evidence supporting this view.

In addition, major structural shifts in the world economy, such as the recovery of Europe and Japan after World War II, or the rise of the newly industrializing countries in the developing world, would be expected to cause permanent shifts in the equilibrium real rate. In Branson (1980) it is argued that the major real devaluation of the U.S. dollar in the 1970s resulted from the change in the structure of the system as Europe and Japan recovered and grew relative to the United States.

6. The data

6.1. Introduction

The asset-market model of sections 2 to 5 implies that unanticipated movements in the money stock, the current-account balance, and relative price levels will cause unanticipated jumps in the exchange rate. In this and the following two sections, we show that the model is consistent with the data on these variables for four major currencies: the U. S. dollar, the Deutsche mark, sterling, and the yen. We study movements in the effective exchange rate of each of these countries, as calculated by the IMF. For each country, movements in the effective rate are related to movements in $M1$ or $M3$, the balance on current account, and an index of relative prices, measured by the Wholesale Price Index (WPI) and weighted by the IMF. The data are described in detail in Table 1.2.

The first step in analyzing the data is to investigate their time-series properties. This provides a compact description of the "facts" and an initial indication of whether the facts are roughly consistent with the theory. The time-series analysis of the data is done in this section. Then in section 7 we focus on the PPP relationship between relative prices and exchange rates. In section 8 we study systems of vector autoregressions, one for each country, to test the relations between unanticipated changes, or innovations, in the variables.

6.2. Time-series analysis

In this section the autoregressive structure of each time series is described by regression equations of the form:

$$X_t = \alpha_0 + \sum_{i=1}^{I} \alpha_i X_{t-i} + \sum_{j=1}^{3} \beta_j D_j + \gamma t + u_t \qquad (10)$$

where X_t is the log of the time series under consideration, X_{t-i} is the

Table 1.2. *Variable definitions and data*

Variable name

e   Effective exchange rate, in units of foreign currency per unit of home currency

$P/\bar{P}$ Relative wholesale prices (ratio of home to competitors indexes)

M1   Narrow money, as defined by the IMF in the *International Financial Statistics* (*IFS*)

M3   Broad money, as defined by the IMF (M1 plus quasi-money) in the *IFS*

CAB   Current-account balance

Countries
United States
United Kingdom
Federal Republic of Germany
Japan

Data

1. All data are quarterly, from IMF sources (in most cases from *IFS*), and cover a sufficiently long time series that autoregressions can be performed over the period 1974-I to 1980-IV.

2. *Exchange rates*: e_t is the log of the average effective exchange rate during quarter t. The units are foreign currency per unit of domestic currency. The index is based on a geometrically weighted average of bilateral rates between the home and thirteen other industrial countries. The weights are the same as those used to calculate $P/\bar{P}$. Base: 1975 = 100. Source: IMF. Note that these are not the Multiple Exchange Rate model (MERM) rates published in *IFS*.

3. *Relative prices*: The index is a log of the ratio of home to foreign quarterly wholesale price indexes. $\bar{P}$ is a composite and uses the same weights as e does. Base = 1975. Source: IMF. This index is not the same as that published in the *IFS*. Our data are based on indexes in local (not a common) currency.

4. *Money*: This is the log of the end of the quarter money stock. Source: *IFS*, line 34 ("money") for M1, lines 34 and 35 ("money" + "quasi-money") for M3.

5. *Current account*: This is the dollar value of the flow during the quarter (not measured in logs). Source: *IFS*. Lines: 77aa (Merchandise: Exports, fob); 77ab (Merchandise: Imports, fob); 77ac (Other Goods, Services, and Income: Credits); 77ad (Other Goods, Services, and Income: Debits); 77ae (Private Unrequited Transfers); 77ag (Official Unrequited Transfers).

---

value of X_t lagged i quarters, D_j is a seasonal dummy, and t is time. Equation (10) is a univariate autoregression of the variable X on its own past values, and the estimated values of the α coefficients give the pattern of response of the time series to a disturbance u_t. The two cases that will appear in our data are first-order autoregression, where only α_1 is significant, and second-order autoregression, where α_1 and α_2 are significant. One purpose of the analysis is simply to describe the data; the second is to see if the time-series structure of the exchange rate data is consistent with that of the money, current account, and relative price data.

For each variable we began with a regression on four lags, seasonal dummies, and a time trend. We then shortened the lags by eliminating insignificant variables at the far end of the lag. The respective results are shown in Tables 1.3 through 1.6. Each column in the tables shows the results of a regression of the indicated variable on lagged values of itself. Coefficients of the time trend and seasonal dummies are not shown. The regressions are performed on quarterly data for the period 1974-I to 1980-IV. The beginning date was chosen because it was after the major period of disequilibrium adjustment in 1971–3, including a major real devaluation of the U.S. dollar (see Branson 1980), and the last date was the most recent for which data were available when we began the study in June 1981.

6.3. Country results

6.3.1. United States: The results for the United States are instructive and serve as an illustration of the technique. In the first two columns of Table 1.3, we show the regressions for the log of the U.S. nominal effective exchange rate e, weighted by the IMF, in foreign currency per dollar. The first column shows the regression with four lags on the exchange rate; only the lag at $t-1$ is significant with a coefficient of 0.86. When the lags at $t-2$ through $t-4$ are eliminated, the standard error of the estimated equation falls a bit, and the coefficient of e_{t-1} is 0.78. Thus, the U.S. effective rate, measured on a quarterly average, can be described as a stable first-order autoregression (AR1). The coefficient of 0.78 on e_{t-1} indicates that a given disturbance u_t will eventually disappear from the time series as its effect is given by increasing powers of 0.78: $\Delta e_t = \Delta u_t$; $\Delta e_{t+1} = 0.78\Delta u_t$; $\Delta e_{t+2} = 0.78^2\Delta_t$; etc. The smaller the coefficient of e_{t-1} in the regression, the faster a disturbance tends to recede.

The third and fourth columns of Table 1.3 show the results for the log of the U.S. relative price index $P/\bar{P}$. This is an index of the U.S. WPI relative to a weighted average of the WPIs of thirteen other industrial countries. The variable $P/e\bar{P}$ is the IMF's measure of relative cost, published in *International Financial Statistics*. It is the inverse of the "real exchange rate" of sections 2 and 3.

The first regression for $P/\bar{P}$ in Table 1.3 gives significant coefficients to the lags at $t-1$ and $t-2$. Elimination of the longer lags results in the second equation, with a standard error only slightly

Table 1.3. *United States: univariate autoregressions (standard errors in parentheses)*

Lags	e		$P/\bar{P}$		$M1$		$M3$		CAB	
$t-1$	0.86^a	0.78^a	1.71^a	1.36^a	0.33	0.55^a	0.70^a	0.78^a	0.92^a	0.80^a
	(0.21)	(0.10)	(0.21)	(0.17)	(0.24)	(0.18)	(0.24)	(0.14)	(0.21)	(0.14)
$t-2$	−0.24	—	−1.41^a	−0.60^a	0.31	—	0.33	—	−0.19	—
	(0.29)		(0.38)	(0.16)	(0.27)		(0.27)		(0.30)	
$t-3$	0.37	—	0.74	—	−0.16	—	−0.22	—	0.13	—
	(0.28)		(0.38)		(0.29)		(0.30)		(0.30)	
$t-4$	−0.24	—	−0.20	—	0.22	—	−0.08	—	−0.20	—
	(0.19)		(0.21)		(0.24)		(0.24)		(0.22)	
Statistics										
R^2	0.86	0.85	0.92	0.90	0.99	0.99	0.99	0.99	0.76	0.74
Durbin-Watson	1.89	1.82	2.16	1.51	1.57	1.96	1.98	2.15	1.86	1.66
SE	0.027	0.026	0.008	0.009	0.012	0.012	0.009	0.008	1.96	1.91

Note: Sample period 1974-I to 1980-IV for dependent variable. All regressions include constant, seasonal dummies, and time trend.
^{a} Coefficient is significant at the 5% level.
Source: International Monetary Fund (but e is not MERM, $P/\bar{P}$ is WPI).

larger than the first. The result for $P/\bar{P}$ is a second-order autoregression (AR2), with a stable cyclical response to a disturbance.[13]

The next two pairs of columns in Table 1.3 show the univariate autoregression results for the two U.S. money stocks, $M1$ and $M3$. In both cases only the lag at $t-1$ is significant. Both are stable first-order autocorrelations.

Finally, the last two columns in Table 1.3 show the autoregressions for the current-account balance. These are run on the level of CAB, rather than its log, since the time series passes through zero. The result is similar to that for the money stocks.

In the case of the United States, then, money stocks, the balance on current account, and the nominal effective exchange rate all follow stable AR1 processes, whereas the relative price series is a cyclical AR2. This suggests that the behavior of money stocks, the current-account balance, and the exchange rate are consistent, at this level, with the theoretical model of sections 2 through 5. These variables all follow stable AR1 processes. However, the relationship between relative price levels and the exchange rate is more complicated. The relative price series exhibits cyclical behavior whereas the exchange rate is monotonically damped. Thus, there is not a one-to-one correspondence between price and exchange rate fluctuations, even in the 1974–80 period.

6.3.2. West Germany: Table 1.4 shows the univariate autoregression results for Germany. The format is exactly the same as for the United States, so the discussion can be brief.

As in the United States, the nominal effective rate, the money stocks, and the balance on current account all follow AR1 processes in Germany. All but $M3$ are stable. German $M3$ has a lag coefficient of unity, indicating that it is a "random walk": The change in $M3$ is (roughly) white noise. The German relative price series is AR2 with a stable cyclical response to disturbances.[14] Thus, the German data are quite similar to those for the United States.

6.3.3. United Kingdom: The results for the United Kingdom are summarized in Table 1.5. Again, the results are broadly similar to

---

[13] The characteristic equation is given by

$$P/\bar{P}_t - 1.36\,P/\bar{P}_{t-1} + 0.60\,P/\bar{P}_{t-2} = 0$$

The roots of this equation are $0.68 \pm 0.37i$, with a modulus of $0.77 = 0.6^{\frac{1}{2}}$.

[14] Note that the German price equation would not invert due to multicolinearity with more than two lags.

Table 1.4. Germany: univariate autoregressions (standard errors in parentheses)

Lags	e		$P/\bar{P}$		$M1$		$M3$		CAB	
$t-1$	0.71[a] (0.20)	0.67[a] (0.18)	—[b]	1.15[a] (0.19)	0.67[a] (0.21)	0.86[a] (0.15)	1.08[a] (0.20)	1.02[a] (0.11)	0.56[a] (0.22)	0.69[a] (0.15)
$t-2$	-0.15 (0.23)	—	—	-0.58[a] (0.19)	0.23 (0.25)	—	-0.10 (0.30)	—	0.30 (0.27)	—
$t-3$	0.37 (0.23)	—	—	—	0.24 (0.24)	—	0.24 (0.30)	—	-0.15 (0.28)	—
$t-4$	-0.29 (0.18)	—	—	—	-0.32 (0.19)	—	-0.50[a] (0.24)	—	0.05 (0.24)	—
Statistics										
R^2	0.96	0.96	—	0.99	0.99	0.99	0.99	0.99	0.82	0.81
Durbin-Watson	1.11	1.43	—	2.50	2.11	2.20	2.06	1.73	1.64	1.95
SE	0.024	0.024	—	0.003	0.020	0.020	0.009	0.009	1.33	1.28

[a] Coefficient is significant at the 5 percent level.
[b] With more than two lags, the autoregression for $P/\bar{P}$ would not invert due to collinearity.

Table 1.5. *United Kingdom: univariate autoregressions (standard errors in parentheses)*

Lags	e		$P/\hat{P}$		$M1$		$M3$		CAB	
$t-1$	1.10^a	1.04^a	1.41^a	1.53^a	1.08^a	0.95^a	0.91^a	0.85^a	0.12	0.12
	(0.22)	(0.07)	(0.22)	(0.17)	(0.21)	(0.12)	(0.24)	(0.16)	(0.23)	(0.21)
$t-2$	0.01	—	−0.48	−0.57	0.21	—	−0.04	—	−0.02	—
	(0.31)		(0.36)	(0.19)	(0.25)		(0.29)		(0.26)	
$t-3$	−0.02	—	0.19	—	−0.62^a	—	−0.03	—	0.02	—
	(0.30)		(0.35)		(0.22)		(0.29)		(0.27)	
$t-4$	−0.10	—	−0.20	—	0.08	—	−0.14	—	0.06	—
	(0.23)		(0.19)		(0.20)		(0.19)		(0.24)	
Statistics										
R^2	0.94	0.94	0.99	0.99	0.99	0.99	0.99	0.99	0.50	0.50
Durbin-Watson	1.7	1.64	1.96	2.09	2.11	1.59	2.11	1.69	1.92	1.96
SE	0.035	0.033	0.012	0.012	0.019	0.024	0.016	0.016	912.71	853.07

^{a} Coefficient is significant at the 5 percent level.

Table 1.6. *Japan: univariate autoregressions (standard errors in parentheses)*

Lags	e		$P/\bar{P}$		$M1$		$M3$		CAB	
$t-1$	1.18[a]	1.33[a]	1.24[a]	1.21[a]	0.79[a]	1.03[a]	1.03[a]	1.10[a]	1.25[a]	1.50[a]
	(0.22)	(0.18)	(0.20)	(0.14)	(0.22)	(0.14)	(0.22)	(0.08)	(0.22)	(0.16)
$t-2$	-0.37	-0.55[a]	-0.85[a]	-0.62[a]	-0.56	—	0.26	—	-0.32	-0.67[a]
	(0.34)	(0.18)	(0.32)	(0.12)	(0.30)		(0.32)		(0.37)	(0.16)
$t-3$	0.12	—	0.45	—	-0.04	—	-0.21	—	0.10	—
	(0.34)		(0.32)		(0.31)		(0.32)		(0.38)	
$t-4$	-0.26	—	-0.27	—	-0.24	—	-0.01	—	-0.34	—
	(0.22)		(0.16)		(0.28)		(0.23)		(0.25)	
Statistics										
R^2	0.91	0.90	0.99	0.99	0.99	0.99	0.99	0.99	0.91	0.90
Durbin-Watson	1.74	2.06	1.82	1.81	1.77	2.42	1.79	1.96	1.85	2.17
SE	0.044	0.044	0.014	0.014	0.023	0.023	0.008	0.008	0.97	1.00

[a] Coefficient is significant at the 5 percent level.

those for the United States and Germany, with one major exception. In the first regression for the current-account balance, there are no significant lag terms. Thus, the U.K. CAB is best described as random around the path described by the trend and seasonal dummy terms. This suggests that innovations in the CAB in the United Kingdom should not be interpreted as conveying information about future movements in the exchange rate.[15] This implication is reinforced by the vector autoregression results in section 8.

Both the nominal effective rate and the $M1$ money stock in the United Kingdom have coefficients of unity on the $t-1$ lag, indicating that they follow a random walk. The relative price series is again AR2, but with a stable monotonic adjustment response to disturbances.

6.3.4. *Japan:* The results for Japan are summarized in Table 1.6. There we see major differences from the other three countries. The nominal effective exchange rate, the relative price series, and the current-account balance are all AR2 with stable cyclical response patterns. The two money stocks are AR1 with unitary lag coefficients. Thus, in the Japanese case the time-series behavior of the exchange rate is consistent with that of relative prices and the current account, but the exchange rate does not follow the random-walk pattern of money.

6.4. *Summary*

The univariate autoregressions of Tables 1.3 through 1.6 provide a useful and compact description of the "facts." Comparing the country results, we see several common points:

1. All weighted relative price series are second-order autoregressions with stable responses to shocks. All but the U.K. series are cyclical.
2. All the money stocks are first-order autoregressions, many with unitary lag coefficients.
3. The exchange rate and current-account series for the United States and Germany are first-order autoregressions; those for Japan are second-order. Thus, movements in the exchange rate are consistent with movements in the current-account balance for these three countries.

---

[15] A moving average specification of the equation for the U.K. CAB was also experimented with, with no improvement in results. The U.K. CAB does seem to be random about its trend.

Table 1.7. PPP *regressions, 1974–80*

Country	Coefficients of			Statistics		
	Constant	Time	$P/\bar{P}$	R^2	ρ	Durbin-Watson
United States	9.71[a]	−0.004	−1.09	0.86	0.65[a]	1.83
	(2.49)	(0.002)	(0.55)		(0.15)	
United	14.06[a]	0.035[a]	−2.20[a]	0.91	0.58[a]	1.52
Kingdom	(1.66)	(0.007)	(0.39)		(0.16)	
Germany	13.57	−0.013	−1.88	0.96	0.83[a]	1.64
	(9.37)	(0.023)	(1.95)		(0.11)	
Japan	14.22[a]	−0.007	−2.06[a]	0.91	0.71[a]	1.43
	(4.10)	(0.009)	(0.86)		(0.14)	

Note: A Cochrane-Orcutt iterative technique with a two-stage least-squares estimation method was used; the instruments are lagged exchange rates, and lag-one and lag-two $P/\bar{P}$, at constant, time, and seasonal dummies.
[a] Coefficient is significant at the 5 percent level.

7.   Purchasing power parity

Before moving on to a vector autoregression analysis of the data for the four countries, it is interesting to look directly at the relationship between exchange rates and relative prices. The IMF data comparing costs and prices provide us with effective exchange rates, e, and weighted relative WPIs using the same weighting system. Thus, we can report regressions testing whether exchange rates followed relative price paths for the four countries in the 1974–80 period. These are summarized in Table 1.7.

In the table, we report regressions of the log of the effective rate on a constant, a time trend, and the log of the effective relative WPI. To allow for simultaneity between prices and exchange rates, the $P/\bar{P}$ term was replaced by an instrumental variable estimate, and the equations were adjusted for first-order serial correlation in the error terms.

If PPP held at all times, the coefficient of time would be zero, and that of $P/\bar{P}$ would be (-1) in Table 1.7. In no case does this pair of conditions hold. The closest case is the United States, where the coefficient of $P/\bar{P}$ is -1.09, but that of time is marginally significant. Even ignoring the difference between the AR1 in the exchange rate and AR2 in $P/\bar{P}$, PPP is violated in the U.S. case during 1974–80 by a divergent trend between e and $P/\bar{P}$. This could be due to measurement biases. In Branson (1980), it was shown that the major jump in the real exchange rate for the United States came in 1970–3; after 1974, a steady trend seems to be the dominant factor.

In the United Kingdom and Japan, the coefficients of $P/\bar{P}$ are well above unity, and quite significantly so in the U.K. case. The United Kingdom also has a very significant time trend. In Germany, neither the time trend nor $P/\bar{P}$ is significant. This is consistent with Frenkel's (1981b) finding that the real exchange rate is AR1.

The regressions of Table 1.7 thus suggest that since 1974 a deviation-from-trend version of PPP may have held in the United States, but that the relationship did not hold in the other three countries. This is consistent with the theoretical view of section 4 that the relative price path is at most a long-run average through the path of nominal exchange rates, even in periods of largely monetary disturbances.

8. Empirical results using vector autoregression

A useful technique for studying the relationships between the innovations in money, the current-account balance, relative price levels, and the exchange rate is vector autoregression (VAR). Here each variable of a system is regressed against the lagged values of all variables (including itself) in the system to extract any information existing in the movements of these variables. The residuals from these vector autoregressions are the innovations – the unanticipated movements – in the variables. We can study the correlations of the residuals to see if they are consistent with the hypotheses implied by the theory of sections 3 to 5. The vector autoregression technique is introduced and justified by Sims (1980). A clear exposition is presented in Sargent (1979). Interesting and instructive applications are discussed in Taylor (1980), Ashenfelter and Card (1981), and Fischer (1981).

Here I estimate systems of VARs for each of the four countries: the United States, the United Kingdom, Germany, and Japan. Two systems are estimated for each country. Both include the effective exchange rate e, the current-account balance CAB, and the effective relative price $P/\bar{P}$; the difference between the two is that one includes $M1$ and the other $M3$. An obvious extension of the research would be to include cross-country effects, particularly of money stocks, but also of the other variables. The difficulty in proceeding in this direction comes from the limited number of quarterly observations: twenty-eight from 1974-I to 1980-IV. Each VAR includes lagged values of four variables, a time trend, and three seasonal dummies.

Table 1.8. *Variables included in vector autoregression systems*

United States, United Kingdom, Germany	Japan
$\ln e_{t-1}$	$\ln e_{t-1}$
$\ln M_{t-1}$	$\ln e_{t-2}$
$\ln P/\bar{P}_{t-1}$	$\ln M_{t-1}$
$\ln P\bar{P}_{t-2}$	$\ln P/\bar{P}_{t-1}$
CAB_{t-2}	$\ln P/\bar{P}_{t-2}$
	CAB_{t-2}
	CAB_{t-3}

Note: Two VAR systems are estimated for each country, one with $M1$, one with $M3$. The equations are estimated on data for 1974-I–1980-IV, described in Table 1.2.

In order to expand the analysis, I am presently moving to a monthly data base.

Before estimating the VARs, one must consider the issue of the timing of the data. The effective exchange rate can be computed from public information on a daily basis. In fact, a U.K. effective rate is published daily in the *Financial Times*. Our data are averages during the quarter. Money stock data are available on a weekly basis, so they are roughly contemporaneous with the exchange rate data. Our money data are end of period. We would expect from section 2 that the weekly changes in M would generate nearly simultaneous movements in e. Thus, the innovation of the average e over a quarter would be most closely connected in our data with the innovation of the end-of-quarter money stock, which is the cumulation of the weekly innovations.

The relative price data are quarterly averages of monthly data, which become known soon after the month finishes. Thus, in our data set, the innovation in e_t would be most closely connected to the innovation in $(P/\bar{P})_t$.

On the other hand, the data on the quarterly balance in current account are not announced until well into the following quarter. Thus, to the extent that the innovation in CAB signals a change in the equilibrium real exchange rate, it is the innovation in CAB_{t-1} that moves e_t.

The VAR residuals to be correlated, then, are those of e_t, M_t,

Table 1.9. *Correlation of exchange rate residuals and other residuals from vector autoregression systems with* M1

Correlation of $\tilde{e}_t$ with own	$\tilde{M}1_t$	$\tilde{CAB}_{t-1}$	$\widetilde{P/\bar{P}}_t$
United States	−0.39	0.36	−0.37
United Kingdom	0.13	−0.14	−0.29
Germany	0.24	0.54	−0.32
Japan	0.03	0.24	0.11

Table 1.10. *Correlation of exchange rate residuals and other residuals from vector autoregression systems with* M3

Correlation of $\tilde{e}_t$ with own	$\tilde{M}3_t$	$\tilde{CAB}_{t-1}$	$\widetilde{P/\bar{P}}_t$
United States	−0.50	0.34	−0.34
United Kingdom	0.11	−0.03	−0.27
Germany	0.47	0.20	−0.50
Japan	0.13	0.39	0.28

$(P/\bar{P})_t$, and CAB_{t-1}. We will use a $\sim$ to designate residuals from the VARs. The variables in each VAR system are listed in Table 1.8. The number of lags included in each variable was determined by the univariate autogressions of Tables 1.3 through 1.6. This constraint provides a convenient way to limit the number of regressors and conserve degrees of freedom. A next step in research would be to reestimate the VAR systems with additional lags to see how much information is lost by application of this constraint.

After the VAR systems are estimated, we correlate their residuals to study the relationship among innovations.[16] The correlations of the exchange rate residuals with those of the VARs for money, CAB, and relative prices are shown in Tables 1.9 and 1.10 for the systems

---

[16] In general, the VAR equations for exchange rates include significant lagged variables other than e_{t-1}. This suggests that the foreign exchange market is inefficient, since e_{t-1} does not summarize all available information relevant to pricing of foreign exchange. Questions of exchange market efficiency are discussed in detail in other chapters in this volume; I leave this note as a side comment here.

using $M1$ and $M3$, respectively. Each row in the tables gives the correlation coefficient r of the exchange rate VAR residual with the VAR residuals of the other three variables. Given the definition of the effective exchange rate as foreign exchange per unit of home currency, we expect the money correlations to be negative – a positive M innovation lends to a depreciation – the CAB correlations to be positive, and the $P/\bar{P}$ correlations to be negative.

In Table 1.9, which presents the correlations using $M1$, the first column shows the correlations of exchange rate and money stock residuals for each country. We see that only for the United States is the sign of the correlation negative. The positive correlations for the United Kingdom and Germany, and the near-zero correlation for Japan, are consistent with "leaning-against-the-wind" policy behavior in which money growth slows when the currency depreciates, and vice versa. This type of policy reaction was discussed in Branson (1976), and policy reaction functions of this form were estimated for Germany by Artus (1976) and by Branson, Halttunen, and Masson (1977). The positive correlation in the case of Germany is thus easy to understand. Similar policy behavior in Japan has been reported in Amano (1979) and could account for the low Japanese $M1$ correlation. A U.K. policy of moving the minimum lending rates to defend the currency would also be consistent with the positive U.K. $M1$ correlation in Table 1.9. When sterling depreciates, interest rates are raised and the rate of money growth is reduced.

The pattern of money correlations in Tables 1.9 and 1.10 reflects an asymmetry in policy behavior between the United States and the other three countries. If U.S. monetary policy is formulated with domestic targets in mind, then U.S. money will be exogenous with respect to the exchange rate. This is the model of section 2 and gives the negative correlation. But monetary policy in the United Kingdom, Germany, and Japan may be reacting to movements in the exchange rate, which would give a positive correlation. Thus, the results are consistent with a view that U.S. monetary policy drives exchange rates, and the others react.

The CAB correlations should be positive, according to the theory of section 5. It should be noted that since we are correlating the VAR residuals of e_t with CAB_{t-1}, the positive correlation will not reflect "J-curve" effects in which a current depreciation in e_t causes a reduction in CAB_t due to low trade elasticities. The small negative correlation in the case of the U. K. CAB is consistent with the univariate autoregression results of Table 1.5. There we saw that the U.K. CAB is approximately random about its trend, so that innovations in CAB do not contain any information about future movements in the real exchange rate. Thus, the expected correlation for the U.K. CAB should be zero, which it approximately is.

The $P/\bar{P}$ correlations should be negative from the theory of section 3 where causation runs from $P/\bar{P}$ to e. However, they would also be negative if causation ran from e to $P/\bar{P}$ through the price of traded goods. Empirical evidence on the importance of this link is presented in Bruno (1978). Thus, the negative correlations for $P/\bar{P}$ for the United States, United Kingdom, and Germany are consistent with the theory of section 3, but could also result from reverse causation. Estimation of the relative strengths of the two effects will require more sophisticated econometrics. The positive correlation in the Japanese case is difficult to understand. The explanation may lie in the divergent behavior of export prices and the WPI in Japan, but analysis of that case will also require further work.

The correlation results of the systems using $M3$ are given in Table 1.10. They are essentially the same as the $M1$ results of Table 1.9. The correlation of the U.K. current-account balance is nearly zero, but the positive correlation for Japanese relative prices is larger than in Table 1.9.

In summary, it appears that the VAR results are (perhaps surprisingly) quite consistent with the theory of sections 2–5, which attempts to integrate money, relative prices, and the current-account balance into one framework explaining movements in exchange rates. The results are clearest for the effects of CAB innovations on exchange rates, supporting Dornbusch (1980). The money causation is less clear because of the plausibility of money reacting continuously to movements in e, as suggested in Branson (1976). The relative price results are consistent with the theory but causation remains ambiguous due to dependence of domestic prices of traded goods on the exchange rate as shown by Bruno (1978). Thus, the empirical results provide support for the theory, but there is much more econometric research to be done.

References

Amano, A. (1979). "Flexible exchange rates and macroeconomic management: a study of the Japanese experience in 1973–1978." Kobe University, mimeographed.

Artus, J. (1976). "Exchange rate stability and managed floating: the experience of the Federal Republic of Germany." *International Monetary Fund Staff Papers* 23, July, 312–33.

Ashenfelter, O., and Card, D. (1981). "Time-series representations of economic variables and alternative models of the labor market." University of Bristol, working paper.

Branson, W. H. (1975). "Comment on M. v. N. Whitman: Global monetarism and the monetary approach to the balance of payments." *Brookings Papers on Economic Activity* 3, 537–42.

Branson, W. H. (1976). "Leaning against the wind as exchange rate policy." Paper presented at Graduate Institute of International Studies, Geneva. Revised 1981 for book publication by the institute.

Branson, W. H. (1977). "Asset markets and relative prices in exchange rate determination." *Sozialwissenschaftliche Annalen* 1, 69–89.

Branson, W. H. (1979a). "Exchange rate dynamics and monetary policy," in A. Lindbeck, ed., *Inflation and employment in open economies* (North-Holland, Amsterdam), 189–224.

Branson, W. H. (1979b). *Macroeconomic theory and policy*, 2nd ed. (Harper & Row, New York).

Branson, W. H. (1980). "Trends in United States international trade and investment since World War II," in M. Feldstein, ed., *The American economy in transition* (University of Chicago Press, Chicago), 183–257.

Branson, W. H., Halttunen, H., and Masson, P. (1977). "Exchange rates in the short run: the dollar-deutschemark rate." *European Economic Review* 10, December, 303–24.

Bruno, M. (1978). "Exchange rates, import costs, and wage-price dynamics." *Journal of Political Economy* 86, June, 379–403.

Dornbusch, R. (1976). "Expectations and exchange rate dynamics." *Journal of Political Economy* 84, December, 1161–76.

Dornbusch, R. (1980). "Exchange rate economics: where do we stand?" *Brookings Papers on Economic Activity* Number 1, 143–86.

Fischer, S. (1981). "Relative shocks, relative price variability and inflation." *Brookings Papers on Economic Activity* Number 2, 381–431.

Frenkel, J. (1981a). "The collapse of purchasing power parities during the 1970's." *European Economic Review* 16, May, 145–65.

Frenkel, J. (1981b). "Flexible exchange rates, prices and the role of news: lessons from the 1970's." *Journal of Political Economy* 89, August, 665–705.

Katseli-Papaefstratiou, L. (1979). "The reemergence of the purchasing power parity doctrine in the 1970's." *Special Papers in International Economics No. 13.* (Princeton University Press, Princeton, N.J.).

Sargent, T. (1979). "Estimating vector autoregressions using methods not based on explicit economic theories." Federal Reserve Bank of Minneapolis *Quarterly Review*, Summer, 8–15.

Sims, C. (1980). "Macroeconomics and reality." *Econometrica* 48, January, 1–48.

Taylor, J. (1980). "Output and price stability: an international comparison." *Journal of Economic Dynamics and Control* 2, February, 109–32.

Perspective: On exchange rate analysis and foreign exchange risk

MARINA v. N. WHITMAN

Perspective on the 1970s

In keeping with the format of this book, my remarks will be more in the nature of a perspective on a broad topic than a specific critique of Professor Branson's chapter. I shall try to survey the development of knowledge about exchange rates and the risks associated with them over the past decade or so from three different perspectives: that of the academic, that of the government policy maker, and that of a decision maker in the corporate world.

Just six years ago our roles were reversed when Professor Branson served as commentator on a paper I gave at the Brookings Panel on Economic Activity. He began by noting, quite correctly, that my paper was "a survey, offering no new results." His chapter can be similarly characterized, although it offers something mine did not, that is, some interesting and imaginative new empirical tests of the theory he surveys. Precisely because they synthesize existing results rather than offering new ones, such discussions are extremely useful in helping us to take the measure of what has been learned about the behavior of exchange rates over the decade of the 1970s, the period that marked the shift from the pegged rates of the Bretton Woods era to the managed floating of today.

Forgive me if I refer back briefly once more to my own paper, entitled "Global Monetarism and the Monetary Approach to the Balance of Payments," because it serves as a convenient symbol of a breakpoint. Written in mid-decade, it described what I termed the "global monetarist revolution," which represented a sharp change in thinking about both the determinants and the effects of exchange rate changes. In essence, the shift was from a Keynesian flow-equilibrium approach to the analysis of the exchange rate – or the balance of payments – to a stock-equilibrium asset-market view. There were several major aspects to this change in approach, which is closely associated with what has come to be widely, if not entirely accurately, termed the "Chicago School."

First, rather than being defined in Keynesian medium-run flow terms, equilibrium is characterized by the requirements of the long-run stationary state, in which not only are there no excess demands or supplies in the system but also in which all stocks of assets are constant.

Second, this approach involved a shift in focus from goods markets to asset markets or, to put it in only slightly oversimplified terms, from the balance of trade to the balance of payments. Rather than concentrating on the trade or current account, the major focus of the Keynesian balance-of-payments analysis on which most economists over forty were raised, it stresses developments in the capital account. An obvious corollary is the shift in emphasis from real variables, including the real terms of trade or relative prices of national outputs, to concern with financial or monetary variables.

Finally, faithful to its Chicago origins, this view stresses the long-run neutrality of money, the maintenance of the so-called purchasing power parity (PPP) relationship via exchange rate changes that mirror differentials in national rates of inflation, and the endogeneity of national money supplies under fixed exchange rates. Under such a regime, a nation's money supply is not under its own control; only under flexible rates does the money supply regain the status of an exogenous or policy-determined variable.

This global monetarist approach has provided a number of important and penetrating new insights. Its major shortcoming, however, is that it assumes away many of the problems that are of interest and concern in the real world, including the problem of foreign exchange risk. For, as Professor Branson noted, if exchange rates move solely in response to changes in the purchasing power parity relationship, such behavior eliminates the risks and uncertainties associated specifically with exchange rates, although it leaves plenty of other risks and uncertainties for us to worry about.

Progress and synthesis

What makes Branson's discussion so interesting is that it reflects, with great imagination and sophistication, advances in thinking about exchange rates that took place during the second half of the 1970s, advances associated with such names as Dornbusch, Frenkel, Isard, Mussa, and a number of others, as well as his own. His analysis represents an integration of the traditional elasticities approach to balance-of-payments analysis − or its dual, exchange rate analysis − and the monetary approach, that is, between a focus on goods markets and a focus on asset markets. In that sense, it can lay truer claim to being a general equilibrium framework than can either of the two approaches taken separately.

Branson notes that it is the asset markets that determine equilibrium exchange rates in the short run. However, because rates at these short-run equilibrium values may be associated with either a surplus or a deficit on current account, the resulting changes restore the Keynesian role of goods markets in the determination of long-run equilibrium rates. Indeed, Branson's synthetic analysis even restores the pivotal role of our old friend the Marshall-Lerner condition, albeit in a "super" (i.e., somewhat modified) form.

The Branson analysis divides the variables that determine exchange rates into two groups, the first reflecting its monetarist and the second its Keynesian heritage. The first category consists of relative inflation rates, which move exchange rates along paths consistent with the requirements of purchasing power parity; the second category pertains to variables that determine changes in *real* exchange rates, that is, changes other than those that simply offset differences in national inflation rates.

Among the variables in the latter category are differentials in interest rates, and particularly in real interest rates. One implication of the analytical framework Branson uses is the ambiguity in the sign of the relationship between interest rate differentials and exchange rates. If a country has a positive interest differential, in other words, an interest rate higher than that of its partner countries, because of a higher expected inflation rate, the impact on its exchange rate will be negative, creating pressure for depreciation. If, on the other hand, the positive interest rate differential is due to some other cause, such as tight monetary conditions or a scarcity of capital for productive investment opportunities, the effect on the exchange rate will be positive, that is, associated with appreciation. In addition, these relationships are affected by the direction and speed with which expectations are changing. All this implies the need to sort things out rather carefully before using interest rate differentials as explanatory variables in empirical work on exchange rates.

Second, real exchange rates are affected by developments in a country's current account (i.e., changes in structural factors). Again, such developments affect exchange rates through two distinct channels. One is the effects of the associated redistribution of wealth; any country with a surplus on current account is gaining wealth, whereas, one with a deficit is losing it. Such changes will generally affect the nature of asset-market equilibrium. The other channel is created by the role of an imbalance on current account in signaling the need for an exchange rate adjustment on the assumption that a surplus or deficit cannot cumulate indefinitely without threatening the stability of the system.

A third group of variables, implicit in Branson's model and also explicit in some other variants of the same basic model, are the risk premia associated with desired portfolio diversification and the relative demand and supply of assets denominated in different currencies.

In addition to integrating the elasticities and monetary approaches, and the explanatory variables associated with them, into a more general framework, Branson's analysis is synthetic in several other aspects as well. First, in its stress on the determination of real and not simply of nominal exchange rates and its emphasis on the durability and importance of deviations from purchasing power parity, it restores to center stage some of the real-world concerns that had temporarily disappeared from the analytical scene, but it brings monetarist insights to bear on old-fashioned Keynesian problems. Branson notes that PPP will prevail, even in the long run, only under certain restrictive assumptions, among which the long-run neutrality of money is a necessary but not a sufficient condition.

Second, this synthetic approach incorporates both short- and medium-run flow equilibria – that is, the clearing of asset and goods markets – and long-run stationary-state stock equilibrium, as well as the dynamics of stock–flow interactions. It traces the characteristics of transition paths and distinguishes between the short-run and the long-run effects of particular disturbances. Finally, it links the present and the future via expectations. More explicitly, the model is driven by the assumption of rational expectations (i.e., that market prices incorporate all existing information about the systematic components of disturbances) plus "surprises" (also called "innovations" or "news"), or the random or unsystematic components of disturbances. Empirical work suggests that the latter tend to dominate the actual movement of exchange rates, at least in recent years.

The academic perspective: the new learning

Let me turn now to an evaluation of what we have learned about exchange rates over the course of a decade, from the three perspectives I mentioned at the beginning. The academic perspective can be quickly summarized, since most of the scholarly or analytical advances have already been discussed in the context of Branson's chapter.

First, we have seen a significant evolution in the definition of equilibrium, in the direction of complexity and comprehensiveness. Current discussions of equilibrium conditions distinguish carefully between flow and stock equilibria, and take account of stock–flow interactions. They also distinguish the determinants and characteristics of short-run and long-run equilibrium, and spell out, in some detail, the transition paths by which a system moves from one to the other. In the case of exchange rates, in particular, the determination of short-run equilibrium values in asset markets is linked, through interest rates and expectations regarding future values of exchange rates, to commodity and factor markets because the variables just mentioned affect income, expenditures, employment, and prices. And because short-term equilibrium values of the exchange rate, given values of these other variables, may yield a nonzero current-account balance, asset flows will occur that in turn affect the long-run stationary-state equilibrium value of the exchange rate, when the current-account balance is zero and all stocks of assets are constant. Indeed, all these variables and interactions will jointly determine whether such a stable long-run equilibrium does in fact exist.

Second, the new models incorporate as explanatory variables not only such monetarist ones as relative rates of inflation or growth rates of the money supply, but also real variables related to the level and composition of demand, or in Keynesian terms, income and current-account balance. Finally, they encompass risk – return considerations related to portfolio diversification, that is, to the relative supplies of and demands for assets denominated in different currencies.

Third, we have learned the importance, in any explanation, not only of the present values of explanatory variables but also of their expected future values as well. The modeling of expectations has also progressed significantly, from assuming static or regressive expectations to the concepts of adaptive and, most recently, rational expectations. Despite all this progress, my own view is that there is a lot more hard work to be done in this area.

Along with recognizing the central role of expectations, we have become acutely aware of the dominant role played by unexpected developments (innovations or news) in determining changes in exchange rates (as well as in the prices of domestic financial assets). A

corollary of this awareness is the importance of distinguishing between anticipated and unanticipated events, including policy actions,
in analyzing their effects. In addition, this approach explains sudden
jumps in exchange rates, and overshooting of long-run equilibrium
values, as being inherent in the system rather than as indications of
inefficient or aberrant market behavior.

One of the implications of these theoretical advances for the
empirical testing of hypotheses is that the appropriate variables for
explaining changes in exchange rates may not be realized magnitudes
– either the levels of explanatory variables or their rates of change
– but rather the residuals, the forecast errors, the measures of how
badly the model builder missed. As one whose responsibilities encompass a good deal of forecasting, this is a rather difficult revelation
to deal with.

These conceptual advances have brought with them significant
changes in the explanation of the observed volatility of exchange
rates. In the Keynesian view, it was "elasticity pessimism," or the
apparent insensitivity of trade flows to changes in relative prices,
that called the stability of the system into question. By the mid-1970s,
more refined estimates yielded higher elasticities and suggestions
that the Marshall-Lerner condition was met and that the system was
indeed stable. That is, it appeared that changes in nominal rates do
affect relative real rates (the terms of trade) and that these, in turn,
do affect trade flows in the direction required for adjustment, albeit
with initial perverse effects (the J curve), substantial lags, and
significant leakages in the form of feedbacks to domestic price levels.
The focus of attention now shifted to market imperfections, including
an insufficiency of stabilizing speculation, as the cause of the volatility
that continued to characterize real-world exchange rates. But, with
the passage of time, an explanation of these imperfections as temporary phenomena characteristic of a transition period, during which
speculators were at a low point on their learning curve and their
views were thus weakly held, became less and less credible.

Most recently, the view has emerged, and is reflected in Branson's
analysis, that such volatility is inherent in the system itself. That is,
it is not due to market imperfections but simply reflects the jumps
caused by rational expectations combined with the importance and
frequency of innovations, or unanticipated exogenous developments.
In this view, *such* volatility is not inconsistent with market efficiency
(although the empirical question of whether such markets are in fact
efficient is currently very much up in the air). More fundamentally,
the question of the long-term stability of the exchange rate system

remains unanswered; almost all of the models incorporating rational expectations, including Branson's, are characterized by the precarious, knife-edged stability of a saddle-point solution.

Lessons for government policy

We come next to the implications of the new learning outlined here for government policies and those who design and try to implement them. First and foremost, these integrative models tell us what most practitioners have painfully learned: Flexible exchange rates do not provide full insulation from foreign disturbances, even of a purely monetary nature, in a world characterized by high capital mobility. And if full insulation is a chimera, so too is full autonomy of domestic economic policies. Interdependence persists in a world of flexible exchange rates, most dramatically for relatively small open economies, but to a lesser degree for large and relatively self-sufficient ones as well.

The constraints of interdependence are most dramatically highlighted in the case of interest rate policy. The evidence regarding the rules that guide such policies is mixed. Some results suggest that capital flows tend to be destabilizing; that is, current and capital-account balances tend to move in the same direction, indicating that interest rate policies are primarily internally rather than externally oriented, whereas other results suggest the opposite. In any case, there clearly are some external constraints on monetary policy under managed floating, at least in the form of a steepened Phillips curve (i.e., a worsened short-run tradeoff between inflation and unemployment) caused by feedbacks from exchange rate changes to domestic price levels or inflation rates. This is the issue often referred to in the literature as the problem of vicious and virtuous circles, of inflation-depreciation-inflation in some countries and deflation-appreciation-deflation in others. All this suggests that, although the nominal money stock is restored to the status of a policy variable under a regime of fully flexible exchange rates, the real money stock may remain endogenous under either system.

Second, whether or not the relevant markets are efficient, governments may still properly be concerned with the social costs of exchange rate volatility and overshooting. But the insights of the 1970s suggest that effective means to reduce these costs may prove elusive. Exchange market intervention is likely to be, at best, marginally helpful. Some scholars argue that, used judiciously and in conjunction with appropriate domestic policies, it may aid adjustment via the expectational effects of "buying credibility," whereas others would deny it even that limited role. The main problem is that, as Branson and others note, PPP is not necessarily an accurate guide to where the equilibrium rate lies, and these models suggest no workable alternative.

Although the issue of whether intervention has a role to play in reducing exchange rate volatility remains unresolved, theoretical insights regarding exchange rate determination provide additional support for the importance of predictability of economic policy in minimizing rate fluctuations and the social costs associated with them. Increased predictability has the effect of reducing the size and frequency of innovations that produce sudden jumps in exchange rates, sharp deviations from PPP to which the real economy is forced to adjust. Beyond that, the critical role played by changes in interest rate differentials suggests a role for international coordination of monetary policies to minimize rate fluctuations, a concept regarding which agreement in principle seems to be as easy as implementation is difficult. But such difficulties have not lessened the intensity of the renewed search for stability, as increasingly sophisticated and comprehensive analytical constructs have reinforced the lessons of experience in the 1970s, namely, that flexible exchange rates, although useful and in a sense inevitable, are no panacea.

Implications for corporate decision making

I turn finally to my third perspective, that of the corporate decision maker, particularly in a large multinational corporation. The advances in knowledge regarding exchange rates over the past decade have confirmed for such practitioners the importance of *real* exchange rates and of the real changes that affect them. Obviously, the concern of major corporations with exchange-related risks has increased tremendously since the shift from pegged exchange rates to managed floating. This concern was both reflected in and reinforced by the issuance in 1976 of FASB 8, a statement of the Financial Accounting Standards Board that made the reported earnings of multinational corporations more vulnerable to short-term fluctuations in exchange rates.[1]

Actually, a multinational company faces not one but three distinct

[1] After prolonged criticism and discussion, the FASB has recently announced new rules (FASB 52) for accounting and translation of foreign operations that should significantly reduce the effect on reported earnings of short-term exchange rate fluctuations.

types of risk associated with changes in exchange rates. One is the short-term risk, affecting commercial transactions and dividend flows, associated with changes in nominal rates over a time period too short to allow for compensating changes in the prices of goods sold abroad. Companies generally try to deal with this category of risk by selective hedging, where possible, in forward markets. Second, there is the so-called translation risk associated with the effect of changes in nominal rates on balance sheet valuations. Firms attempt to reduce these accounting fluctuations by balancing financial assets and liabilities in a particular currency. Such matching efforts are often limited, however, by legal or institutional constraints, as well as by transactions costs and the underlying operating requirements of the business. Finally, and most important, there is the risk arising from changes in competitive relationships between alternative foreign locations that arise from changes in real exchange rates. Such risks are associated with the location of production and cannot be reduced by strategies affecting the sources of financing. For that reason, most major corporations, including my own, try to focus on forecasts of real rather than nominal exchange rates in making decisions regarding the location of foreign production and investment.

One of the implications for corporate practitioners of recent advances in theorizing about the behavior of exchange rates is a negative one; that is, the apparent domination of exchange rate movements by surprises, which are by nature unsystematic and therefore unpredictable, bodes a poor batting average for those who attempt such forecasts. At the same time, there is mounting theoretical evidence to support what corporations indicate by their behavior (e.g., selective hedging) that they believe intuitively, namely, that forward rates are very poor (though not necessarily biased) predictors of future spot rates. More broadly, the jury is still out on whether exchange markets are indeed fully efficient, or whether there are not gains, in the form of reduced risk, to be had from collecting the best possible information in order to "beat the market" with expertise.

Although the definition and analysis of exchange rate behavior and the associated risks have become both more refined and more comprehensive, the desired fruits of these insights remain tantalizingly elusive. And so the search goes on, on the part of governments for ways to provide insulation against external disturbances and restore domestic policy autonomy without sacrificing the significant benefits of economic interdependence, and on the part of multinational corporations for ways to manage risk and reduce uncertainty, tasks that are the focus of this volume.

CHAPTER 2

Modeling exchange rate fluctuations and international disturbances

LAWRENCE R. KLEIN

We live in constant fear of massive worldwide complications in the smooth working of the international economy. Domino effects from a sequence of loan defaults, supply interruptions of basic materials (food and fuel in recent years), strongly synchronized business cycle downturns, and military conflagration are all examples of risky events that could plunge the world into economic disorder. It is not only the risks of a general debacle, but also the risk of something adverse happening in a single country or in a single enterprise, without strong ripple effects, that interest us as well. These are the kinds of things that come to mind when we consider the subject of international risk.

As economists we must be prepared to contribute to the solution of the problems that occur in risky situations. We do not know, from economic analysis alone, when risky events will materialize or where they will occur. We do not even have a firm judgment about which items in the economy are going to be directly affected. At best, we can develop methods for helping us to decide what to do when a risky event has become a reality.

If the living laboratory of economics were filled with frequently replicated case histories, we could hope to use the laws of probability, applied to empirical relative frequencies. But my experience to date, meager as it is, is that there is not enough regularity or information that would lead to repetitive occurrence in the risky areas we have selected for investigation. We would have had to have been studying the international economic scene and observed replicated occurrences of risky situations with stable relative frequencies about the outcomes in order to make direct inferences from observation.

Unfortunately, the systematic study of risky situations does not have large data collections from which to estimate stable distributions or relative frequencies that would tell one what to expect, on average.

Thanks are due to S. Fardoust, V. Filatov, and other researchers on the staff of Project LINK for very helpful research contributions on energy prices and related markets.

85

In contrast to the adoption of a strict probability calculus for analyzing risk, I want to describe a system for coping with risk, among the many other troubled areas of the economy.

We shall not try to anticipate major risky events, and we shall not try to form expected value functions, using intuitive probability levels, for making a "rational" calculus.

Using an econometric model, or combinations of several models, we shall not be able to anticipate most risky situations, but once we have seen the occurrence of a major event, it will be useful and essential to try to interpret the economy's situation in the face of the risky event. This is a principal use of an econometric model and is the appropriate way to use it when the full force of a risky situation appears on the horizon.

1.   Some contingency simulations

Two major worldwide disturbances have occurred in large enough magnitudes and frequently enough to lead us, as students of international economics, to try to anticipate recurrences. These two disturbances are harvest failures and oil supply interruptions. Both have had their ultimate manifestation in world trade prices – price increases in food and fuel items. To some extent, there were physical allocations or other adjustments, but price rises and generation of associated market fears about uncertainties were also part of the overall economic adjustment. In addition, there were both direct and indirect effects of the massive price changes. Direct effects can be quickly estimated, often by the arithmetic of price index construction based on the relative importance of the commodities concerned. The indirect effects have been substantial. These included price rises in related lines, general inflationary pressures, balance-of-payments adjustments, exchange rate movements, and reequipping of the capital structures of the economy.

The important indirect effects cannot be easily treated by simple arithmetic rules. These effects are more subtle and ought to be worked out through complete model simulation. *Complete* is the appropriate concept since these events had economywide repercussions.

There were at least two major oil supply disturbances in recent years: the oil embargo of 1973–4 and the Iranian Revolution, which was responsible for a cutback in 1979–80. The Iran – Iraq War may be regarded either as an additional supply interruption or merely as an extension of the Iranian Revolution.

The first of the recent shortfalls in grain supply was the sequence of events associated with the Soviet harvest failure of 1972..That event was serious because the USSR purchased such a large amount of U.S. reserves that our stocks were virtually depleted during 1973. After the full recognition of this, prices rose considerably. A large harvest failure occurred again in the USSR in 1975, and smaller shortfalls have become apparent in other years.

There will be more supply interruptions in the future in these two markets, oil and grain. We do not know where or when they will occur, but we should have learned enough about their general nature from the previous encounters that we can simulate their effects on the world economy as a whole, and by strategic parts.

It is also likely that entirely new kinds of disturbances will occur. The next major disturbances of the order of magnitude of fuel and food disturbances of the past may well originate in a totally unsuspected segment of the economy. We can think about that as a possible future and simulate it, but it could also prove to be an entirely false lead. One of the frequently discussed possibilities is a wave of payments defaults in international lending. This could take the form of bankruptcy or simply restructuring of debt. Usually, application of the latter technique is interpreted as having been sufficient policy action to have averted a serious disturbance to the economy.

It is not easy to quantify bankruptcies. The cases we have had – Herstatt and Franklin National Bank – are examples of situations that bordered on being significant. They were very important for those involved, but not very illuminating. On the whole, neither case had a big societal impact. Debt default on a large scale will clearly be informative, if unpleasant, because it will tell us much about personal and social adaptation to risk that became failure.

We are, in this chapter, concentrating attention on fuel and food supply interruptions. Let us first consider oil supply cutoffs. Apart from attempting to construct, on our best judgment, trajectories of the world economy on the basis of assumed time paths of oil prices, we have computed multiplier responses to general oil price changes. These are for use as rules of thumb in judging effects quickly in new situations. The second kind of analysis is that associated with disaster scenarios. These are "What if?" calculations, based on assumptions of drastic and sudden reductions of oil supplies, presumably because of a military invasion into producing areas. The cases considered have been 50 percent and 20 percent limitations on supply, as a result of a military – political dispute. Simulations of these low-probability events are used for evaluation of risks to the

Table 2.1. *Effects of a 10 percent sustained oil price increase (nominal) over the baseline*

		1981		1980–5		1985–90		1980–90	
		Base	Shock	Base	Shock	Base	Shock	Base	Shock
OECD (13 LINK)	GDP	2.4	2.0	3.6	3.5	3.27	3.27	3.42	3.40
	PC	8.3	8.8	6.5	6.6	5.1	5.2	5.8	5.9
	X	2.3	1.5	5.2	5.2	5.5	5.4	5.3	5.3
	M	1.8	1.0	4.2	4.2	5.2	5.2	4.7	4.7
	TB	−38.0	−59.4	−7.5	−34.8	62.3	1.5	27.4	−16.7
Developing (non–oil)	GDP	4.7	4.2	5.0	4.8	5.2	5.1	5.1	5.0
	PC	30.2	32.4	20.8	21.2	11.1	11.1	15.8	16.1
	X	2.7	2.6	3.0	3.3	5.3	5.3	4.2	4.3
	M	1.6	−3.1	2.9	2.0	3.2	3.2	3.0	8.6
	TB	−80.7	−79.6	−111.9	−111.5	−218.9	−220.4	−165.4	−165.9
Developing (oil; OPEC)	GDP	5.3	5.3	5.3	5.3	6.3	6.8	5.8	5.8
	PC	18.2	18.7	10.3	10.4	7.0	7.0	8.6	8.7
	X	−2.0	−4.6	−0.3	−0.9	−0.1	0.2	−0.2	−0.3
	M	9.4	14.4	9.0	10.0	6.4	6.1	7.7	8.1
	TB	135.7	154.7	141.5	166.8	161.0	219.6	151.3	193.2
Centrally planned	GDP	3.4	3.4	4.2	4.2	4.6	4.6	4.4	4.4
	PC	—	—	—	—	—	—	—	—
	X	1.5	2.7	6.4	6.9	7.7	7.9	7.1	7.4
	M	1.4	1.9	4.2	4.4	6.9	7.0	5.5	5.7
	TB	−12.4	−11.2	−5.8	−3.8	1.1	5.6	−2.4	0.9

Note: Trade balances are in $U.S. billions; all other figures are real growth rates. In both solutions flexible exchange rates (purchasing power parity model) are used. GDP, gross domestic product; PC, consumption price deflator; X, exports of goods; M, imports of goods; TB, merchandise trade balance.

Table 2.2. *Effects of a 10 percent oil price increase in two models (growth rate derivations from baseline case)*

	1981	1982	1983	1984	1985
(Interlink) OECD					
Domestic demand	−0.4	−0.2			
Exports	−0.2	−0.1			
Imports	−0.7	−0.4			
GDP	−0.3	−0.1			
PGDP	0.4	0.5			
PC	0.7	0.5			
LINK (13 OECD countries)					
Merchandise exports		−0.8	−1.0	−1.0	−0.4
Merchandise imports		−0.6	−1.0	−0.8	−0.1
GDP		−0.4	−0.5	−0.5	−0.4
PGDP		0.1	0.2	0.2	0.0
PC		0.5	0.6	0.7	0.5

Note: These results differ from those in Table 2.1 by being obtained in a mode of exogenous exchange rates. LINK results are based on constrained 10 percent oil price increases. GDP, gross domestic product; PGDP, gross domestic product price deflator; PC, consumption price deflator.

world economy if there were price changes of the magnitude being studied (100 percent or more).

In many applications, under various combinations of initial conditions, we have found the economic responses to world oil price changes shown in Table 2.1.

These figures suggest that a 10 percent increase in crude oil prices lowers world growth prospects by about 0.25 percent, raises world inflation by about 0.25 percent, and reduces the volume of world trade by about 0.75 percent. If, instead of a 10 percent change, we were confronted by a 50 percent change, as in 1979–80, we could multiply the figures in Table 2.1 by a factor of 5.0 in order to get a quick estimate of some leading results. More complete tables and fresh system simulations with new prices could probably bring forth a better estimate of the effects, but the use of multiplier tables can be quite helpful.

These are only indicative of the results that could be tabulated. Complete listings, country by country, across a rich collection of variables can be obtained.

These results are evaluated from Project LINK under the imposition of a purchasing power parity (PPP) rule; therefore, secondary effects on payments balances, inflation, and exchange rate variation are implicitly taken into account (Klein, Fardoust, and Filatov 1981a). The system is not linear. On the other hand, it is not so nonlinear that the results are greatly sensitive to the size of the price change or to the direction of the change. The results in Table 2.1 are to be used for first approximations only; therefore, they should be interpreted only as preliminary indicators.

The results obtained in Table 2.1 from simulations of the LINK system are subject to the usual amounts of error involved in such econometric exercises. But to reduce the risk involved in such evaluations of uncertain situations, the LINK findings have been compared with similar findings from other models that have been independently specified, estimated, and simulated (Table 2.2). There is a tendency for results from a few different models to be quite similar, and this reduces the risk of relying on any one of them.

The calculations in Tables 2.1 and 2.2 are fairly standardized. More careful risk assessments have been carried out from the LINK model simulated under more specialized sets of input assumptions. To assess the risk involved in a major interruption of oil supplies, we introduce not only price changes but also physical supply limitations, where appropriate. Guidelines for these are taken from the experience gained in trying to simulate the effects of the oil embargo of 1973–4. In macromodels, with strong orientation toward analysis of aggregate demand, the main quantitative adjustment occurs in inventory change. In large-scale supply interruptions, we also introduced somewhat smaller changes for countries supplying coal or other fuels.

The main lessons to be learned from the simulation of severe cutbacks in oil supplies are as follows:

1. With a 50 percent disappearance of Middle East crude supplies to the world market, there would be a sharp depression in the industrial world; an economic interest in security of supplies seems wholly justified.

2. With a 20 percent disappearance of Middle East crude supplies to the world market under the conditions prevailing in 1981 (when countries learned to adjust better to energy shortfalls), there would be a world slowdown, but one that would stop short of a genuine synchronized recession. The quantitative dimensions of this case are laid out in Table 2.3 by main areas of the world. In the first scenario (S_1) the nominal price of oil comes back below its 1981 level by 1985 as the supply of oil from the Middle East returns to its original level of 1981. In the second scenario (S_2) the nominal price of oil stays at its 1982 level. For example, the compound

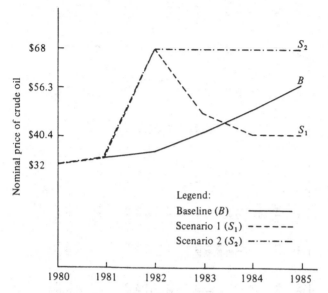

Figure 2.1.   Oil price paths in response to supply levels

average growth rate of nominal oil prices for 1981–5 in baseline, S_1, and S_2 is 12.7, 5.5, and 17.0 percent, respectively. Figure 2.1 depicts the three oil price paths.

Energy shortfalls and energy price rises of the size that have taken place during the 1970s contributed markedly to a general worldwide slowdown of a lasting nature. It certainly persists in LINK model simulations for the whole decade, 1981–90. By contrast, a harvest failure scenario is not so permanent (Table 2.4). A remarkable result of the depletion of U.S. grain reserves of 1973 was that idle acreage was brought back into cultivation through the use of economic incentives, and by 1975, if not sooner, the reserves were rebuilt. Thus, the full economic impact of a harvest failure is expected to be shorter than that of an energy supply interruption.

This kind of disturbance is not likely to create a world recession. It does not hit the import and production requirements of a whole block of industrial countries all at once. It is more temporary and dispersed. It has an impact, but one that is apparently different in kind from energy supply interruptions. We do not have, as in the case of energy scenarios, a set of similar calculations from other models that would allow us to establish extra confidence in the results.

In a more general approach to the modeling of risk in the international economy, it seems advisable to compute outcomes both aggregative for the world as a whole, and also by country or area

Table 2.3. *The effect of an oil supply shortfall on the world economy*

	1982			1983			1984			1985			1981–5 (annual rate)		
	B	S_1	S_2	B	S_1	S_2	B	S_1	S_2	B	S_1	S_2	B	S_1	S_2
Change in nominal oil prices	(10.0)	100.0	100.0	(12.7)	−30.0	100.0	(15.2)	−15.0	0.0	(16.0)	0.0	0.0	(12.7)	5.5	17.0
Change in Middle East oil exports	(−2.1)	−22.6	−22.6	(−1.4)	−8.5	−22.6	(−1.0)	5.2	−10.2	(−1.4)	6.1	6.3	(−2.0)	−5.1	−4.7
OECD (LINK 13)															
GDP	4.7	1.7	1.7	3.9	5.2	1.7	3.5	5.4	3.7	3.0	4.9	3.7	3.5	3.7	3.4
PC	6.3	9.0	9.0	6.0	4.8	9.0	5.9	5.0	6.5	5.8	5.4	5.0	6.4	6.3	6.8
X	9.7	2.7	2.7	4.3	8.5	2.7	4.5	10.5	5.7	4.4	8.6	9.3	5.1	6.8	6.1
M	5.3	−1.0	−1.0	4.3	6.9	−1.0	4.8	11.4	4.1	3.8	9.0	8.2	4.1	5.5	4.8
TB	31.0	−106.1	−106.1	23.5	43.1	−106.1	7.5	104.2	−55.1	−1.0	−36.3	157.9	7.8	35.9	−43.5
Developing (non–oil)															
GNP	5.2	2.2	2.2	5.3	7.5	2.2	5.0	6.7	5.4	4.9	5.3	6.7	5.1	5.6	4.8
PC	21.5	34.5	34.5	19.8	11.3	34.5	17.4	12.3	18.2	14.4	15.7	10.6	20.3	19.0	21.2
X	3.7	0.5	0.5	3.4	6.9	0.5	2.5	7.5	4.3	2.6	5.6	6.8	3.2	5.1	4.3
M	3.6	−22.6	−22.6	3.4	37.9	−22.6	0.0	13.4	14.4	0.4	6.6	12.6	2.6	7.6	2.8
TB	−94.2	−87.4	−87.4	−111.4	−119.2	−87.4	−122.9	−128.5	−113.6	−138.7	−123.6	−160.9	−109.8	−115.5	−112.2
Developing (oil)															
GDP	5.3	5.3	5.3	5.3	5.3	5.3	5.3	5.3	5.3	5.3	5.3	5.3	5.3	5.3	5.3
PC	8.3	10.5	10.5	7.9	8.6	10.5	7.5	5.7	9.9	7.3	7.4	5.5	9.7	9.5	10.3
X	−1.3	−19.1	−19.1	−1.0	−2.4	−19.1	0.2	7.5	−1.7	0.2	8.8	2.8	−0.8	−3.2	−2.5
M	9.0	30.8	30.8	10.0	−7.0	30.8	10.5	2.2	10.0	9.6	10.8	4.7	8.8	6.4	11.7
TB	114.7	210.7	210.7	116.8	75.5	210.7	127.1	27.6	161.1	141.4	153.0	8.1	124.0	88.2	158.8

Centrally planned

GDP	4.2	4.2	4.2	4.4	4.5	4.5	4.6	4.7	4.7	4.4	4.3	4.5	4.2	4.2	4.2
X	4.3	10.0	10.0	7.8	4.8	9.7	8.4	5.9	9.9	8.0	6.5	8.5	5.8	5.5	7.6
M	2.3	4.8	4.8	4.4	2.1	4.0	6.4	5.2	6.6	6.2	5.7	6.4	4.0	3.7	4.5
TB	−10.2	−4.3	−4.3	−6.6	−5.9	0.5	−4.6	−6.1	4.1	−2.4	−4.7	6.9	−7.4	−6.9	−1.3

World

GDP	4.6	2.3	2.3	4.2	5.3	4.1	3.9	5.4	4.9	3.5	4.2	4.4	3.9	4.1	3.8
PC	8.8	13.1	13.1	8.3	5.9	8.5	7.8	6.2	7.1	7.2	5.9	6.1	8.7	8.5	9.2
X (total)	5.5	1.7	1.7	5.1	6.6	5.8	5.0	9.7	8.5	4.5	8.4	8.7	4.5	5.8	5.4
X (fuel)	4.6	−3.7	−3.7	3.9	6.2	4.8	3.6	7.5	6.7	3.2	5.8	6.1	2.3	2.3	1.9

Note: All figures are percentage real growth rates over previous year. B, baseline; S₁, scenario 1; S₂, scenario 2; GDP, gross domestic product base 1970; PC, consumption price deflator; X, exports of goods; M, imports of goods; TB, merchandise trade balance, in $U.S. billions.

Table 2.4. *Harvest failure scenario (reduction of grain supply by 30 percent and doubling of price; differences from baseline case)*

Effects on	1978	1979	1980
OECD GDP growth	−0.15	−0.35	−0.67
OECD inflation rate (PC)	0.28	0.07	0.12
Volume of world trade	−0.8	0.81	−2.26

Note: Figures represent percentage real growth rate. GDP, gross domestic product; PC, consumption price deflator.

for different levels of disturbance and also for different patterns of disturbance. Some different patterns that have been considered are (a) a repeated sequence of harvest failures, say, one every two or three years, and (b) a path for oil prices that represents smooth growth up to a point, followed by a jump, and then maintenance of a plateau level from that point forward.

The first large harvest failure of the 1970s caught the world by surprise, especially at the marketing level, but the depletions of supply were quickly made up. After that time, there were frequent recurrences, with some good years in between. In the event, the world marketing organizations learned to adapt to this harvest cycle sequence. The subsequent shortfalls were, for the most part, more modest than the 1972 failure, and the world economy absorbed the sequence without a great deal of trouble. This would not be the case for any size failure, but it did work out all right for those that occurred and the system was not strained to its limits. The worst thing about the 1972–3 episode was that it was unexpected.

As for the oil price scenarios with a smooth path and a jump, one would generally expect to find that the smooth path is preferable. We may distinguish two cases, depicted in Figure 2.2.

If prices start at $30/barrel at point A and rise to $50 at point B (see Figure 2.2A) according to the smooth path of AB or the kinked path of ACB, we conclude that the latter is better for the consuming world, even though it takes a jump. This is evident because throughout the whole period, up to T, the price is lower along the kinked path. If, however, the kink occurs as in Figure 2.2B, it is likely to turn out that the smooth path is preferred. The kink here is much like that of 1973–9.

We have become accustomed to seeing oil prices go in only one direction − up. Events during the oil glut of 1981–2 have indicated that prices can in fact go down and that imposition of production limits is necessary to keep prices from falling. But even that may not

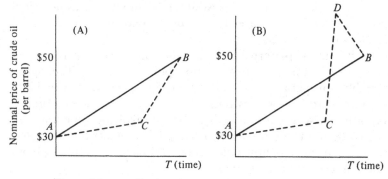

Figure 2.2. (A) Single price step; (B) double price step

be workable. Given that price declines are possible, do they deserve separate analysis? Are the effects of price declines symmetrical with increases?

The answer to the second question, after some reflection, is no, and this makes the analysis of price declines interesting, with significant international risk under present conditions. The reasons that price declines essentially are different from increases are as follows.

The decline, if occurring during the worldwide recession of 1981–2, could have a negative multiplier impact for some industrial countries who also had negative impacts from price rises. It appears that the United States, although benefiting from the antiinflationary consequences of an oil price decline, would lose so much in export volume to OPEC countries that the international repercussions would outweigh domestic benefits. This is true of other large exporting countries in the OECD group.

Many oil-exporting countries, not only those in OPEC, have geared development plans to a continued rise in oil prices, indefinitely into the future. Countries that would be adversely affected, in a direct way, from oil price declines are Mexico, Nigeria, Indonesia, the United Kingdom, the Soviet Union and Norway. These are only some noteworthy examples; others would also be hurt. At any rate, the group of exporters could pose serious problems as credit risks because they have borrowed heavily and incurred large debt service burdens in the expectation of steady increases in oil revenues. Mexico and Nigeria could pose serious questions for world financial stability in the event of a large protracted price decline. The United Kingdom may face serious balance-of-payments adjustments without the buffering effects of the revenues from the North Sea. Other oil exporters have been more prudent in their commitments: Some have large financial reserves, and some have highly diversified economies. These more favorably situated countries would, in symmetrical fashion, feel the adverse effects of a price decline but would, in all probability, not be thrown into a crisis.

Obviously, many patterns are plausible and worth considering separately. Given a model, specific entry points for strategic exogenous variables or parameters, and an on-line simulation capability from a state of readiness, it is possible to respond to the emergence of risky situations. As soon as a disturbance involving potential risk becomes evident, the model can be activated to simulate the estimated results. This, in short, is how risk can be evaluated and studied from international econometric models.

2.   Risks in statistical analysis

Risky situations have been analyzed through the workings of Project LINK and other models of the international economy. Apart from the practice of comparing estimates from alternative models to get a better idea of the range of error to be expected in the risk analyses, we may directly consider the possible error sources in using models in the indicated way.

What are the sources of error that introduce risk into the entire exercise? There are two possible errors in (a) estimated coefficients, (b) additive disturbances, (c) data inaccuracy, and (d) specification.

It is well known that the statistical equations used in econometric models have estimated coefficients that are subject to error. The LINK model, in that respect, is no exception. The errors are essentially sampling errors involved in determining the coefficients by standard statistical techniques from relatively small samples of data. There is thus a sampling error component. In a formal sense, it is possible to compute confidence regions for the joint coefficients of the models and to use these in evaluating the formulas for the standard error of forecast. The simulations are, in a general sense, forecasts. They extend the model beyond the sample in extrapolation exercises. If the formulas for the standard error of forecast are difficult to compute for a system as large and complicated as LINK, it is also possible to make replicated stochastic simulations to obtain estimates of the ranges within which it would lie. This has been done for individual country models, in particular for the U.S. component of LINK, the Wharton model, but it is such a massive data-intensive calculation that it has not been done on a broad scale for the system as a whole (Schink 1971).

Stochastic simulation of linked systems is very complicated because it must take into account the variance and covariance of error across different relationships not only within a single country model, but also between countries. There are some apparent correlations between errors of the same economic process in related but separate countries. These country covariances have an effect on the simulation outcome of system response to disturbance (Sterbenz 1981).

The formulas or numerical estimates of standard error of forecast include both sampling errors of estimated reaction coefficient and additive random disturbance. There is another source of error, and that is in the very data used to construct models and simulate them. Data accuracy is severely limited, in the best of circumstances, in countries that have outstanding data collection and distribution services. But in world modeling, the sources of data are highly variable. The degree of accuracy is not uniform.

At the top of the scale, we have the major industrial countries, where extensive data collections based on complete accounting systems are of long standing. Many researchers automatically put the United States at the top of the list in terms of overall data quality, in terms of both accuracy and comprehensiveness. The United States provides vast quantities of annual economic data, as well as many on a quarterly, monthly, weekly, or even daily basis. This is important because exchange rate analysis in the context of capital flows involves markets where the situation can change markedly from one hour to the next. Data for Germany, Japan, the United Kingdom, France, and other Western nations are of high quality and steadily improving. In many individual cases, these may have outstripped U.S. data.

But what appears to be satisfactory for the major countries is far from satisfactory for many of the smaller countries of Europe. They often lack quarterly, monthly, or other refined data series, although in analyzing problems of uncertainty, or even normal problems, short-run data on exchange rates and capital flows are of utmost significance. The data problem for the OECD countries, even in the case of ill-equipped small countries, is manageable, especially in building systems for the economic analysis of world trade and payments components. The more serious problems arise in the cases of the developing countries and the centrally planned economies. In these cases, data are sparse, sometimes poorly collected, and not generally available without a great deal of specialized research effort. This is more understandable for the poor and struggling developing countries than for the centrally planned economies. It might have been thought that the latter are "rich" in data because so much information is needed for technicians who participate in state planning ministries (GOSPLAN) for executing orders that do in fact run the Soviet system. In many respects centrally planned economies are like developing countries, and in the matter of data, they are quite similar. Centrally planned economies are only now realizing the difficulty of their tasks and the need for large amounts of detailed data on production or consumption operations in order to improve the performance of their countries. Undoubtedly, the data deficiencies of the centrally planned economies will be rectified, but it will take some time.

A notorious source of error in the world economy as a whole, including both developed and developing areas, is the failure of the sum of current-account balances around the world to add to zero! At present they add to a large discrepancy of more than $20–$30 billion per year. There are hypotheses about this observational discrepancy, but it does show that economic life can go forward with much vigor, even in the face of large international discrepancies.

At the individual country and bilateral level, there are significant data discrepancies. Country i's exports to country j are not equal to j's imports from country i, both measured for the same time period. This is due to valuation differences and some timing differences. If there is uncertainty in the trade data for individual country exchanges, then there is bound to be uncertainty at the global level. As a percentage of country activity, however, many of the observed discrepancies in the international data are large. In this sense, the errors can be more important for individual countries than for the nation because the global totals are so large that percentage errors will be small. Also, there is some error cancellation in aggregating country errors into global errors.

There are significant discrepancies not only in the trade flows, but also in the payments flows. The uncertainty in the flows of capital payments are a consequence of the same kinds of inconsistencies associated with the merchandise flows as well as a consequence of lack of reporting. Some countries report capital flows on a net basis – funds in minus funds out. Others provide detailed data on gross flows – flows in and flows out. In a few cases, bilateral capital flows, from country i to country j, and vice versa, are reported, but such data collections are not yet the rule. This gives rise to a great deal of data uncertainty.

The errors of statistical inference – sampling errors and residual variances – are straightforward, if a bit tedious to evaluate and larger than is desired, in many situations. Similarly, the errors of observation are capable of being given an order of magnitude. But another kind of error is generally recognized to be a possible source of uncertainty, though not at all easy to evaluate, either in principle or in practice. This is the error of specification: We never know if we are working with the right model. This can be a significant source of uncertainty, and it is why so many sceptics ask first, "What is your track record?" If specification error is quite serious, we would not be able to do a credible job in forecasting, and that is where forecast error is ascertainable and regularly monitored. Personally, I like the objective error analyses of Dr. Stephen McNees of the Federal Reserve Bank of Boston. Dr. McNees regularly keeps scores of errors by several different models and several different variables for each case. It is only by experimenting, testing, and using some commonsense reasoning that any tendencies toward specification error can be detected and changed. If uncertainty is to be reduced, or suppressed, it is advisable to continue monitoring systems and changing them where needed.

3. Exchange rate markets

Equally significant as the occurrence of large disturbances (oil shortfalls and harvest failures) in creating international risk has been another major event of world proportions, namely, the breakdown of the system of fixed exchange rate parities first established at Bretton Woods and administered through the International Monetary Fund. In 1971, President Nixon closed the Gold Window and later devalued the dollar. Following the Smithsonian Agreement of December 1971, the dollar was subsequently devalued again and allowed to float together with other leading currencies in the spring of 1973.

From this point forward a new element of risk, as well as a new degree of freedom in helping to establish international balance-of-payments equilibrium, was introduced into the world economy. Exporters and importers had to take into account the risk of exchange rate fluctuation in addition to the usual price, demand, and supply fluctuations when completing deals in international commerce.[1]

This risk was vividly brought home to me on the occasion of being awarded the Nobel Prize of 880,000 Swedish kronor, announced on October 15, 1980. On that day, the world press immediately reported the value of the prize in various local currencies at the prevailing exchange rate. The U.S. press made it $212,000 at a rate of 4.15 Swedish kronor per U.S. dollar. The money was handed over on December 11, 1980, and the Swedish krona had depreciated to 4.40 per dollar, making the prize worth $200,000 at time of payment. Some of the other recipients were shocked to learn about the depreciation of their expected winnings. Swedish economists noted that I should have anticipated this risk and covered it by dealing in forward markets on October 15.

Just as we try to model other endogenous variables in international economics such as exports, imports, and their respective prices, we now face the problem of providing an explanation of exchange rates. The issue does not stop at this point, however, because we shall find that in order to model exchange rates, it will be necessary to explain some particular interest rates, several kinds of associated capital flows, international reserve movements, and other closely related variables.

The biggest single problem and challenge facing Project LINK now is the inclusion of endogenous exchange rates in the system. The uncertainties of modeling exchange rates are serious and visible. The uncertainties about exchange rate projections are also just as serious. The problem with the treatment of exchange rates as endogenous variables is that it is a new and poorly understood process in the present managed float regime. Not only is the endogenous process ill understood, but it also lacks an adequate sample. Because the present system has been in effect only since 1973, a sample of annual data is much too small for making strong inferences. It is not even a very large sample at the quarterly or monthly level, when serial correlation properties are taken into account. The short-run process demands data at a short interval, but other data for the international economy are available only in an annual time frame. This is especially true of OPEC and other LDC national economy performances. Within Project LINK, we have learned to combine data of different reporting frequencies, and quarterly or monthly exchange rate models thus can be integrated with annual real models, although not without difficulty.

Exchange rate movements seem to reflect, in the extreme, emotional swings of public sentiment concerning many noneconomic events, for example, military outbreaks, crop failures, OPEC surpluses, energy restrictions, assassinations, and other disturbances to the smooth working of markets. Exchange rate projections from equation systems are likely to contain a fair amount of error, to make wide swings, and to be generally troublesome economic variables – more troublesome than projections of consumer prices, real activity, and trade flows. Thus, a new degree of freedom has been added to international economic or financial calculations, and this new degree of freedom is going to be very difficult to analyze.

The provision of two kinds of information about the functioning of exchange markets could facilitate the modeling of exchange rate movements. First, it would be useful to have more information about "intervention" in operating the managed float. How do top decision makers come to a firm conclusion? What sources of funding are they going to use?

Second, it is important to have more detailed information, at shorter intervals, about international financial flows, especially with regard to the currency denomination of transactions. Both stocks and flows are needed. It will be first necessary to build a model of international capital, one that describes transactions or distributions. Then this model, through interest rate changes and financial flow changes, will have an effect on exchange rates. That process must be modeled, but in addition, a reliable data base must be made available for a wide range of countries.

Experiments on predictive ability provide series of replicated results that enable us to sift through different performance indexes to see if some methods or persons can be found who predict endogenous exchange rates well. Risk will be measured, in part at least, by these associated error statistics, and as more knowledge and experience are gained about exchange markets we shall be able to reduce some of the risks. At the present time, we are building up a fund of experience in exchange rate forecasting, and the preliminary results look promising (Levich 1981, 1982).

At least three different approaches have been followed for introducing and generating exchange rates in the LINK system.[2] First, to make up for a scarcity of degrees of freedom, a pooled time-series and cross-sectional (cross-country) sample has been prepared in terms of normalized data (unit free variables that have the same meaning in different countries). This system consists of three equations, namely, a reserve identity, the net demand for capital flows, and an exchange rate adjustment equation. Second, a system of quarterly single-equation estimates has been prepared for each major country's (bilateral) dollar rate. Third, a system of nine detailed capital flow equations in a time-series, cross-sectional sample, together with an exchange rate equation and a reserve identity, has been estimated.

1. The use of cross-sectional data means that for each year there are as many observations as there are countries in the analysis (less one for the numeraire country, which is the United States). Multiplying the number of cross-nation estimates by the number of time periods, we find a respectable sample size, 12×4 (time periods) in the case at hand. A time indicator is used for each year, and if this is introduced simply as a variation of the constant term in the

[2] Individual country-model operators have also introduced some different approaches for their own national systems.

equation, there is loss of only one degree of freedom. If individual year dummy variables are used, a few more degrees of freedom may be lost, and if dummy variables are used to interact with response variables ("slope" coefficient changes) more degrees of freedom will be lost in the estimation process.

Individual countries may have been disturbed by singular events that could have impacted strongly on either exchange rate or capital flow. In order not to distort the average relationship a country dummy variable can be introduced. Use of general time, year, or country dummy variables cuts into the available degrees of freedom; so they must be introduced sparingly. But if a moderately large sample is available at the outset, this need not be a serious problem.

A price is paid, nevertheless, for the added degrees of freedom in a combined time-series, cross-sectional approach, namely, that the reaction coefficients in each relationship are common to all countries.

The explanatory variables used are interest rate differentials (domestic less foreign), inflation rate differentials (domestic less foreign), growth rate differentials (domestic less foreign), and the ratio of current-account balance to total reserves to explain fluctuations (from country to country and period to period) in net capital flows expressed as a percentage of total reserves. All variables are ratios or percentages. The same variables are used to explain exchange rates, but reserves are expressed as a ratio to GDP in their role as an explanatory variable. This small system is indicative and can easily be used together with the reserve identity to complement the LINK system with just three more equations. Although the equations are the same for each country, the right-hand-side variables differ for each case; therefore, different exchange rates and capital flows are estimated.

2. The small three-equation system is usable. It has provided reasonable exchange rate projections, but there is so much short-run activity taking place in foreign exchange markets that it is necessary to use a much shorter unit of account, either a quarter or a month. Quarterly equations have been estimated for each major LINK country and appended to the model. These are single equations to explain exchange rates directly and must be functions only of variables generated within the LINK system. These variables are local export price relative to the numeraire export price (typically the U.S. dollar price), interest rate differentials, (domestic less the U.S. rate), and current-account balance as a ratio to GDP.

In each case, the exchange rate is regressed against these variables for individual countries over quarterly time-series samples. An interesting aspect of these quarterly exchange rate equations is that the coefficient of relative prices – the coefficient of the logarithm of the average export price in local currency divided by the average export price of the United States in dollars – is greater than unity for some countries and less than unity for others (in absolute value) but averages to about unity across countries. This result holds for both unweighted and trade-weighted averages. A unit coefficient in a bilogarithmic equation would be indicative of the principle of purchasing power parity. In the investigation of these separate exchange rate equations, for individual countries, and in medium-term investigations from pooled cross-country, time-series samples over an entire decade (by years) we also find evidence in support of medium-to-long-term PPP. For short-run variation and accurate (to the extent possible) predictions of exchange rates, it is necessary to go beyond PPP concepts. In a sense, however, interest rate movements and balance-of-payment disequilibria are necessary concepts to explain the significant deviations that occur in the short run above and below PPP movements.

3. Something is missing from short-run and longer-term disequilibrium analysis in the list of variables considered for the direct exchange rate equations, namely, capital flows. In a superficial way, capital flows are taken into account in the small three-equation system described in (1), but that approach was used only as a first step in exchange rate analysis and a more detailed treatment of capital flows has recently been undertaken.

Some nine types of capital flows in this expanded effort are estimated as functions of relative inflation rates (again finding PPP to be an equilibrium base), interest differentials, current-account and balance-of-payment variables. Because these detailed statistics are available only on a limited basis, only the five largest countries are considered and annual data are used at this stage. To stretch the degrees of freedom as broadly as possible, a time series of cross sections makes up the sample. For the purposes of cross-sectional analysis, the data are scaled, and total net foreign assets are used as the standard scaling factor in the denominator of ratio variables. Also, the interest rate differential is adjusted for possible future variation in exchange rates. Forward and spot rates are combined to give a covered interest differential.

These capital flow equations appear to fit the sample data fairly well and provide an exhaustive set of relationships to estimate the complete balance of payments. An exchange rate equation of the usual sort with capital flow variables from the other equations completes the system and offers some hope that we may be able to account for detailed capital movements in the determination of exchange rates.

Quantitative analysis of exchange rates is clearly expanding as an area of interest and activity. As the sample experience expands, the data become ever more available and we gain more understanding of these international markets, we shall undoubtedly be able to do a better job in forecasting exchange rates and in understanding them. This element of risk in international economics will never be eliminated, but it can probably be reduced.

There are many approaches to exchange rate model construction, and, as the preceding discussion shows, many of them are being tried for use in the LINK system. Eventually the analysis will have to be quarterly in order to capture some of the short-run fluctuations that do occur. But, apart from that line of development, all the different approaches rely on some configuration or other of the same concepts and magnitudes – inflation rates, interest rates, growth rates, foreign reserves, and trade or payments balances. Simple rules such as PPP or interest parity have important contributions to make, but they cannot explain the whole of short-run movement. Somewhere in the process, official intervention must also be accounted for, because although we have the interesting market situation of a "float," which lays the groundwork for statistical variance analysis, we do not have a clean float. It is a managed float and official intervention is associated with the attempts to manage.

It should be apparent that whatever approach is ultimately adopted for generating, estimating, or explaining exchange rate movements, a great deal of the analysis will depend on monetary factors – directly through interest rate differentials and indirectly through monetary effects on inflation rates or balance-of-payments disequilibria. In addition, if the portfolio composition is directly involved, through the separate analysis of each major component of the balance of payments, we have even more direct linkage to the monetary sector. People's choices between holding domestic and foreign assets will be involved in getting finally at exchange rates.

In any event, the domestic monetary sector of each constituent model in Project LINK will be used in the explanation of exchange rates. Originally, the LINK system focused main attention on trade flows and real consumer or producer behavior. Gradually, the more elaborate country models, for the largest industrial countries, incorporated more detailed interrelationships with their own financial sectors. Now, the trend of analysis is to interrelate the financial sectors across countries, and the risks of exchange rate movements are important ingredients in the explanation of that process.

From an analytical point of view, the best results in these new research ventures are expected to come from the attempts to explain international financial capital flows, the estimation of reserve balances, and their effect on exchange rates, with all the related expectations variables and dynamics. To have exchange rates depend on capital flows may mean that we introduce uncertainty through our inability to give an accurate accounting of capital flows, either because of measurement inadequacies or because of the volatility of behavior in this area. That may lead us to rely more on single semireduced form equations for each currency that express exchange rates as direct functions of a few strategic variables. We may generate more accurate predictions this way, but we will lack some of the understanding that goes with the more elaborate portfolio analysis. We must carry out both lines of research simultaneously within Project LINK so that even if we have rather simple exchange rate equations for each major country model, we know at least the implied intricacies by which these exchange rate values are being generated within the more complete system. The ultimate system based on *bilateral* capital flows patterned, by analogy, on our present system of bilateral goods flows cannot be investigated at this stage because of data inadequacies, but the estimation of main asset and liability equations in the international sphere is a step forward in our attempts to deal with the problem of understanding exchange rate risk.

Whatever equations, either singly or in systems, are ultimately adopted, attention will have to be paid to prevailing institutions. At the present time, one of the most important constraints on the working of the system of exchange rates is the European Monetary System (EMS). In applications of single equations for direct exchange rate estimation within the context of the LINK system, we have found that some of the estimates (1981–3) for individual countries violated the bounds imposed by the EMS. Subsequently, the bounds were, in fact, broadened (in October 1981) and are very likely to be changed again in the direction indicated by the LINK forecasts. In this respect, we have not been displeased with the projections that have already been made, for events tended to bear out the results.

There is, however, an interesting methodological issue raised by the existence of institutional constraints such as the rules of the EMS. In this case, the interesting problem is to estimate the response coefficients of the equations under the restriction that the equation projections lie within the limits set by the EMS rules. This problem is solvable and is in the process of being worked out, but it has not yet been applied.

4.   Conclusions

Econometric model building often proceeds as though the system is operating in a "benign" environment. Although change and variability are important for being able to pin down econometric estimates of reaction coefficients, too much change can be troublesome. At least, many researchers act that way. They exclude "outlying" observations, either by redefining a sample in a direct sense, or by introducing "dummy" variables to explain unusual events. These treatments are special to the observation period. In the application period, pertinent to model extrapolation, assumptions are usually made that exogenous factors are going to be normal or that no major disturbing events are going to occur. Normal weather for crops, supplies of basic resources, no military disturbances, and no natural disasters are generally assumed. As I have argued, these assumptions should be made only for the baseline case. It is also important to have computed a number of alternatives.

The environment for the economy is rarely benign. In every decade since the end of World War II, there have been one or more explosive developments that had great repercussions on the economy. The 1970s seem to have been particularly turbulent and created a great deal of economic risk. For international economic analysis it was important to have modeling capability for dealing specifically with food and fuel shortages (high prices) and variable exchange rates. Fortunately for the LINK system, world trading relationships were split into Standard International Trade Classification groups that singled out O–1 (food, beverages, and tobacco) and 3 (mineral fuels) for separate treatment. This meant that prices, quantities, exports, and imports of food and fuel were separately available and estimated from their "own" equations.

Within the United States alone, the Wharton model anticipated the surge in oil imports as early as 1971. It did not have an appropriate estimate of the strength of OPEC in raising prices, but soon after 1973 an entire energy complex was built into the Wharton model to deal with the whole sector in the context of the macroeconomy. The same was true of agriculture, but the date of completion of the agricultural sector was 1976. At the national level and the international level, the risks generated as a result of supply–demand imbalances in food and energy were eventually incorporated into models as integral components. This enabled us to simulate risks of further shortfalls and extreme price fluctuations and also to study more gradual adaptation, especially in energy consumption.

The breakdown of the Bretton Woods system and the floating of exchange rates caused model builders to construct new sectors to explain exchange rate movements and the associated financial factors that are closely related. This meant that the component national models of Project LINK had to prepare more elaborate financial sectors with a spectrum of interest rates, monetary aggregates, and international financial capital flows. These were wanted in their own right and were being discussed for model-building purposes even before the establishment of the floating rate system, but their use in models became even more urgent after 1972 and again after 1973. Now we have endogenous exchange rates, which depend on interest rate differentials, inflation differentials, current-account balances, capital flows, and official intervention. This work is in the early stages and is sure to flourish, and it is stimulated by the need to bring exchange risk under control or, at least, under comprehension.

In the LINK system, some attention is already being paid to capital transfers to developing and socialist countries. Loans, unilateral capital transfers, remittances, and debt burdens are used to one degree or another in the various models. Capital transfer from developed to developing countries has figured importantly in Brazilian growth. Various forms of capital assistance have been prominent in getting South Korea and other Pacific economies to import a great deal in the form of capital goods (for growth) and soft consumer goods (for survival).

Primary importance must be attached to the efforts to explain exchange rate fluctuations in the advanced industrial economies. This work is progressing at a rapid pace, but attention must eventually be turned to the explanation of exchange rate behavior in the developing countries, too. For the most part, developing countries peg their rates to one or more large industrial countries with whom close economic ties are maintained. This is not always advantageous, especially when large industrial countries go into prolonged periods of over- or undervaluation of their currency. Witness the high dollar rates of 1981–2 and the consequent difficulties for countries who have pegged their currencies to the dollar.

Yet currency rates do show diverse movements among developing countries. Some have steady moderate depreciation policies, and some follow "maxi-" devaluations periodically when the situation becomes very demanding. Others hold their rates quite steady. An analysis of exchange rate behavior among developing countries, in both a normative and descriptive vein, is a high priority for future research.

Bibliography

Amano, A. "FLEXI: A Quarterly Model of the Japanese Flexible Exchange Rate System." *The Annals of the School of Business Administration*, no. 23. Kobe University, 1979.

Armington, P., "A Model of Exchange Rate Movement in the Short Run Under Conditions of Managed Floating." Paper presented to meeting of Project LINK, Venice, September 1976.

Armington, P., "A Closed Multilateral Model of the International Adjustment Process With No Sectoral Disaggregation." Paper presented to the International Workshop on Exchange Rates in Multicountry Econometric Models, University of Leuven, Belgium, November 1981.

Ball, R. J., ed. *The International Linkage of National Economic Models* (Amsterdam: North-Holland, 1973).

Berner, R., et al. "A Multicountry Model of International Influences on the U.S. Economy: Preliminary Results." International Finance Discussion Paper no. 115, Board of Governors of the Federal Reserve System, December 1977.

Helliwell, J. F., "Policy Modeling of Foreign Exchange Rates." *Journal of Policy Modeling* 1, 3(1979), 425–444.

Hickman, B. G., "Exchange Rates in Project LINK." Paper presented to the International Workshop on Exchange Rates in Multicountry Econometric Models, University of Leuven, Belgium, November 1981.

Hickman, B. G., & L. R. Klein. "A Decade of Research by Project LINK." *ITEMS*, Social Science Research Council, N.Y. (December 1979), 49–56.

Klein, L. R., & V. Filatov. "A Quick LINK Short Run Exchange Rate Model." Paper presented to meeting of Project LINK, La Hulpe, Belgium, September 1971.

Klein, L. R., S. Fardoust, & V. Filatov. "Indexation of Oil Prices in Medium-Term Simulations of the LINK System." Paper presented to the Stanford Conference on global international economic models, June 1981a.

Klein, L.R., S. Fardoust, & V. Filatov. "Oil Price Simulations with Fixed and Flexible Exchange Rates in the Decade of the 1980s." Paper presented to the symposium of World and Latin America Economic Projections, Caracas, Venezuela, December 1981b.

Klein, L. R., S. Fardoust, & V. Filatov. "Purchasing Power Parity in Medium Term Simulation of the World Economy." *Scandinavian Journal of Economics* 83(1981c), 479–96.

Klein, L. R., S. Fardoust, & V. Filatov. "Endogenous Exchange Rates in the Medium Term, a Weak Law of Purchasing Power Parity." To be published in a volume of essays in honor of Ivor Pearce, Southampton University, in press.

Levich, Richard M. "How to Compare Chance with Forecasting Expertise." *Euromoney* (August 1981), 61–78.

Levich, Richard M. "How the Rise of the Dollar Took Forecasters by Surprise." *Euromoney* (August 1982), 98–111.

Marwan, K., & L. R. Klein. "A Model of Foreign Exchange Markets: Estimating Capital

Flows and Exchange Rates." Paper presented at the meeting of Project LINK, United Nations, N.Y., March 1982.

Sawyer, J., ed. *Modeling the International Transmission Mechanism* (Amsterdam: North-Holland, 1979).

Schink, George. "Small Sample Estimates of the Variance-Covariance Matrix of Forecast Error for Large Econometric Models: The Stochastic Simulation Technique." Doctoral thesis, University of Pennsylvania, Philadelphia, 1971.

Sterbenz, Fred. "Stochastic Simulation of the Linkage of Macroeconomic Models and Techniques for Generating Pseudo-Random Vectors with Desirable Properties." Doctoral thesis, University of Pennsylvania, Philadelphia, 1981.

Waelbroeck, J., ed. *The Models of Project LINK* (Amsterdam: North-Holland, 1976).

Perspective: Problems in modeling international risks

PETER B. KENEN

I shall review what seem to me the contributions and limitations of Professor Klein's approach to modeling international risks and then address the specific simulations and the solutions to some problems raised by his approach. Klein begins by drawing a very important distinction between what we might call garden variety or ordinary forms of uncertainty, on the one hand, and extraordinary forms of uncertainty, on the other. Economic actors, whether they be firms, households, or governments, and economic analysts must deal continuously with the ordinary forms of uncertainty. Economic actors must make decisions without knowing exactly how the world will look tomorrow. Economic analysts must make forecasts and recommendations without knowing exactly how the economy functions.

In technical terms, our forecasts and recommendations are or ought to be presented as best guesses, but they should be accompanied by some indication of the likelihood that we are right or wrong and of the extent to which we may be wrong. The best advice I have received came from a policy maker years ago. I had written a paper and appended a long technical memorandum. "I don't need all that," he said. "I just want to know one thing: What happens to me if I take your advice and you turn out to be wrong? You want me to climb out on a limb. I want to know how high and long that limb is." In most instances, we can make useful statements about the likelihood that we are wrong and about the consequences of being wrong. Reverting to the jargon once again, we know something about the error terms that attach to our equations and thus the error terms that surround our forecasts.

The events of the last decade, however, have caused us to worry about the extraordinary forms of uncertainty: surprises that are very large and different from previous experience. They are extraordinary in two ways: It is hard to judge from previous experience how frequently they will occur and almost impossible to judge when they will occur. It is also very hard to judge from previous experience how economies will respond to them. In his chapter, Klein deals mainly with the second problem. He tries to judge from experience how the economy is likely to respond to a very large and unpleasant shock. He uses what we know about economic behavior – the information embodied in a large econometric model – to domesticate extraordinary shocks and get some feel for the ways in which these events are digested by the economy. That is essentially what a simulation does. It permits us to replicate in a controlled framework an event that lies outside previous experience.

This approach is useful, and Klein is a master of the technique. But I have misgivings about the quality of the information that the method can provide. I can best present my main reservation by asking you to pretend that you are back in the first week of October 1973. You awake and are told that war will break out in the Middle East within twenty-four hours, that it will result in a partial embargo of oil exports to the United States and the Netherlands, and that it will be followed within three months by an extraordinarily large increase in the price of oil. Had you run to your computer to ask about the consequences of these shocks, how much would you have learned? Could you have conducted a simulation of the sort that Professor Klein has run, using a model of 1973 vintage?

I am not an expert on the history of the LINK model. What little I know, however, leads me to believe that, groping for a handle on the problem in 1973, it would have been hard for Professor Klein to locate an appropriate entry point for the shocks themselves. The model probably did not contain an adequate energy sector in 1973. Had there been one, moreover, it would probably have underestimated supply and demand responses.

Let me put my point thus: If Professor Klein were to resurrect the LINK model of 1973 vintage and run the sorts of simulations he describes, the model might not tell a story comparable to the one told in Table 2.1 of his chapter.

Econometric models summarize experience. In consequence, we cannot expect them to describe precisely the effects of shocks that have not happened previously. The economy has not been forced to cope with them. Econometricians have not been inspired to allow for them. Once a shock occurs, of course, two learning processes are set in motion. First, economic actors learn from the experience and position themselves to deal more effectively with a repetition of the shock. In that sense, an event that was once extraordinary becomes quasi-ordinary. We store it in our memories and take measures to minimize its costs. Second, econometricians learn from the experience, revising not only the parameters but also the structure of their models in order to be able to domesticate the disturbance and treat it henceforth as part of the environment with which we normally deal.

Consider another shock to which Professor Klein alludes. If we were to awake tomorrow and learn that the six largest LDC debtors had sent out telexes saying that they could no longer service their debts, how would we go about modeling the consequences? We would know how to do it in 1990, but only because of our experience in 1982.

The approach that Professor Klein describes is useful once the unexpected has occurred and we have some sort of handle on the problem of modeling and responding to it. It is less useful for dealing with these disturbances that pose the gravest dangers. Is there a solution to the problem? I am not sure. It would perhaps be useful to assemble a team consisting of professional Cassandras and skillful econometricians and ask them to model the worst of all possible worlds. Seriously, the task of dealing with the first occurrence of a shock may be the most challenging task that faces us as we think about the future uses of large-scale models.

I turn now to some smaller points and some of the issues that Professor Klein has raised. He has told us that the effects of a 50 percent increase in the price of oil would be about five times as large as those of a 10 percent increase. In other words, his model is approximately log linear. I wonder whether this describes the world well. When dealing with fairly small disturbances, we can achieve simplicity at small cost by imposing linearity or approximate linearity on our behavioral relationships. When departing from the range of previous experience, we should perhaps try hard to introduce nonlinearities deliberately, rather than try to avoid them. I find it difficult to believe that a 100 percent increase in the oil price can be described as being ten times as large as a 10 percent increase. I do not know when nonlinearities begin to creep in. I do think we should try to capture them.

I have another question. To whom is this sort of simulation useful? Whose anxiety is reduced by reading Table 2.1? The anxiety of the private-sector actor is not much reduced by the information it provides. The anxiety of the public-sector actor, by contrast, may be much reduced because the table says something about the steps that must be taken to minimize or mitigate the costs of a large shock. Putting my point in different terms, private-sector actors need to know not only what an oil price shock can do to the world economy with all other things held constant. They also need to know how the policy maker will respond to that shock. They may be interested in knowing that the growth rate of the GNP will fall by one-half of 1 percent in the absence of a policy response, but they are more interested in knowing by how much it will change after the policy response has occurred.

My point is quite general, and it is one that has bothered me for a long time. When we engage in economic forecasting, even in projections as distinct from predictions, our largest problems arise in modeling policy responses and feeding them in as quasi-endogenous reactions to exogenous disturbances. At one point, Professor Klein refers to the track records of various models. I would be interested in the reasons for good and bad track records. When a particular model does badly, it seems to me important to ask whether it did badly because the underlying structure of the model was inadequate or because the model was fed bad guesses about the exogenous variables and particularly about policy variables. A perfectly good model will make absolutely absurd predictions if it is told that a policy maker has absolutely absurd intentions. In short-term macroeconomic forecasting, of course, the greatest uncertainties frequently attach to the policy variables. Will the Federal Reserve speed up the growth rate of the money supply?

I am not suggesting that one can completely endogenize Mr. Volcker. That would be a tall order. I am suggesting that, from a standpoint of risk reduction for the private sector, two-stage simulations are needed. One would tell the oil price story. The other would describe the consequences under various policies: the accommodating policies of 1973–4 and the nonaccommodating policies of 1979–80. This suggestion does not diminish the contribution of Table 2.1. It contains the essential first stage. We cannot begin to ask what sort of policy response is necessary until we have taken that step. There is a distinction to be drawn, however, between projections that are useful for public policy purposes and those that are useful for risk reduction on the part of private economic actors.

Professor Klein ends with an interesting discussion of a problem that requires much more attention. How should we endogenize floating exchange rates? I am unhappy with what we have been doing. We have paid too much attention to short-term fluctuations. Sensible experts in finance would not try to forecast bond prices or stock prices from week to week or month to month. Those same experts, however, have been trying to forecast exchange rates on this same short-term basis. Having failed rather badly, moreover, they have covered their defeat with seemingly profound assertions about the importance of "news" and the need for predictable monetary policies. They are right, of course, about the short run. But we knew that all along. What is worse, they have been misled by their own findings. Having failed to predict short-run changes in exchange rates, they should not stop trying to identify the forces that influence exchange rates in the long run or, for that matter, in the medium run emphasized by most macroeconomic models.

The emphasis on short-term forecasting is perhaps symptomatic of a larger problem. In my view, we have put too much emphasis on forecasting at the expense of hypothesis testing. We tend to conduct our hypothesis testing as a by-product of our forecasting. We tend then to say that a particular hypothesis is acceptable because it satisfies some overall measure of goodness of fit, and we hope that it will continue to work two periods from now. Hypothesis testing should go forward separately, using techniques somewhat different from those we use to choose between forecasting equations. Hypothesis testing, for example, can use cross-sectional techniques.

There has been some work of the sort I seek. Some interesting work has been done, for example, on the existence and size of risk premia – on the substitutability between assets denominated in different currencies. There has been some interesting work on the effects of official intervention. But much more work is needed. Professor Klein and his colleagues cannot wait until this work is finished. They need exchange rate equations to close the LINK model. I am a bit unhappy, however, about the way in which exchange rates are determined in Klein's simulation. When dealing with a real disturbance, such as an increase in the price of oil, one should not suppose that purchasing power parity will hold, even in the long run. If I understand matters correctly, moreover, the simulations tell a rather strange story. The exchange rate between the U.S. dollar and the Saudi riyal must move eventually to offset the difference between the increase in Saudi export prices (which is, of course, the increase in the price of oil) and the increase in U.S. export prices. Is this a sensible prediction? What are its implications for the price and current-account effects of an increase in the price of oil? I should like to see another simulation, one with fixed exchange rates, to understand completely what is happening here.

CHAPTER 3

International portfolio diversification

HAIM LEVY AND MARSHALL SARNAT

1. Introduction

The purpose of this chapter is to assess the degree to which international portfolio diversification can reduce risk. Clearly, the potential gain depends, inter alia, on the correlations among the security returns of various countries, which in turn is a function of the degree of integration between their capital markets. Similarly, the size of the gain also depends on the country of residence (i.e., currency viewpoint) of the investor.

Although fluctuations in foreign exchange have always been a source of potential financial risk, the two decades prior to 1970 were characterized by relatively stable exchange rates between the highly developed nations. Under the Bretton Woods system, changes in exchange rates tended to be relatively large, but infrequent. Today almost all the major currencies are free to fluctuate (at least to some extent) against the U.S. dollar. This underlying change in the international monetary order has significant implications for international portfolio investment, and in order to reflect the influence of floating exchange rates our empirical study focuses on a comparison of the 1960s (the Bretton Woods period) with the 1970s (a period of sharply fluctuating exchange rates).

The nominal and real (i.e., inflation-adjusted) returns of an international cross section of currencies, short-term debt instruments, and risky securities and their correlations have been estimated for the two decades in question from the viewpoints of American and foreign investors. These returns were then used to estimate the potential gains from international diversification among foreign securities for highly developed countries, for example, the United States and West Germany, as well as for countries with less-developed capital markets, such as Israel.

2. Risk and the return on holding foreign currency

The fluctuations in the exchange rates of eight major currencies (sterling, Swiss francs, Italian lire, French francs, Japanese yen,

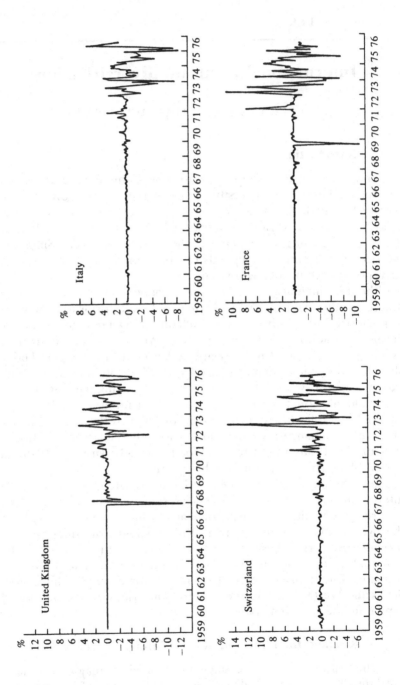

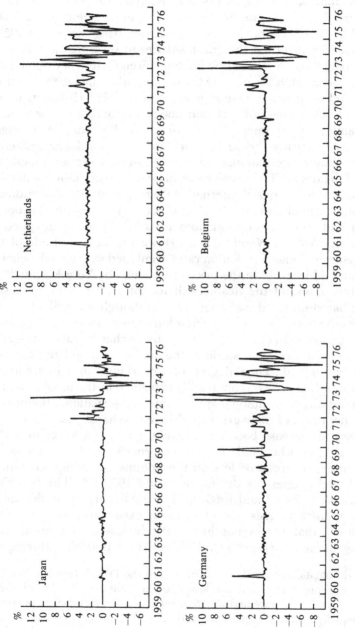

Figure 3.1. Monthly percentage change in exchange rate relative to the dollar

German marks, Dutch guilders, and Belgian francs) are illustrated in Figure 3.1, which graphs the monthly percentage gains or losses earned by U.S. holders of those currencies during the period 1959–76. A cursory glance at the graph suffices to show that a significant return could not be earned by holding foreign currency during the decade of the 1960s because the fluctuations in exchange rates during the period in question were in general negligible.[1] However, under the combined impact of inflation and a weakening of the dollar's acceptability as an international currency, this situation changed dramatically during the 1970s. Early in 1970, the dollar weakened and the major international markets began to sense an impending crisis of the dollar. The massive speculative currency movements that followed led to a series of international agreements (the Smithsonian, the Committee of Twenty, the Committee of Ten, and the European Snake) and successive devaluations of the U.S. dollar designed to salvage the Bretton Woods system. However, the magnitude of the divergence in domestic inflation rates, combined with the oil embargo and fourfold increase in the price of oil after the Yom Kippur War, appeared to sound the death knell for an international monetary system based on fixed exchange rates. Although it is still a bit early to assess the performance of the new international monetary arrangements, the subsequent instability of the exchange rates of several leading currencies (e.g., sterling, the Italian lira, and the German mark) has introduced a degree of uncertainty into international economic relations that is not readily explained by the usual economic considerations or traditional approaches to international finance.

The net result of these greatly enhanced exchange rate movements has been to increase both the potential gains and losses to a U.S. dollar investor who holds foreign currencies. Table 3.1 quantifies the cumulative profit or loss on the holding of foreign currencies for selected subperiods during the years 1959–73. The two early subperiods, 1959–61 and 1966–8, illustrate the argument that, prior to the monetary crisis, the changes in exchange rates were of a magnitude that would not justify the inclusion of non–interest-bearing foreign currency in a U.S. investor's portfolio. During the

---

[1] The devaluation of sterling in 1967 and of the French franc in 1969, of course, represents significant losses to the American holder of those currencies. These once-and-for-all losses cancel for all practical purposes the equally sporadic gains from holding marks and guilders, so that the average monthly rate of return on a balanced portfolio of the eight currencies during the period in question is not significantly different from zero, even when transaction costs are ignored.

Table 3.1. *Total gain or loss to a U. S. investor from the holding of non–interest-bearing foreign currencies, selected periods, 1959–1973 (in percent)*

Currency	Feb. 1959–Dec. 1961	Jan. 1966–Dec. 1968	Jan. 1971–July 1973	Aug. 1973–Dec. 1973	Jan. 1971–Dec. 1973
Belgian francs	0.44	−1.00	38.49	−13.9	20.22
French francs	0.00	−1.01	33.72	−12.32	17.25
German marks	4.50	0.25	55.10	−12.99	34.96
Italian lire	0.13	0.19	6.50	−3.78	2.48
Japanese yen	−0.50	0.89	35.76	−5.91	27.73
Dutch guilders	4.72	0.00	38.40	−7.97	27.37
Swiss francs	−0.23	0.47	50.59	−11.65	33.05
U.K. pounds	0.00	−14.29	4.98	−7.55	−2.95

two-year period from 1971 to 1973, an American investor could have earned a significant profit by holding all but one of the eight foreign currencies included in our sample. However, in the last five months of 1973, the holding of foreign currencies produced a loss to an American investor in all cases. The fluctuations in foreign exchange rates did not abate after 1973. Indeed, the uncertainty regarding both the magnitude and direction of exchange rate fluctuations has continued to be a significant factor in international investment.

In order to isolate the risk–return characteristics of exchange rate fluctuations, monthly rates of return on the holding of eight foreign currencies, from the viewpoint of an American investor, were calculated as follows:

$$R_{jt} = \frac{M_{jt} - M_{jt+1}}{M_{jt}}.$$

where M_{jt} denotes the exchange rate of the jth country in month t expressed in terms of that currency per U.S. dollar and R_{jt} denotes the rate of return earned by an American investor from holding the jth country's currency in month t. A correlation matrix among the monthly rates of return of the eight countries was calculated, and the variances and covariances were used in all subsequent computations.

Mean monthly rates of return and standard deviations for the currencies of eight countries are given in Table 3.2. In the two time periods prior to 1970, the return to an American investor on the holding of foreign currencies was either negligible or negative.

Table 3.2. *Mean monthly rates of return and standard deviations of foreign currencies, selected periods, 1965–1973 (in percent)*

Currency	Oct. 1965–April 1968		May 1968–Oct. 1970		Nov. 1970–April 1973		July 1971–Dec. 1973	
	Mean rate of return	Standard deviation	Mean rate of return	Standard deviation	Mean rate of return	Standard deviation	Mean rate of return	Standard deviation
Belgian francs	0.00	0.17	0.00	0.29	0.72	2.20	0.67	3.23
French francs	−0.04	0.22	−0.36	1.90	0.66	2.29	0.58	3.20
German marks	0.01	0.24	0.32	1.43	0.85	2.12	0.92	3.63
Italian lire	0.01	0.10	0.01	0.29	0.18	0.99	0.10	1.59
Japanese yen	0.00	0.82	0.04	0.15	1.02	2.37	0.85	2.60
Dutch guilders	−0.02	0.19	0.02	0.27	0.67	2.32	0.84	3.47
Swiss francs	−0.02	0.25	0.01	0.35	1.02	3.15	0.84	3.60
U.K. pounds	−0.47	2.22	0.00	0.27	0.15	1.76	−0.11	2.13

Note: Mean rate of return is expressed as arithmetic mean.

However, during the thirty-month period from November 1970 to April 1973, the mean monthly rate of return generated by exchange rate fluctuations was significantly positive for all currencies with the exception of sterling, reaching an annual rate of over 10 percent in some cases. The magnitude of the return on holding foreign currency can be placed in better perspective by comparing it with the rate of return earned by investors in the portfolio of common stocks represented by the Standard and Poors' Common Stock Index. In the period from November 1970 to April 1972, the monthly return on the Standard and Poors' stocks was relatively high (1 percent), but even in this case, the same return could have been earned by simply holding *non–interest-bearing* bank accounts of Japanese yen or Swiss francs. In the other period examined (July 1971–December 1973), all currencies (with the exception of sterling) provided a higher rate of return than did the Standard and Poors' Index.

3. The gains from currency diversification

To this point we have treated the various currencies as *mutually exclusive* options confronting a potential American investor. It is the essence of portfolio theory, however, that risk can be reduced by combining a number of investment options in a portfolio. Thus, even though the mean rate of return and standard deviation on holding U.S. dollars are zero from the viewpoint of American investors, they might still benefit from holding a diversified currency portfolio comprised of dollars and various foreign currencies. Following Markowitz (1952), overall portfolio risk (variance) can be reduced, with the degree of risk reduction being inversely related to the degree of correlation. Thus, the covariances among alternative returns, and not just their own dispersions, are germane to the portfolio problem. In order to carry out an empirical simulation of the potential benefits from the diversification of non–interest-bearing currency holdings, we first calculate the set of *efficient* portfolios; an efficient foreign currency portfolio is defined as a combination of currencies of various countries that maximizes the rate of return for a given variance (standard deviation). The locus of all such points comprises the efficiency curve, with each point on the curve representing a particular combination of investment proportions in various countries' currencies.[2]

---

[2] The locus of efficient points (portfolios) was found by deriving the investment proportions X_i, which minimize the variance of the portfolio for given expected rates of return. Formally the problem can be stated as

Table 3.3. *Composition of optimal foreign currency portfolios for selected periods (in percent)*

	Portfolio A (1968–1970)	Portfolio B (1970–1973)	Portfolio C (1971–1973)
German marks	7	29	18
Japanese yen	81	71	82
Dutch guilders	4	—	—
Swiss francs	8	—	—
Mean monthly rate of return	0.06	0.97	0.86
Standard deviation	0.14	2.23	2.57

If we now offer the American investor the further opportunity of holding U.S. dollars, the locus of efficient foreign currency portfolios, following Tobin (1958) (see section 5), can be reduced to a single *optimal* portfolio. Such a portfolio represents the *optimal* combinations of risky foreign currency in each period for those investors who also decide to hold some proportion of their cash assets in U.S. dollars.

Table 3.3 gives the composition of the optimal foreign currency portfolios in each of the three periods studied. During the early 1970s, the optimal foreign currency portfolio was comprised of varying proportions of only two currencies – the Japanese yen and the German mark. This represents a significant change relative to the period before the monetary crisis. Although the portfolio for the 1968–70 period also includes a high proportion of Japanese currency (81 percent), the remainder of the portfolio is made up of Swiss

follows. Find the vector X that minimizes the portfolio variance $\sigma_R^2 = X'\Sigma X$ subject to the following constraints:

$$X_i \geqq 0_{(i = 1, 2, \ldots, 8)}$$
$$X'R = E$$
$$X'1 = 100$$

where X_i denotes the proportion of the portfolio invested in the ith country's currency, Σ denotes the variance–covariance matrix of the rates of return on holding the currencies of countries $i, j(i, j = 1, 2, \ldots, 8)$, and R_i denotes the average rate of return on holding the ith country's currency, so that $X'R$ represents the portfolio rate of return for a given vector of investment proportions X. The final constraint, $X'1 = 100$, ensures that the investment proportions of the portfolio of foreign currencies add to 100 percent. The latter constraint is tantamount to assuming the absence of short sales.

Table 3.4. *Intercurrency correlation coefficients for the period November 1970–April 1973 (in percent)*

	1	2	3	4	5	6	7	8
1. Belgium	1.000	0.890	0.919	0.740	0.927	0.969	0.870	0.593
2. France		1.000	0.849	0.707	0.586	0.839	0.809	0.586
3. Germany			1.000	0.558	0.867	0.928	0.931	0.530
4. Italy				1.000	0.629	0.727	0.593	0.477
5. Japan					1.000	0.882	0.784	0.529
6. Netherlands						1.000	0.928	0.501
7. Switzerland							1.000	0.451
8. United Kingdom								1.000

francs, German marks, and Dutch guilders. But as we have already noted, the return on foreign currency during this early period was negligible: The mean monthly rate of return of the optimal portfolio was only 0.06 percent (i.e., an annual return of less than 1 percent).

The post–monetary crisis portfolios B and C are more representative of current exchange rate fluctuations; the expected rate of return on each of these portfolios is about 1 percent a month. At first glance, it is surprising that such strong currencies as the Swiss franc and Dutch guilder are not included in the optimal portfolio. Looking back at Table 3.2, it can be seen that in the period 1970–73 (portfolio B) the average monthly rate of return on both the Swiss franc and the Dutch guilder was 0.84 percent, that is, almost the same rate of return as the yen. But, despite these relatively high returns, the guilder and the Swiss franc are not included, even in small proportions, in the optimal portfolios B and C.

An explanation for this somewhat paradoxical result can be found by examining the co-movements of the exchange rates. Table 3.4 sets out the intercountry correlation coefficients for the period November 1970–April 1973. The coefficient of correlation between the rates of return of the German mark and the Dutch guilder was 0.928, whereas that for both the mark and the Swiss franc was 0.931. (The relevant figures for the period July 1971–December 1973 are 0.913 and 0.823, respectively.) Thus, there was an almost perfect positive correlation among the returns from holding marks, Swiss francs, and guilders. In such cases, only one representative of the group will, in general, be included in the efficient portfolio, because the inclusion of the others would not significantly reduce the portfolio's risk.

4.   The gains from currency diversification: interest-bearing deposits

To this point we have limited the analysis to combinations of non–interest-bearing currencies held by U.S. investors. Clearly both of these assumptions are unduly restrictive. Broadly speaking, investors in all countries are (or should be) concerned with the potential benefits from international diversification; independent of their countries of origin, individual investors (or companies) who hold foreign currency typically receive interest on their deposits and a capital gain (or loss) as a result of exchange rate fluctuations.

Let us now denote by $M_{ij,t}$ the exchange rate between currencies i and j at time t, expressed in units of currency j per one unit of currency i. The first index, i, designates the investor's country of origin (viewpoint currency) and the second index, j, designates the foreign currency. Now suppose that investor i decides to hold foreign currency j. One unit of currency i will purchase $M_{ij,t}$ units of currency j in period t. After one holding period the investor converts back to the domestic currency and receives $M_{ij,t}/M_{ij,t+1}$. Thus, the rate of return from exchange rate fluctuations is

$$R^c_{ij,\,t} = \frac{M_{ij,\,t} - M_{ij,\,t+1}}{M_{ij,\,t+1}}$$

where the superscript c denotes capital gain (or loss). However, if we further assume that the holding of foreign currency earns interest at the rate of $R_{j,t}$ the unit of foreign currency holdings increases (in terms of the foreign currency j) to $M_{ij,t}(1 + R_{j,t})$ during the period. When this end-of-period amount is converted into domestic currency i at the rate $M_{ij,t+1}$, the investor nets a *total* return of

$$R_{ij,\,t} = \frac{M_{ij,\,t}(1 + R_{j,t})}{M_{ij,\,t+1}} - 1$$

$$= \left(\frac{M_{ij,\,t}}{M_{ij,\,t+1}} - 1\right)(1 + R_{j,\,t}) + R_{j,\,t}$$

$$= R^c_{ij,\,t}(1 + R_{j,\,t}) + R_{j,\,t}$$

$$= R^c_{ij,\,t} + R_{j,\,t} + R^c_{ij,\,t}\,R_{j,\,t}$$

Thus, the total return is the sum of the exchange rate capital gains return $R^c_{ij,\,t}$, the interest rate on currency j for the holding period $R_{j,t}$, and the cross product $R^c_{ij,\,t}\,R_{j,t}$, which represents the exchange rate gain (or loss) on interest income (see Levy 1981).

Monthly and quarterly rates of return were then calculated for a sample fifteen currencies, from the various country viewpoints, with each investor permitted to diversify holdings over fourteen foreign currencies.[3] The data on exchange rates and representative domestic interest rates for each country were taken from the IMF *International Finance Statistics*.

Table 3.5 sets out the mean monthly rate of return on interest-bearing holdings· of foreign currency for the period 1970–8 from the viewpoints of U.S. and Israeli investors.[4] In the case of U.S. investor holdings of domestic currency, the average rate of interest earned on U.S. Treasury bills during the period was 0.48 percent. It is noteworthy that in all instances the U.S. investor could have increased returns by holding foreign currency deposits: The rate of return to a U.S. investor on such deposits, in all but three countries, exceeded the domestic U.S. interest rate. The exceptions were Brazil, Israel, and South Africa. However, the increase in return could be obtained only by increasing the risks of exchange rate fluctuations, which of course creates the necessary conditions for diversifying over foreign currencies.

The impact of the exchange rate on the return earned by holders of foreign currencies can be clearly discerned by examining the last two columns of Table 3.5, which set out the mean monthly returns (and standard deviations) on the holdings of interest-bearing foreign currency deposits from the viewpoint of an Israeli investor. Although the domestic interest rates remain the same independent of an investor's country of origin, the return to an Israeli investor was considerably higher than that earned by an American holding the same foreign currency deposit. Thus, an Israeli earned a monthly return from the holding of Swiss franc deposits of over 3 percent per month (!) during the period 1970–8, compared with the 1.34 percent return enjoyed by American holders of the same deposits of Swiss francs. Clearly the enhanced returns, and standard deviations from the Israeli investor's viewpoint, reflect the greater volatility of the Israeli currency.

These viewpoint returns on interest-bearing deposits were used as

---

[3] The sample includes the eight currencies included in Tables 3.1–3.4, plus the United States, Australia, Brazil, Israel, Norway, South Africa, and Sweden. The reader should note that for *each* country viewpoint only fourteen of the fifteen currencies are "foreign," the remaining currency unit representing that country's domestic currency.

[4] The same data from the viewpoints of the remaining thirteen countries are given in the Appendix.

inputs to generate the mean–variance set of efficient foreign currency portfolios for the investors of various countries. In order to reduce each investor's efficient set to a single optimal portfolio choice, each investor was also given the opportunity to hold a riskless domestic asset (e.g., U.S. Treasury bills for American investors, U.K. Treasury bills for English investors, and so on) in addition to the opportunity of holding risky deposits of foreign currencies. As Sharpe (1964) and Lintner (1965) have shown (see section 5), the inclusion of riskless lending and borrowing opportunities reduces the efficient locus to a single "optimal" point.

Table 3.6 sets out the composition of the optimal portfolios of interest-bearing foreign currency holdings from the viewpoints of the investors of six countries, the United States, Belgium, France, Italy, the Netherlands, and the United Kingdom, using the 1970–8 returns (interest plus exchange rate gains or losses) for our sample of deposits in fourteen countries.[5]

In all instances a diversified portfolio strategy is optimal, which again illustrates the importance and desirability of risk reduction. Although six different viewpoints are considered, the optimal portfolios of all countries are concentrated in three currencies: German marks, Japanese yen, and Swiss francs. In most instances the mark and Swiss franc comprised over 85 percent of the portfolio with the remainder in yen. U.S. investors are somewhat of an exception to this pattern: The yen comprised 21 percent of the optimal portfolio from their viewpoint.

5.   The gains from diversification: risky securities

To this point we have examined the increase in risk and uncertainty generated by the enhanced fluctuations that have characterized the exchange rates of even the leading industrial nations since the beginning of the decade of the 1970s. Clearly, exchange risk presents a challenge to financial managers, and many firms have responded to this challenge by diversifying their foreign currency holdings.

In this section we turn to a parallel challenge that confronts investors in risky securities, that is, in common stock. For simplicity let us define the rate of return on risky investments in each country

[5] Once again, note that the "foreign currency" portfolio of each of the countries does *not* include its own domestic currency. Thus, in each case the relevant opportunity set is comprised of only fourteen of the fifteen currencies included in the sample.

Table 3.5. *Mean monthly rates of return and standard deviations on interest-bearing foreign currency holdings from U.S. and Israeli investors' viewpoints, 1970–1978 (in percent)*

Currency	U.S. viewpoint		Israeli viewpoint	
	Rate of return	Standard deviation	Rate of return	Standard deviation
Belgian francs	1.06	3.00	2.84	7.47
French francs	0.95	2.85	2.72	7.26
German marks	1.17	3.11	2.96	7.64
Italian lire	0.54	2.31	2.32	7.22
Japanese yen	1.24	4.65	3.03	8.40
Dutch guilders	1.07	3.05	2.85	7.53
Swiss francs	1.34	3.42	3.15	8.09
U. K. pounds	0.49	2.39	2.25	6.99
U. S. dollars	—	—	2.25	6.68
Australian dollars	0.66	2.71	2.43	7.26
Brazilian cruzeiros	0.27	5.43	2.04	8.66
Canadian dollars	0.43	1.11	2.20	6.80
Israeli shekels	−0.15	4.83	—	—
Norwegian kroner	0.99	2.57	2.78	7.38
South African rand	0.32	2.38	2.08	6.98
Swedish kronor	0.85	2.64	3.62	7.23

Table 3.6. *Composition of optimal foreign currency portfolios for selected investor viewpoints (in percent)*

Portfolio components	Investor viewpoint					
	U.S.	Belgium	France	Italy	Netherlands	U.K.
German marks	11.6	49.3	19.9	11.7	49.8	28.8
Japanese yen	20.9	4.5	7.2	11.0	3.3	12.6
Swiss francs	67.5	46.2	72.9	77.30	46.9	58.6
Portfolio mean	1.3	0.72	1.03	1.57	0.66	1.49
Portfolio standard deviation	3.09	1.22	2.73	2.93	1.25	2.67

as the dividend received plus the percentage change in the value of its index of common stocks.

$$r_{j(t)} = \frac{D_{jt} + I_{j(t)} - I_{j(t-1)}}{I_{j(t-1)}}$$

where D_{jt} is the average dividend received on the common stock included in the ordinary share index of the jth country, $I_{j(t)}$ is the

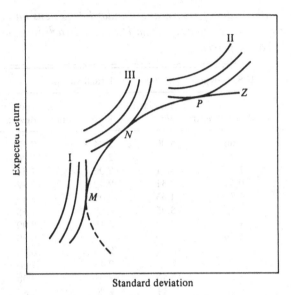

Figure 3.2.   Locus of efficient portfolios

value of the jth country's share index at the end of year t, and $r_{j(t)}$ is
the rate of return on the domestic share index of country j.

With respect to domestic risky assets in general, and common stock
in particular, Markowitz (1952) has demonstrated that for a number
of significant cases, risk-averse investors who maximize their expected
utility *inevitably* choose their optimal portfolio out of the mean–
variance efficient set. Figure 3.2 sets out the locus of efficient
portfolios, that is, attainable combinations of securities that maximize
the expected return for a given variance. The efficient set is represented by the envelope curve MZ. It should be noted that each point
on this curve represents a particular combination of investment
proportions in the risky securities that are assumed to comprise the
market. The minimum-risk portfolio lies at the southwest corner of
the curve at point M; as we move in a northeasterly direction up the
efficiency locus, all other attainable portfolios have both higher
standard deviations and higher expected returns. On the other hand,
all points to the right and below this curve represent inefficient
alternatives, since the investor can always achieve higher levels of
expected utility by moving from such an option to a portfolio located
on the efficiency curve. To illustrate this proposition, the indifference
curves of three hypothetical risk-averse investors have been superimposed on the efficiency locus; *optimal* solutions exist at points M,

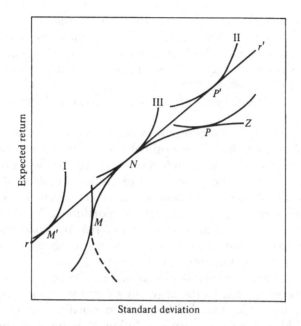

Figure 3.3. Efficient frontier with a riskless asset

N, and P, respectively. Clearly the optimal portfolio is not unique, and it depends not only on the investment alternatives (efficient set) confronting investors but also on their preferences (i.e., their subjective tradeoff between return and risk).

Tobin (1958) has shown that, given the existence of a "riskless" asset (in his example, cash), the investment decision can be dichotomized: Investors first isolate those alternatives that are efficient, independent of their preferences; their subjective tradeoff between risk and return becomes operative only in the second stage in which the optimal portfolio is selected. Sharpe (1964) and Lintner (1965) have extended Tobin's "Separation Theorem" to the problem of determining equilibrium prices for risky assets. They show that the array of alternative efficient portfolios can be reduced to a single optimal choice, independent of individual investors' marginal rates of substitution between risk and return, by introducing the additional assumption of borrowing and lending at a riskless interest rate, r. The model is illustrated in Figure 3.3, which reproduces the efficiency locus of Figure 3.2. The market opportunity line rr', which is tangent to the efficiency locus at point N, sets out all the alternative combinations of the risk portfolio N with riskless bonds (the segment from point r to point N includes these mixed portfolios); levered portfolios (combinations of N with riskless loans) are represented by points along the line beyond point N. The portfolio of risky assets designated by N in Figure 3.3 is optimal since, given the opportunity of borrowing or lending at rate r, it allows the investor to reach the highest attainable market line, and hence the highest possible indifference curve.

The Sharpe-Lintner model dichotomizes the investment decision. The proportions of portfolio N are optimal for all investors, independent of their tastes; individuals' indifference curves are operative only at a later stage when the proportion of riskless bonds in the overall portfolio, or the degree of leverage, is determined. In the first stage the composition of the optimal risk portfolio is fixed; in the second stage the optimal mix between the risk portfolio and riskless bonds (loans) is determined by finding the tangent of the market line to an individual investor's indifference curve.

Three types of solutions can be distinguished in Figure 3.3. If an indifference curve is tangent to the segment rN of the market line (e.g., point M'), the individual holds a mixed portfolio of risky securities and riskless bonds; a corner solution at point r on the vertical axis would represent an extreme case of risk aversion in which the investor placed all wealth in riskless assets. Tangency solutions that occur on the segment of the market line above point N (e.g., point P') represent levered portfolios, that is, cases in which the risk portfolio N is financed in part by borrowing. Finally, if the indifference curve is tangent to point N itself, the investor neither lends nor borrows, placing all resources in the risk portfolio. Thus, by postulating a perfect capital market in which unlimited lending and borrowing are possible at a given riskless interest rate, the optimal proportions of an unlevered portfolio of risky assets can be uniquely determined for all investors, independent of their tastes.[6]

However, given the current magnitude of worldwide inflation yet another type of risk, in this instance the purchasing power risk generated by inflation, must be considered when analyzing the gains from international diversification among risky assets such as common stock. Imperfectly anticipated rises in the price level can generate massive, and often socially undesirable, shifts in the allocation of wealth between the buyers and sellers of some goods and services and between debtors and creditors. And although these gains and

---

[6] These two separation theorems were employed in the previous section to identify the optimal investment proportions of foreign currency holdings.

Table 3.7. *Mean quarterly real rates of return on domestic
investments and their standard deviations (in percent)*

Country	1960–1969		1970–1979	
	Rates of return	Standard deviation	Rates of return	Standard deviation
Belgium	0.3	5.8	0.5	7.2
Canada	2.1	6.2	1.0	9.5
Germany	1.7	10.9	−0.2	7.9
France	0.4	8.5	0.4	11.1
Italy	0.6	10.9	−3.2	11.8
Japan	2.3	8.6	1.2	8.9
United Kingdom	1.6	7.4	0.1	17.0
United States	1.5	6.6	0.1	9.0

Note: Arithmetic mean used.

losses cancel in the aggregate, this provides little solace to individual investors who find themselves unwilling "victims" of the inflationary process. Rational decision making, therefore, must take the impact of inflation explicitly into account, and to this end the nominal rate of return on common stock must be further adjusted to reflect changes in the purchasing power of money.

This can be accomplished by redefining the nominal (i.e., money) rates of return in *real* terms (i.e., in terms of constant purchasing power).[7]

$$1 + m_{j(t)} = \frac{1 + r_{j(t)}}{1 + g_{j(t)}}$$

where $m_{j(t)}$ is the real rate of return on the common stock of country j, $r_{j(t)}$ is the nominal rate of return on the common stock of country j, and $g_{j(t)}$ is the percentage change in the general level of prices of country j.

Dropping the subscripts and cross multiplying this equation yields

$$m = r - g - mg$$

which reduces to the familiar rule of thumb when m and g are small:

$$m = r - g$$

Table 3.7 uses this formula to set out the mean quarterly *real* rates

[7] We owe this distinction to Irving Fisher (1907); the algebraic formulation is taken from Patinkin (1965).

of return on domestic common stocks, and their standard deviations, for a cross section of eight industrial nations before and after the monetary crisis that took place at the beginning of the 1970s. The countries included are Belgium, Canada, Germany, France, Italy, Japan, the United Kingdom, and the United States. The mean rates of return and the standard deviations have been estimated from quarterly data over the periods 1960–9 and 1970–9. Since they are based on the common stock index, the risk–return data of Table 3.7 provide a convenient proxy for the real return on a well-diversified portfolio of risky assets in each of these countries. In what follows we shall use these figures as a benchmark for the return and risk confronting local investors in these countries, on the assumption that they are constrained to domestic investment.

Several noteworthy features of Table 3.7 should be mentioned:

1. In both periods Japan had the highest *real* rate of return on risky investments. On an annual basis, the real return on Japanese common stock was 9.5 percent during the period 1960–9 and a little less than 5 percent (4.9 percent) during the decade of the 1970s.
2. Reflecting the stagnation of the 1970s, the real rate of return on common stock declined dramatically in the period 1970–9 relative to the decade of the 1960s. Particularly striking is the decline in return in Italy, Canada, Germany, the United Kingdom, and the United States.
3. Using the variability of returns (standard deviation) as our measure of risk, the uncertainty of investment in the 1970s increased in all of the countries with the exception of Germany. Once again these results are readily explainable in terms of the economic conditions that prevailed during most of this turbulent period.

Several interesting conceptual problems arise when the Sharpe-Lintner asset-pricing model is applied to international investments. If all countries had a common currency unit and efficient capital markets, international investment decisions would not differ conceptually from their domestic counterparts, and all investors, independent of their country of origin, would hold exactly the same proportions of risky assets in their portfolios. In such a case the capital markets of the n countries would comprise, in effect, a single integrated world market, and all investment decisions, international or otherwise, would be reached solely on the basis of the expected returns, variances, and covariances of the alternatives confronting the investor. But when the restriction to a common currency unit is relaxed, the possibility of changes in the external value of a country's currency unit (exchange rate) can, and often does, create differing sets of international investment opportunities for investors in different countries so that the optimal investment proportions of an internationally diversified portfolio can no longer be assumed to be the same in all countries.

In order to analyze international investment we first measure the nominal rate of return on foreign investment *from the viewpoint* of, say, an American investor. As was true of currency deposits, the rate of return must be adjusted to reflect any changes in exchange rates during the period. Consider the concrete example of an American who invested $100 in the securities of a foreign country, say, Israel, and earned a 20 percent *nominal* rate of return in Israeli shekels on the investment. Let us also assume that the exchange was one dollar to one Israeli shekel at the time of the initial investment and that during the year the market value of the shekel fell to 1.80 Israeli shekels to the dollar. Taking the currency devaluation into account, the rate of return *in dollars* is negative: minus 33 percent.[8]

The nominal rates of return in foreign securities, from the American investor's viewpoint, were then reduced to real terms using the general price level of the *investor's home country* – in our example, the United States:

$$1 + m_{i,\,j(t)} = \frac{1 + r_{i,\,j(t)}}{1 + g_{i(t)}}$$

[8] The required adjustment is illustrated in the following diagram:

		Exchange rate IS 1 to $1	
Beginning of year	$100	⟶	IS 100
			20% nominal rate of return
End of year	$67	⟵	IS 120
		Exchange rate IS 1.80 to $1	

At the beginning of the year the U.S. investor acquired IS 100 for $100 at the prevailing exchange rate and invested this sum in Israeli securities (represented by that country's index of common stock prices). At the end of the year the investor liquidated the Israeli investment and received IS 120 (i.e., a rate of return of 20 percent in local currency); however, owing to the devaluation, the IS 120 could be converted into only $67 ($120 ÷ 1.80 = $67), so that the *dollar-adjusted* rate of return is negative: minus 33 percent.

Table 3.8. *Mean quarterly real rates of return and standard deviations to U.S. investors in the common stock of selected countries (in percent)*

Country	1960–1969		1970–1979	
	Rates of return	Standard deviation	Rates of return	Standard deviation
Belgium	0.3	5.7	2.0	9.1
Canada	1.8	7.0	0.9	9.7
Germany	2.0	10.9	1.4	10.7
France	0.4	8.6	1.9	13.9
Italy	0.9	10.7	−2.4	13.2
Japan	3.1	8.6	2.8	10.7
United Kingdom	1.5	7.3	2.1	19.2
United States	1.5	6.6	0.1	9.0

Note: Arithmetic mean used.

where $m_{i,j(t)}$ is the real rate of return to the investors of country i in the securities of country j, $r_{i,j(t)}$ is the nominal rate of return on the investment in country j's securities from the viewpoint of country i's investors, and $g_{i(t)}$ is the percentage change in the general price level of country i.

Since we assume that the investment in risky assets is motivated by the desire to secure command over future consumption goods, these *real* "viewpoint" returns comprise the relevant variables for the international portfolio selection process.[9] Therefore, for the remainder of this section we shall concentrate our attention on the potential *real* gain to the investors from the holding of internationally diversified portfolios of common stock.

Mean quarterly *real* rates of return and standard deviations on the investment in the common stocks of each of the eight countries included in our sample are given in Table 3.8 from the *viewpoint* of American investors. Note therefore, that the last line of Table 3.8 is

---

[9] We are implicitly assuming that the "point of view" refers to the base currency being used exclusively by the investor. For example, if a U.S. investor consumes 20 percent German imports and 80 percent U.S. goods, a new base, accounting for the German proportion, should be used as the "domestic" currency. We ignore this problem and assume that a U.S. investor exclusively uses dollars for consumption. The analysis, however, could readily be generalized to handle the more complex case of a mixed consumption basket.

simply the real domestic return and standard deviation on U.S. common stock. The figures for the other countries deviate from their domestic counterparts since they represent the nominal return to U.S. investors in the shares of those countries, deflated by the rise in the U.S. general price level. A comparison of Tables 3.7 and 3.8 reveals a striking increase in the real U.S. viewpoint returns on foreign investment relative to their real domestic counterparts in the period 1970–9. This reflects the weakening of the U.S. dollar vis-à-vis the major European currencies during that period. As the data of Table 3.8 show, the fall in the value of the dollar went beyond that which can be explained by differentials in inflation rates. As a result, the mean *real* return to U.S. investors in Japanese stocks was 11.7 percent on an annual basis. The relevant figure for U.S. investments in German stocks, for example, was 5.7 percent. To put these returns into their proper perspective it should be recalled that the mean annual real return on U.S. common stock was less than 0.5 percent during this same period.

Even a cursory glance at Table 3.8 suffices to show that the increase in mean return from foreign investment was accompanied by an increase in risk (standard deviation). However, to this point we have implicitly restricted the U.S. investor to placements in the securities of a single foreign country. As we have already noted, it is the essence of modern risk analysis that uncertainty can be reduced by combining securities in a portfolio. Hence, in order to make an empirical test of the benefits from an internationally diversified portfolio of risky securities, we must once again calculate the set of efficient portfolios, in this instance, a combination of investments in the common stock of the various countries included in our sample.

Each point along the locus of efficient points (portfolios) represents a particular combination of investment proportions in the securities of the various countries included in the opportunity set. Here, too, the efficiency curve can be reduced to a single optimal point (portfolio) by considering a particular real riskless interest rate.

Tables 3.9 and 3.10 set out the optimal portfolios of common stock from the viewpoints of U.S., German, Israeli, Italian, Canadian, French, Belgian, Japanese, and English investors for 1960–9 using a 3 percent annual real rate of interest and for 1970–9 using a zero riskless annual real rate of interest. In the earlier period the portfolios are largely comprised of varying proportions of the securities of four countries: Japan, Germany, the United States, and Canada. The Japanese and German portfolios do not include U.S. shares, whereas the optimal Israeli portfolio is made up solely of Japanese and

Table 3.9. *Composition of optimal portfolios of common stock from various investor viewpoints 1960–1969 (in percent)*

Common stock of country	Investor viewpoint								
	U.S.	German	Israeli	Italian	Canadian	French	Belgian	Japanese	U.K.
Canada	6	16	—	11	11	2	9	1	20
Germany	19	19	45	18	18	18	17	21	15
Japan	57	65	55	63	47	59	59	78	60
United States	18	—	—	8	24	21	15	—	5
Portfolio return	2.5	2.3	4.0	2.3	2.6	2.5	2.5	2.1	2.7
Standard deviation	5.6	5.95	11.6	6.1	4.8	6.1	5.9	6.9	6.1

Note: Portfolio compiled for an annual 3 percent real interest rate and quarterly holding period.

Table 3.10. *Composition of optimal portfolios of common stock from various investor viewpoints 1970–1979 (in percent)*

| | Investor viewpoint | | | | | | | | | |
Common stock of country	U.S.	German	Israeli	Italian	Canadian	French	Belgian	Japanese	U.K.
Belgium	37	7	18	21	21	18	6	3	7
Japan	63	93	82	79	79	82	94	97	93
Portfolio return	2.5	1.3	2.7	2.0	2.8	1.3	1.4	2.1	1.6
Standard deviation	9.0	9.3	11.2	9.9	10.0	8.6	9.9	6.9	10.6

Note: Portfolio designed for an annual zero real interest rate and quarterly holding period.

German shares in roughly equal proportion, 55 percent and 45 percent, respectively. In this context it should be recalled that during the 1960s Israel was effectively isolated from the world capital market by an unconvertible currency and stringent exchange controls.

The striking feature of Table 3.10, which sets out the optimal portfolios for the period 1970–9, is the broad similarity of the composition of the *real* optimal portfolios, independent of the viewpoint adopted. In all cases they are comprised of combinations of Belgian and Japanese shares, with Japan accounting for most of the portfolio – the proportion of Japanese shares varying from a low of 63 percent for U.S. investors to fully 97 percent in the case of Japanese investors.

Some additional insight into these results can be gained by examining Tables 3.11 and 3.12, which set out the intercountry correlation matrix for the real U.S. viewpoint returns in 1960–9 and 1970–9, respectively.[10] In the pre–monetary crisis decade of the 1960s the real returns to a U.S. investor in Japanese stock had near-zero correlation with the returns with U.S. stocks, a slightly negative correlation with German shares, and relatively low positive correlation coefficients with the other countries. The inclusion of high proportions of Japanese and German shares in the optimal portfolio for 1960–9 is, therefore, readily understandable. Similarly, the reduction of the optimal portfolios to two countries – the shares of Japan and Belgium – reflects the sharp overall rise in the intercountry correlation coefficients during the 1970s. This, in turn, suggests that the floating exchange rates of the 1970s have led to a greater degree of integration among the world's capital markets. Particularly striking is the disappearance in the 1970s of the very low correlation between Japan and the remaining member of the set that characterized the earlier period. The rise in the correlation coefficients also suggests that the degree of benefit from international diversification may have declined somewhat in the latter period.

Table 3.13 sets out two measures of the gains from international diversification from the viewpoint of U.S. investors in the two periods under study. Holding risk constant at the level for domestic investment (standard deviation of 6.621 percent and 9.050 percent in 1960–9 and 1970–9, respectively) a substantial increase in return could have been earned on an efficient internationally diversified portfolio without incurring additional risk. The increment in the

---

[10] The correlation matrices from the viewpoints of the other countries are roughly similar to those for the United States.

Table 3.11. *Intercountry correlation coefficients for the real returns on common stock from an American investor's viewpoint, 1960–1969 (in percent)*

	1	2	3	4	5	6	7	8
1. Belgium	1.00	0.55	0.43	0.59	0.26	0.08	0.44	0.56
2. Canada		1.00	0.24	0.22	0.13	0.19	0.45	0.87
3. Germany			1.00	0.34	0.37	-0.09	0.12	0.36
4. France				1.00	0.35	0.08	0.26	0.16
5. Italy					1.00	0.29	0.14	0.01
6. Japan						1.00	0.22	0.02
7. United Kingdom							1.00	0.53
8. United States								1.00

Table 3.12. *Intercountry correlation coefficients for the real returns on common stock from an American investor's viewpoint, 1970–1979 (in percent)*

	1	2	3	4	5	6	7	8
1. Belgium	1.00	0.40	0.79	0.76	0.55	0.58	0.53	0.51
2. Canada		1.00	0.31	0.37	0.28	0.40	0.46	0.75
3. Germany			1.00	0.76	0.39	0.63	0.44	0.50
4. France				1.00	0.57	0.52	0.43	0.44
5. Italy					1.00	0.36	0.35	0.27
6. Japan						1.00	0.38	0.55
7. United Kingdom							1.00	0.61
8. United States								1.00

Table 3.13. *Gains from efficient international diversification for U.S. investors (in percent per quarter)*

	1960–1969		1970–1979	
	Expected return	Standard deviation	Expected return	Standard deviation
On domestic investment	1.536	6.621	0.113	9.050
On constant risk portfolio	1.9	6.621	2.49	9.050
On constant return portfolio	1.536	4.57	0.113	7.78
Increase in return	+0.36		+2.38	
Decrease in risk (standard deviation)		-2.05		-1.27

mean quarterly return for 1960–9 is 0.36 percent; the relevant figure for 1970–9 is 2.38 percent. The greater increase in the 1970s reflects, of course, the very poor performance of the U.S. stock market during this period. Hence, permitting U.S. investors to diversify their portfolios internationally leads to a very substantial increase in *real* returns.

Alternatively, if we hold the level of return constant at the mean returns on domestic investment (1.536 percent per quarter in 1960–9 and 0.113 percent per quarter in 1970–9) we can measure the degree of *risk reduction* from international diversification. Once again, the gain from international diversification, in this instance, the reduction of risk (standard deviation), is substantial in both periods. However, as we might have surmised from the correlation matrices, the risk reduction is greater in the earlier period.[11] Efficient international diversification reduces the standard deviation in 1960–9 by 2.05 percentage points; the relevant figure for 1970–9 is a reduction of 1.27 percentage points.

6.   Concluding remarks

The decade of the 1970s witnessed a remarkable change in the international economic order. The system of fixed exchange rates was replaced by freely or semifreely fluctuating exchange values. This shift has not only created problems, but has also opened new investment opportunities. For example, most international firms that hold large quantities of cash assets tend to use, albeit not always explicitly, the type of portfolio diversification techniques we have discussed. Similarly, investors in risky assets are confronted with the need to diversify their holdings internationally if they are to take maximum advantage of the opportunities afforded by the capital market for risk reduction. In this context, the rise of internationally diversified mutual funds, commodity funds, and, of course, the investment in precious metals all reflect, in part, the quest for risk reduction through diversification in a world characterized by serious inflation.

Finally, one final caveat may be appropriate. Throughout we have used ex post data to demonstrate the gain from diversification.[12]

---

[11] This pattern holds true for the investor (viewpoints) of Belgium, Canada, Germany, and Italy as well. France and the United Kingdom, which had very high standard deviations on their domestic portfolios, are exceptions to this rule.

[12] The construction of the mean–variance efficient frontier with ex post data creates a sampling bias in favor of assets that are characterized by a

Clearly, actual decisions should be based on ex ante estimates; however, we feel that the best estimates of the intercountry correlations are likely to be those calculated from observed data. Although return estimates may vary widely, the principal motive for diversification will remain, and the techniques we have outlined can be used to derive the optimal portfolio of foreign currency holdings and securities. As is true of ex post data, in employing ex ante data one may expect that the efficient portfolios will generally depend on the "point of view" of investors and that significant benefits from proper diversification among various currencies and securities can be expected.[13]

References

Fisher, Irving. *The Rate of Interest.* New York: Macmillan, 1907.

Friend, Irwin, and Losq, Etienne. "Advantages and Limitations of International Portfolio Diversification," in Marshall Sarnat and Giorgio P. Szego (eds.), *International Finance and Trade*, vol. 2. Cambridge, Mass.: Ballinger, 1979.

IMF, *International Financial Statistics*, 1968–80.

Levy, Haim. "Optimal Portfolio of Foreign Currencies with Borrowing and Lending." *Journal of Money, Credit and Banking* (August 1981), pp. 325–41.

Levy, Haim, and Sarnat, Marshall. "International Diversification of Investment Portfolios." *American Economic Review* (September 1970), pp. 668–75.

Levy, Haim, and Sarnat, Marshall. "Exchange Rate Risk and the Optimal Diversification of Foreign Currency Holdings." *Journal of Money, Credit and Banking* (November 1978), pp. 453–63.

Lintner, John. "Security Prices, Risk and Maximal Gain from Diversification." *Journal of Finance* (December 1965), pp. 587–616.

Markowitz, Harry M. "Portfolio Selection." *Journal of Finance* (March 1952), pp. 77–91.

Patinkin, Don. *Money, Interest and Prices*, 2nd ed. New York: Harper & Row, 1965.

Sharpe, William F. "Capital Asset Prices: A Theory of Market Equilibrium Under Conditions of Risk." *Journal of Finance* (September 1964), pp. 425–42.

Tobin, James. "Liquidity Preference as Behavior Towards Risk." *Review of Economic Studies* (February 1958), pp. 65–86.

low variance (or a high mean) in the sample. Nevertheless, we believe that our main conclusions are unaffected by this bias. Obviously, for actual investment decisions, one should use ex ante predictions. Thus, the quantitative results do not necessarily determine the optimal investment policy for the future; they only indicate the potential gain from diversification. Investors can, and often do, adjust ex post data in order to find their optimal investment strategy.

[13] For a detailed critique of the theoretical and empirical literature regarding the gains from diversification see Friend and Losq (1979). They note, inter alia, the almost universal neglect of differential taxation when quantifying the gains from diversification and, in this respect, this chapter is no exception.

Appendix: *Mean monthly rates of return and standard deviations on interest-bearing foreign currency holdings from various investors' viewpoints, 1970–1978 (in percent) (standard deviations in parentheses)*

Currency	Belgium	Brazil	Canada	France	Germany	Israel	Italy	Japan	Netherlands	Norway	S. Africa	Sweden	Switzerland	U.K.	U.S.A.
Belgium	— (—)	3.43 (10.47)	1.17 (3.07)	0.79 (1.78)	0.38 (1.00)	2.84 (7.47)	1.32 (2.79)	0.58 (4.54)	0.46 (0.81)	0.71 (1.43)	1.25 (3.34)	0.87 (1.55)	0.16 (2.02)	1.27 (2.50)	1.06 (3.00)
Brazil	-0.17 (6.21)	— (—)	0.38 (5.56)	0.07 (6.14)	-0.31 (6.24)	2.04 (8.66)	0.57 (5.89)	-0.16 (7.05)	-0.24 (6.20)	-0.01 (5.95)	0.49 (6.09)	0.15 (6.08)	-0.54 (6.42)	0.53 (5.98)	0.27 (5.43)
Canada	-0.02 (3.03)	2.79 (10.09)	— (—)	0.22 (3.00)	-0.16 (3.12)	2.20 (6.80)	0.73 (2.78)	0.00 (4.79)	-0.08 (3.08)	0.14 (2.67)	0.64 (2.91)	0.30 (2.83)	-0.38 (3.56)	0.68 (2.67)	0.43 (1.11)
France	0.43 (1.71)	3.32 (10.41)	1.06 (3.03)	— (—)	0.29 (1.83)	2.72 (7.26)	1.21 (2.40)	0.48 (4.56)	0.37 (1.76)	0.61 (1.75)	1.14 (3.37)	0.77 (1.92)	0.07 (2.37)	1.16 (2.46)	0.95 (2.85)
Germany	0.63 (1.02)	3.56 (10.52)	1.28 (3.20)	0.90 (1.88)	— (—)	2.96 (7.64)	1.44 (2.93)	0.69 (4.55)	0.57 (0.99)	0.82 (1.49)	1.36 (3.33)	0.98 (1.61)	0.27 (1.98)	1.38 (2.70)	1.17 (3.11)
Israel	-0.59 (5.62)	2.21 (11.20)	-0.03 (5.00)	-0.35 (5.49)	-0.73 (5.72)	— (—)	0.15 (5.43)	-0.57 (6.69)	-0.65 (5.66)	-0.42 (5.48)	0.05 (5.14)	-0.27 (5.44)	-0.94 (6.06)	0.10 (5.31)	-0.15 (4.83)
Italy	0.06 (2.69)	2.90 (10.23)	0.66 (2.70)	0.30 (2.34)	-0.08 (2.79)	2.32 (7.22)	— (—)	0.08 (4.32)	0.00 (2.62)	0.24 (2.55)	0.75 (3.29)	0.39 (2.55)	-0.31 (2.97)	0.77 (2.46)	0.54 (2.31)
Japan	0.74 (4.53)	3.62 (11.11)	1.35 (4.80)	1.00 (4.77)	0.59 (4.51)	3.03 (8.40)	1.52 (5.17)	— (—)	0.68 (4.61)	0.91 (4.46)	1.44 (5.09)	1.07 (4.61)	0.36 (4.67)	1.46 (4.89)	1.24 (4.65)
Netherlands	0.53 (0.80)	3.44 (10.43)	1.18 (3.14)	0.80 (1.81)	0.39 (0.98)	2.85 (7.53)	1.33 (2.74)	0.59 (4.57)	— (—)	0.72 (1.58)	1.26 (3.32)	0.88 (1.67)	0.17 (2.06)	1.28 (2.59)	1.07 (3.05)
Norway	0.48 (1.42)	3.36 (10.24)	1.10 (2.70)	0.73 (1.83)	0.33 (1.48)	2.78 (7.38)	1.27 (2.66)	0.52 (4.50)	0.42 (1.58)	— (—)	1.19 (3.10)	0.81 (1.33)	0.11 (2.23)	1.21 (2.49)	0.99 (2.57)
S. Africa	-0.14 (3.18)	2.69 (10.41)	0.44 (2.65)	0.10 (3.20)	-0.29 (3.20)	2.08 (6.98)	0.61 (3.18)	-0.12 (4.93)	-0.21 (3.18)	0.03 (2.94)	— (—)	0.19 (3.20)	-0.51 (3.58)	0.56 (3.02)	0.32 (2.38)
Sweden	0.33 (1.46)	3.22 (10.32)	0.96 (2.79)	0.59 (1.86)	0.19 (1.52)	2.62 (7.23)	1.12 (2.53)	0.38 (4.55)	0.27 (1.58)	0.51 (1.27)	1.05 (3.29)	— (—)	-0.03 (2.35)	1.07 (2.50)	0.85 (2.64)
Switzerland	0.81 (2.01)	3.72 (10.59)	1.45 (3.60)	1.07 (2.43)	0.67 (1.95)	3.15 (8.09)	1.60 (3.11)	0.86 (4.74)	0.75 (2.05)	0.99 (2.22)	1.53 (3.67)	1.16 (2.45)	— (—)	1.55 (3.00)	1.34 (3.42)
U.K.	0.00 (2.40)	2.86 (10.45)	0.60 (2.66)	0.25 (2.39)	-0.14 (2.57)	2.25 (6.99)	0.76 (2.44)	0.02 (4.38)	-0.06 (2.47)	0.17 (2.35)	0.69 (3.15)	0.33 (2.49)	-0.37 (2.90)	— (—)	0.49 (2.39)
U.S.A.	0.03 (2.95)	2.84 (9.98)	0.59 (1.15)	0.28 (2.81)	-0.11 (3.02)	2.25 (6.68)	0.78 (2.41)	0.05 (4.62)	-0.03 (2.98)	0.20 (2.55)	0.69 (2.64)	0.36 (2.70)	-0.33 (2.90)	0.73 (2.44)	— (—)

Perspective: International portfolio diversification: a practitioner's point of view

HENK A. KLEIN HANEVELD

The financial literature has flourished since the transplantation of the portfolio concept to the arena of national and international financial analysis and decision making. Introduced in the early 1950s by Markowitz, portfolio theory was applied during the 1960s to the analysis of the behavior of investors within the context of a single-equity market. It was only during the last decade that the portfolio concept was used to provide a theoretical framework for the international approach to investment management, which had rapidly gained acceptance following the general elimination of exchange and capital controls.

In their chapter, Haim Levy and Marshall Sarnat evaluate in a clear and systematic way two important characteristics of international portfolio diversification:

1. A relatively low degree of co-movement between the returns of different assets or markets enables investors to reduce the variability of their overall performance by shifting their investment strategy from a single market–asset approach toward diversification into several markets or assets.
2. The composition of an "optimally" diversified portfolio is not unique: It depends on investors' points of view (their base currency) and also fluctuates over time due to the instability of the correlations of returns of different markets or assets.

In this perspective we shall focus on some aspects of their discussion from the point of view of an investment manager who is responsible for funds that are diversified internationally both by market and by asset. At times a more theoretical comment may also be presented, as many of the ideas and principles of international diversification have been the subject of internal research within the Morgan Bank.

Levy and Sarnat provide a very systematic *tour d'horizon* of the various markets in which international diversification can be applied: exchange markets, money markets, and equity markets. But as is more often true with statistically oriented academic literature, the study lags the developments in the real world by not including in the analysis the rapidly growing share of the global investment market that is accounted for by multicurrency bond portfolios. In this respect Levy and Sarnat's discussion shares the problem of many academic studies that are constrained in their coverage by the lack of easily available data on the historical performance of investment markets that should logically be included in the analysis. Fortunately, statistical material on the major international bond market sector(s) has become available in recent years, and future academic research will undoubtedly incorporate fixed-income markets, the worldwide capitalization of which is at least twice that of equity markets. In the meantime, initial studies have shown that many of the conclusions Levy and Sarnat reach on international portfolio diversification apply to bonds as much as to currencies, money market investments, and equities.[1]

Nevertheless, the lack of historical data continues to frustrate the analysis of international portfolio diversification in several respects. In terms of coverage, the inclusion of real estate or property investments will have to wait until acceptable international performance figures have been constructed. Regarding the analysis of equity markets, the lack of consistent national return data for sectors and/ or industries within the individual equity markets hampers the analysis and understanding of the observed behavior of diversified portfolios. Last, Levy and Sarnat join many others in only focusing on a single asset category at a time, rather than extending the analysis to the behavior of internationally diversified, multiasset (e.g., bonds, cash, and equities) portfolios. The interactions between the different assets may well prove to be the more interesting aspect of international portfolio diversification.

As Levy and Sarnat utilize the Markowitz framework for creating an "optimally" diversified portfolio, it is an interesting question whether the real world permits using this methodology for investment decision making. In this context the authors illustrate the very important point that correlations between returns in different markets are unstable over time. This should not be a surprise. The performance of individual markets is influenced in varying degrees by financial (interest rates, capital flows), economic (oil prices, industrial trends), and policy (monetary, budget, and exchange rate policies) variables, which are subject to both regular fluctuations and irregular shocks.

See Klein Haneveld, "Investing Internationally: The Role of Foreign Currency Bonds in U.S. Dollar-based Portfolios" (London: Morgan Guaranty Trust Company, 1981).

Also, the differing structure of the various markets (e.g., industry weighting, institutional framework) makes them react differently to any shift in the external variables. This state of affairs ensures not only that the resulting correlations are rather complex, but also that they tend to vary over time, as is partly evidenced by the statistical analysis in Chapter 3. In passing, it should be emphasized that for similar reasons the returns themselves, and their volatility ("risk"), fluctuate over time and contribute to a rather unstable set of parameters with which to optimize prospectively (rather than retrospectively) within the Markowitz framework. What is therefore needed is a follow-up to the statistical evidence confirming that all major variables are unstable, that is, an attempt to analyze and interpret the reasons for the level and pattern of returns, volatilities, and correlations. For instance, the correlations between market returns may be high due not only to a close geographical proximity, but also to a great similarity in their economic or industrial structure (both Canada and Australia are influenced by the same energy and commodity trends), or in their financial policies (similar currency policies, such as "basket managers" vs. "U.S. dollar linkups," create similar influences on financial variables and market performance, ceteris paribus). Perhaps economic history and comparative economic analysis could make a useful contribution to the thus far rather statistical approach to the understanding of international portfolio diversification.

In this context, it is our experience that a flexible, research-based approach is a necessary condition for realizing the potential benefits from a multimarket, multiasset investment strategy, whereas an active management style is needed to respond to the rapidly changing economic and financial variables that underlie the instability of returns, volatilities, and correlations. Nevertheless, in spite of the difficulties in using the Markowitz framework prospectively for short-term investment decision making, a partial usage of this approach can add value, for example, to test the validity and consistency of any global investment strategy. Also, alternative optimization methodologies (e.g., based on multiple objective and goal programming) have been developed to cope with some of the less plausible assumptions of the Markowitz model.

Levy and Sarnat go further than most studies on international portfolio diversification by focusing on the proper objective of investors: inflation-adjusted "real" returns rather than nominal returns. Many investors have learned to look through nominal returns to the underlying real performance, as they realized that the objectives of their funds are inflation-adjusted as well. For instance, in many countries benefits paid out by pension funds have some form of indexation to consumer price and/or wage–cost inflation. Also, although the liabilities of insurance companies tend to be in nominal terms, even they have to achieve a real return on their capital and reserves if they do not want to see their capital base effectively reduced by the cumulative impact of persistent inflation.

Levy and Sarnat also emphasize another aspect of international portfolio diversification that many global investment managers have learned on the job: A universally optimal portfolio composition does not exist. Instead, the authors show that the country of residence of the investor (the "base currency") is an important variable that helps to produce different optimal portfolios for investors who are based in different currencies. This characteristic of international portfolio diversification appears to be due to the fact that (using Markowitz's terms) the choice of the currency impacts the correlations and volatilities used in the optimization process.

On a more fundamental level, experience with managing funds internationally shows that a thorough analysis of the objectives and constraints of the ultimate client is, at a minimum, a necessary (but by no means a sufficient) condition for a satisfactory manager–client relationship. Such analysis often reveals that the concept of risk, and the tolerance of it, varies widely among clients. For those whose pattern of future liabilities allows a longer-term view, short-term volatility may be irrelevant and secondary to long-term real returns. Others, with near-term liabilities and/or a weaker capital base, have to incorporate explicit guidelines on the maximum degree of acceptable volatility. In view of this phenomenon of diverging objectives it has proven useful to establish, in consultation with the client, (1) a so-called normal or baseline portfolio composition on the basis of longer-term return and risk patterns of the relevant assets, and (2) guidelines for the degree to which the manager can deviate from this baseline. The latter constraint tries to harmonize the historical and prospective return and risk characteristics of the chosen investment assets, and the corresponding portfolio risk profile, with the manager's ability to use insights into markets and assets for achieving superior results by making prudent "bets." It is in the context of this client-counseling process that Markowitz's and other optimization techniques have proven very useful in spite of their already mentioned inherent weaknesses.

As a final comment, Levy and Sarnat mention in their footnotes that their analysis does not focus on the more practical aspects of real-life international portfolio diversification: taxation, transaction costs, market liquidity, administrative details such as custody and accounting, and so on. It should be stressed, however, that this does not invalidate the basic conclusions of their analysis. In fact, the performance of actively managed, internationally diversified investment portfolios over a substantial number of years has confirmed that diversification does indeed reduce portfolio volatility while often enhancing realized returns. These practical considerations only help to emphasize the crucial fact that successful international portfolio results can only be achieved by an investment strategy that is client oriented, based on active but prudent management supported by sound research of financial and economic trends, and founded on sufficient experience with the imperfections of the real world as well as with the latest techniques and systems to overcome them.

CHAPTER 4

The evaluation and use of foreign exchange rate forecasting services

JOHN F. O. BILSON

The output of a foreign exchange management program is a set of open positions in foreign currencies; the inputs are typically a set of forecasts of future foreign exchange rates and a set of corporate constraints. The purpose of this chapter is to describe a variety of techniques – a production function – for transforming the inputs into the output in a cost- and risk-minimizing fashion. In the first stage, the forecasts are evaluated on the basis of their historical record, and a composite forecast for each currency is created. In the next stage, optimal open positions are estimated on the basis of both the expected profit and the risk of the position. Finally, procedures are described that allow for the imposition of constraints dictated by corporate policy. These techniques are illustrated in an evaluation of the forecasts of Predex Corporation.

1.   Introduction

Many commercial foreign exchange forecasting services are now available to the international currency manager, and a subsidiary industry of evaluators of forecasting services is also growing rapidly.[1] The available statistical evidence, and the fact that many services have survived in an extremely competitive marketplace, suggests that the forecasts provided by the services may be superior to the forward exchange rate and that an active international cash management strategy may be justified. But a great deal of work must be completed before the benefits of an active strategy are realized:

This research was undertaken while the author was a National Fellow at the Hoover Institution, Stanford, California, and was partially funded by a grant from the National Science Foundation. I am grateful to Dr. Charles Ramond of Predex Corporation for providing me with the data used in this chapter. The views expressed are solely the responsibility of the author and are not necessarily shared by the sponsoring institutions.

[1] The two most important papers on the evaluation of foreign exchange advisory services are Goodman (1979) and Levich (1980).

One or more of the services must be chosen on the basis of an *evaluation* of their methodologies and historical performance.

The forecasts must be combined into a consensus or composite forecast.

An open position must be taken on the basis of the composite forecast.

These three steps may be complicated by other factors. First, since most exchange rates move together against the dollar, it is necessary to take account of this covariation in the construction of an open position. For example, a short position of 10 million Deutsche marks may not be very risky if it is balanced by a long position of 10 million Swiss francs because the $/DM rate and the $/SF rate tend to move together. Second, the open position may involve a number of maturities, and it may not be profitable to match maturities if the bias in the forward rate's forecast of the future spot rate differs across the maturity spectrum. Finally, it is necessary to take account of top-level constraints on exposure management. Most managers, for example, are prohibited from either reversing or extending a natural position. Put simply, this means that if the corporation will receive 1 million pounds in six months' time, the amount to be sold in the forward market must lie within the range from zero to 1 million pounds.

The foreign currency manager consequently must deal with multiple forecasting services, multiple currencies, multiple maturities, and a variety of constraints. Obviously, the task of turning a set of forecasts into an open position is not an easy one. Fortunately, however, the problem is amenable to systematic analysis and, once the system is established, the operation of the system is simple and straightforward. And although the use of a systematic approach does not guarantee the absence of losses from exposed positions in foreign currencies, it does provide a structure that relates the risk of a position to its potential profit. The empirical analysis presented here suggests, in fact, that the risk–return tradeoff has been very favorable during the past few years.

2.   Reasons for an active strategy

Given that the practice of maintaining open positions in foreign currencies is risky and unpopular, we must begin by asking why a corporation should engage in it. The alternative – a passive strategy – simply involves selling off all foreign currency receivables in the forward market. This procedure converts foreign currency cash flows into known dollar flows and hence removes the exchange risk. The passive strategy has at least three favorable characteristics. First, the fees charged by the forecasting services do not have to be paid and administrative costs are reduced. Second, if the forward price is an unbiased forecast of the future spot price, the costs of the passive strategy tend to zero over time. Third, the corporation avoids the embarrassment of having to report either large foreign currency gains or losses on the quarterly income statement. All things considered, the passive strategy has much to recommend it.

The case for an active strategy begins with the supposition that it is more profitable than a passive strategy. The emerging consensus of academic opinion is that there are alternative forecasts that are superior to the forward exchange rate. Richard Levich (1980, p. 122) summarizes his own extensive work on the topic in the following statement:

Based on the analysis of mean squared errors, our results suggest that most forecasts are not as accurate as the forward rate. Our analysis of the speculative returns and the fraction of "correct" forecasts, however, does suggest that advisory services have beaten the forward rate in the past. The record of correct forecasts and percent of perfect information profits are too good for some services to be explained by chance. These unusual profits are more convincing for services with a long track record.

The position taken by Stephen Goodman, another prominent evaluator of forecasting services, is that technical services are superior to the forward rate whereas econometric and judgmental services are not. In fact, Goodman (1980, pp. 81-2) finds that

the return on capital employed for the speculator or investor using the technical services averages a phenomenal 243% annually excluding the Canadian dollar and French franc, assuming an average margin of 5% and cost of .5% per transaction representing the spread between the bid and asked price in the interbank market or the brokerage commission in the currency futures market. Including the Canadian dollar and French franc, the return on capital employed is still a remarkable 195% annually.

The potential profit from open positions in foreign currencies is the most important consideration in the decision to adopt an active strategy. The research by Levich, Goodman, and others suggests that an active management strategy can be profitable if the good forecasting services can be identified and if their information is used correctly. Unfortunately, neither Levich nor Goodman combines his evaluation procedures with a multi-currency portfolio-based management strategy. As we shall see, this failure greatly lessens the value of their research.

Although less important than direct speculative profits, differential transactions costs and the thinness of forward and future foreign currency markets also may be used to justify an active management strategy. On average, the bid–ask spread in the twelve–month forward market is about four times the bid–ask spread in the spot market. Hence, even if the forward price is an unbiased forecast of the future spot price, it will still be more profitable in the long run to trade in the spot market rather than the forward market. And if large sums are being transacted, the published spreads may greatly underestimate the true spreads paid by the corporation when dealing in the forward market.

What about risk? In this regard, the most important distinction that must be made is between diversifiable and nondiversifiable risk. In portfolio analysis, this distinction is now widely accepted: When the decision to include a stock in a portfolio is made, the risk is judged not by the volatility of the stock's price but by the contribution the stock makes to the volatility of the whole portfolio. A stock whose return is very volatile but whose price tends to move against the market – gold is a good example – may actually reduce the volatility of the return on the portfolio. In their search for such "low beta" stocks, many portfolio managers have engaged in international portfolio diversification as a risk-reducing device. In part, international diversification reduces risk because the price of the dollar and the price of U.S. stocks and bonds tend to move together, so that the dollar value of a foreign equity will increase when the dollar value of a domestic equity falls.

The trend toward international portfolio diversification holds an important lesson for the executive who is concerned about the problem of foreign exchange exposure: one person's foreign exchange exposure is another's international portfolio diversification. If the profits from the active international cash management strategy tend to occur when the traditional sources of profit are depressed, then an active strategy may actually be considered to be less risky, from the viewpoint of the entire corporation, than the passive strategy. The total earnings risk may be reduced by adding some foreign exchange risk to the earnings portfolio.

On a less esoteric level, the passive strategy may also be riskier than the active strategy if the foreign cash flows are themselves uncertain. Consider the example of a corporation that sets a price list on a quarterly basis and that makes an estimate of the sales in, say, Germany and France on the basis of this price list. During the quarter, the French franc devalues by a substantial amount against the Deutsche mark so that German customers find it worthwhile to buy the product in France rather than Germany. The fall in the value of the franc is matched by an increase in sales, and the increase in the value of the Deutsche mark is offset by a decline in sales. Under these circumstances, the passive strategy will only minimize the foreign exchange exposure by chance. In general, an active strategy can be used to reduce the level of risk.

In the following example, we assume that the decision to consider an active strategy has been made. A corporation is assumed to have cash flows from five countries – Canada, France, Germany (Federal Republic), Japan, and the United Kingdom – and these cash flows are divided into maturities of three, six, and twelve months. As forecasts, the corporation uses the forward exchange rate, the current spot rate, and the forecast provided by Predex Corporation. All of the data are taken from the *Predex Forecast* bulletin, which has been sent to clients of the corporation on a monthly basis over the period from September 1976 to the present. Our sample ends in January 1981. The current spot rate is included as a forecast because of the suggestion that exchange rates, as a first approximation, follow a random walk. If this characterization is correct, the current spot rate should be a forecast of the future spot rate. A more explicit definition of what is meant by the spot rate in a multi-maturity environment will be given in the following section. For methodological purposes, the spot rate may also be considered an additional forecasting service – Random Walk Consulting – that must be evaluated.

3.   Evaluation of the forecasting services

In this section, two different approaches to the evaluation of forecasting services are compared. The first approach, which is similar to that followed by Levich and Goodman, evaluates each service relative to the forward rate on a currency-by-currency basis. The alternative, which I shall call a portfolio approach, calculates the contribution of each service to a composite forecast in a multi-currency, multi-maturity environment.

The evaluation is based upon the following information. Each month, the *Predex Forecast* provides forecasts for the five currencies for three-, six-, and twelve-month maturities. In addition, the exchange rates for the currencies for the spot, three-, six-, and twelve-month maturities are provided. Finally, a nine-month forward rate is constructed as the arithmetic average of the six- and twelve-month maturities.

We assume that the manager operates on the basis of a three-month planning horizon: The profits (losses) from the operation will be realized each quarter by the purchase or sale of an offsetting contract. For the three-month contract, a short position today will be closed by the purchase of foreign exchange in the spot market in three months' time. If the future spot price is below the current forward price, a profit will be realized.

The same principle applies for the longer maturities. A six-month contract will be realized by an offsetting three-month contract in three months' time. If foreign currency is sold six months forward, a profit will be realized if the three-month forward price is below the six-month forward price that existed three months previously. With the three-month horizon, we therefore have the following:

A.   The three-month forecast predicts the spot price in three months' time.
B.   The six-month forecast predicts the three-month forward rate in three months' time.
C.   The twelve-month forecast predicts the nine-month forward in three months' time.

For each maturity, there are three forecasts of the price at which the contract will be realized: the forward price, the spot price, and the Predex forecast. For the spot rate forecast for the longer maturities, the current value of the forward rate for that maturity is employed. In other words, today's spot rate forecasts the spot rate in three months' time; today's three-month forward rate predicts the three-month forward rate in three months' time; and today's twelve-month forward rate predicts the twelve-month forward rate in three months' time. To save time, all of these forecasts are referred to as "spot" forecasts, because they are based upon the idea that the best forecast of any future price is its current value.

The standard horizon approach appears to have a number of advantages over the alternative of using the natural horizon for each forecast. No forecasting service actually believes that a client should stick to an old twelve-month forecast for a year: If the service revises its forecast, it expects that its customers will revise their positions. The standard horizon also allows for a better analysis of cross-maturity spreads, since all of the maturities are realized at the same date, and it reduces the problems associated with the evaluation of overlapping forecasts. On the second point, if twelve-month forecasts were used, only two or three independent observations could be used for the whole sample, whereas the standard horizon approach allows for four independent forecasts per year.

3.1   The right side of the market approach

Having decided what the forecasts are forecasting, it is now possible to proceed with the evaluation. As a first step, a variant of the traditional form of evaluation will be explored. This form, which I shall call the "right side of the market test" (RSOM), is a method for evaluating the probability that the service will predict the correct open position. Suppose, for example, that the three-month forward rate for the DM is fifty cents, and the service predicts a value of forty-five cents for the spot rate in three months' time. On the basis of this forecast, the customer would sell DM in today's forward market in the hope of buying DM in the future spot market at a lower price. If the actual price turned out to be thirty-five cents, the service has placed the client on the right side of the market, and a score of 100 points is given to that observation. On the other hand, suppose that the actual spot rate turned out to be fifty-two cents. Even though the outcome is closer to the forecast, the forecast still placed the client on the wrong side of the market and a score of − 100 would be given for that forecast. When the scores are averaged over all of the observations, the average forms the basis for the evaluation. An average score of 100 implies a perfect record in choosing the position, an average score of zero implies a state of no knowledge, and an average score of − 100 indicates that the service is always wrong.

The scores for the two services (spot and Predex) are presented in Table 4.1. The results yield a number of interesting patterns. First, both services appear to be proficient in predicting the forward rate bias in the French franc and the pound sterling, but they have little or no expertise in the Canadian dollar and the Japanese yen. For the DM, the spot service appears to be predictably wrong whereas Predex has a creditable track record. On the basis of these results, an analyst might make the following decisions:

> Find another service for the Canadian dollar and the yen.
> Use Predex for the Deutsche mark.
> Give 50 percent of the exposure in the French franc and sterling
>   to each service.

This type of analysis represents a common approach to the evaluation of forecasting services.

Table 4.1. *Right side of the market score*

Currency	Spot	Predex
C$-3	−25	−3
C$-6	−18	−8
C$-12	2	−23
FF-3	46	64
FF-6	54	59
FF-12	69	51
DM-3	−18	38
DM-6	−18	44
DM-12	−23	44
BP-3	54	33
BP-6	49	59
BP-12	59	49
JY-3	−3	−23
JY-6	−5	−12
JY-12	3	28

Note: The service scores 100 points if the forecast is closer to the future spot rate than the forward rate, and − 100 if it is not. The statistics given are the average value of the score.

Before proceeding to the portfolio approach, we should note the limitations of the RSOM approach. Since the test only compares each service against the forward rate, we have no way of knowing how the services compare against each other. More important, there is no way of knowing whether some combination of the two services – say, 50 percent of spot and 50 percent of Predex – would be superior to either service by itself. Second, notice that there is a tendency for the services to be "good" at the same currencies (the DM is an exception), and hence it is likely that the forecasts from the two services are correlated. It may be that the two services often recommend the same positions, and it may consequently not be worthwhile to purchase both services. Although it may appear that the risk is being diversified when the exposure is allocated among a number of services, the reduction in risk may be very small if the forecasts of the two services are highly correlated.

The most important limitation of the RSOM approach is, however, that it neglects the possibilities for either cross-currency or cross-maturity spreading.[2] The typical manager is not simply interested in the movement in a single rate against the dollar, but rather in the return from the entire open position. The RSOM test does not tell us if a service is accurate in predicting the evolution of the SF–DM rate, for example, or the bias in the three-month market relative to the six-month market.

This point is related to another statistical aspect of portfolio theory: the difference between diversifiable and nondiversifiable forecast errors. Basically, the situation considered in the RSOM test is a speculator operating in a single currency. For this speculator, the important consideration *is* whether the service predicts the correct position as described in the RSOM test. Suppose, however, that the speculator is primarily interested in the SF–DM spreads already mentioned. The forecast error for the spread cannot be computed from the information given in Table 4.1.

3.2   The portfolio, composite forecast approach

We now turn to the portfolio approach. We begin by constructing a composite forecast of the future price, S, from the market forecasts implicit in the forward price, F, the spot forecast, Z, and the Predex forecast, X. These composite forecasts are constructed for each currency and each maturity. The typical equation has the following structure:

$$S_{nmt+1} = (1 - w_{nz} - w_{nx})\, F_{nmt}$$
$$+ w_{nz}\, Z_{nmt} + w_{nx}\, X_{nmt} + u_{nmt+1} \quad (1)$$

In this equation, the subscript n represents the currency, the subscript m represents the maturity, and the subscript t represents the time period. Hence, S_{nmt+1} is the price of currency n and maturity m in period $t + 1$. The weights w_{nz} and w_{nx}, are estimates of the weight given to forecasts Z and X in the composite forecast. The econometric techniques used to estimate the weights are discussed in Appendix A. For the moment, all that is necessary is to note that the weights are assumed to be the same for each maturity – an assumption that

[2] "Spreading" refers to the practice of taking offsetting positions in two currency contracts. Selling one three-month Deutsche mark contract and buying one three-month Swiss franc contract is an example of a cross-currency spread.

Table 4.2. *Weight in composite forecast*

Currency	Spot	Predex
C$	0.41	0.05
	(5.52)	(3.20)
FF	1.07	0.03
	(8.99)	(2.14)
DM	1.13	0.05
	(11.29)	(2.91)
BP	0.65	−0.02
	(8.19)	(1.93)
JY	0.83	0.02
	(10.51)	(0.96)

Note: The numbers in parentheses are *t*-statistics. See Appendix A for details concerning the estimation procedure.

can be relaxed – and that the weights represent a true measure of the incremental value of the forecasting service.

The composite forecast approach has a number of advantages over the RSOM model. First, it allows for the "efficient market" outcome in which the forward rate represents all of the information that is available about the future spot rate. In fact, a test of the hypothesis that all of the weights are zero could be used as a test of the efficiency of the foreign exchange market. Second, note that we are not running a horse race between the two services. In principle, there is no reason why a significant weight should not be given to both services. However, if the forecasts of the two services are similar, the weights will not be measured with a great deal of precision. Imprecise weights tell the analyst that both services are not necessary. Third, using the methodology developed in the next section, the composite forecasts may be directly used to construct a portfolio of open positions in all currencies and maturities.

The estimated weights are presented in Table 4.2. Remember that we are constructing a weighted average of the three available forecasts. For example, in the case of the Canadian dollar, a 41 percent weight is assigned to the spot forecast and a 5 percent weight is assigned to Predex. The residual weight, 54 percent, is given to the forward rate. In this case, it is interesting to note that the composite forecast approach gives a statistically significant weight to both forecasts even though they failed the RSOM test. This is simply one example of a case in which a combination of forecasts is superior to any one of its components.

The numbers in parentheses beneath the coefficients in Table 4.2 are *t*-statistics. If the *t*-statistic is greater than 2, statistical theory suggests that there are fewer than 5 chances in 100 that the true weight on the forecast is zero. In the case of the spot forecast, the weight in the composite forecast is significantly greater than zero in every case. With the exception of the Canadian dollar, the estimated weight on the spot forecast is over three-quarters of the total weight. The weights given to Predex are typically smaller and are not as precisely estimated. The main reason for this result is that the spot forecasts are less volatile than the Predex forecasts when expressed as a deviation from the forward rate. The statistical model corrects for this volatility by giving a small weight to the forecast. Despite this volatility, the Predex forecast is statistically greater than zero for three of the five currencies.

It is noticeable that the Predex forecast receives a negative weight in the case of the pound sterling. This is analogous to the case in which a particular stock is sold short in conventional portfolio analysis. This result does not necessarily imply anything about the absolute forecasting ability of the service, since it could be due to the possibility that the Predex forecast offers valuable diversification potential in conjunction with the other forecasts in this instance. In this regard, it is noticeable that the Predex forecast does quite well in the RSOM score on the pound. It is also important to note that the forward rate receives a negative weight in the composite forecast in the French franc and Deutsche mark examples.

There are two major lessons to be learned from these results. First, the fact that the weights on the alternative forecasts are greater than zero confirms the earlier evidence from Levich, Goodman, and others that it is possible to beat the forward exchange rate as a forecast of the future spot rate. This does not necessarily mean that the foreign exchange market is "inefficient" since the predictable returns could be simply compensating for the risk associated with foreign exchange speculation. Still, the results as they stand suggest that a properly managed active strategy would be profitable.

The second major lesson arises from the difference between the conclusions reached on the basis of the two methods of evaluation. On the basis of the RSOM model, the Predex forecast did well in the French franc, the Deutsche mark, and sterling and poorly in the Canadian dollar and the yen. The spot forecast did poorly in the Canadian dollar, the Deutsche mark, and the yen and was comparable to Predex in the French franc and sterling. Hence, on the basis of the RSOM test, a corporation would be justified in concluding that the spot forecast was not worth the money (!) and that the Predex forecast should not be used in the case of the Canadian dollar and the yen. Both of these conclusions are strongly refuted by the composite forecast analysis: The spot forecast is shown to be preferable in general, and Predex is shown to have significant predictive power in the case of the Canadian dollar, the French franc, and the Deutsche mark.

There is, however, another advantage of the composite forecast approach. The RSOM approach does not offer any real guidance on the use of the services that have been selected, but the output from the composite forecast model provides all of the necessary information for the choice of the optimal open position by currency and maturity. The procedures for constructing the portfolio are discussed in the next section.

4.   Construction of the portfolio

From the statistical evaluation of the forecasting services, two important inputs for the portfolio model are derived. The first is the predicted bias, based on information available today, in the forward rate as a forecast of the future spot rate. A predicted bias is available in each planning period for each currency and each maturity. The second input is the covariance matrix of the forecast errors. The covariance matrix may be decomposed into the variance of the forecast error for each currency and maturity and into the correlation between the forecast errors for each currency and maturity. Most of the forecast errors are highly correlated. This is particularly the case for the errors in forecasting the different maturities of a single currency. If there is, for example, an unanticipated increase in the spot rate for Deutsche marks, there is almost certain to be an approximately equal increase in the price of Deutsche marks for delivery in three months' time. To a lesser extent, the forecast errors for the different currencies are also generally positively correlated. In part, this is because U.S. shocks influence all the exchange rates in the same direction: If the current U.S. money supply statistics are "bad," the dollar will depreciate against all the European currencies. In addition, arrangements like the European Monetary System also lead to coincident movements in the European currencies.

Although this correlation between forecast errors has been known for some time, it is generally not considered by currency managers

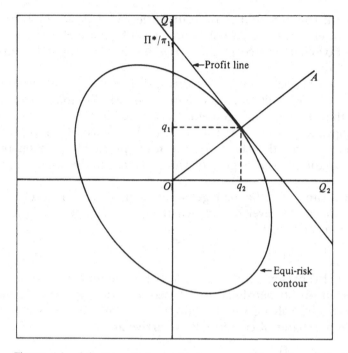

Figure 4.1. Selection of the optimal open position. The profit line is extended from the origin until it reaches a tangency with the equi-risk contour. This tangency gives the position, represented by the purchases q_1 and q_2, which yields the maximum level of profit for the given degree of risk.

or forecasting services in the formulation of a hedging strategy. The technical details of the procedures for constructing a speculative portfolio are described in Appendix B. The general principles of the approach are illustrated in Figure 4.1. The exposition in Figure 4.1 is simplified by considering only two currencies, but computer programs are available that are capable of handling a large number of currencies and maturities.

In Figure 4.1, the oval shape is an equi-risk contour that defines the same level of risk for all possible positions in the two currencies. Notice, for example, that the equi-risk contour cuts the vertical and horizontal axes at equal distances from the origin. This result follows from the fact that the forecast error is independent of whether the manager takes a long or a short position; if the position is the same size (in absolute value), the level of risk will be the same. The correlation between the forecast errors influences the shape of the equi-risk contour: If the two currencies have positively correlated forecast errors, the equi-risk contour will be more elongated. In the case of two perfectly correlated series, it will be a straight line through the origin.

For every level of risk, there is a different equi-risk contour. A riskier contour will be larger than a less risky contour. Seen in this way, the currency management decision reduces to a question of the appropriate degree of risk to take – the choice of an appropriate contour – and the choice of the most profitable position on the contour for a given degree of risk.[3] We tackle the second problem first.

We assume that the manager wants to maximize the level of profit for some given level of risk. In the two-currency case, the profit function is defined by

$$\Pi = \pi_1 Q_1 + \pi_2 Q_2 \tag{2}$$

where Π represents the total expected profit and π_1 and π_2 are the expected profits per dollar purchased of currency 1 and currency 2, respectively. Solving for the purchases of currency 1 as a function of the purchases of currency 2, we arrive at

$$Q_1 = \frac{\Pi}{\pi_1} - \frac{\pi_2}{\pi_1} Q_2 \tag{3}$$

Equation (3) is represented in Figure 4.1 as the profit line. If π_1 and π_2 have the same sign, the profit line will be downward sloping. Clearly, the profit line associated with a zero total profit will go through the origin. If Π_1 is positive, higher levels of the profit line will be associated with higher levels of profit. The highest level of profit that can be attained subject to the risk constraint is the level Π^* where the profit line is tangent to the equi-risk contour. At this optimum point, the desired position is to purchase q_1 units of currency 1 and q_2 units of currency 2.

Certain features of this solution are noteworthy. First, the ratio of purchases or sales of the currencies, as represented by the ray OA in Figure 4.1, is independent of the scale of the operation. This is a characteristic of most pure speculative models: If you double the bets, you double both the risk and the expected return. Second, the

---

[3] See Appendix B for an algebraic derivation of the portfolio weights. The algorithm minimizes the variance of profit subject to the constraint that expected profit is equal to target profit. Bilson (1981) discusses the technical details of the approach in more detail.

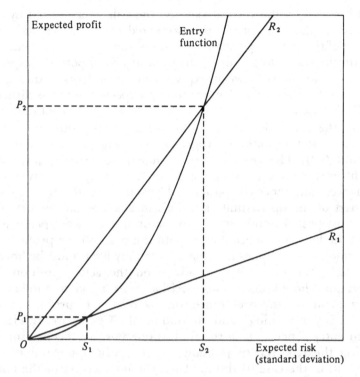

Figure 4.2. The opportunity set and the entry function. The rays OR_1 and OR_2 represent the tradeoff between risk and profit predicted by the model. The entry function represents the risk-return preferences of the portfolio manager. The actual position taken is determined by the intersection of the opportunity set and the entry function.

simple two-currency model may easily be extended to handle a very large number of currencies and maturities.

The most important lesson to be learned from the solution illustrated in Figure 4.1 is that the position in one currency is not independent of the position in all other currencies. For example, suppose the expected profit in the second currency, π_2, increases. Within the terms of Figure 4.1, this change would make the profit line more steeply sloped, and the new solution would involve larger purchases of currency 2 and smaller purchases in currency 1. The position in the first currency changes despite the fact that neither the potential profit nor the risk in that currency has changed.

The position for the entire portfolio is illustrated in Figure 4.2 in terms of the familiar risk–return tradeoff diagram. The expected profit is scaled on the vertical axis and the risk, as measured by the standard deviation of profit, is represented on the horizontal axis. Because of the purely speculative nature of the exercise, the tradeoff diagram differs from the usual diagram in two important respects. First, the tradeoff is between expected profit and risk rather than expected return and risk. The concept of expected return is difficult to define in the purely speculative case because capital is not required to enter the game. Second, the tradeoff between profit and risk is linear; two tradeoff lines are represented in Figure 4.2 by the rays OR_1 and OR_2. The reasons for the linear opportunity locus are straightforward. It is always possible for the manager to stay out of the market, and hence the position of zero profit and zero risk must be a part of the opportunity set. This means that the opportunity locus must pass through the origin. Second, it is always possible to double the bets and hence double both the risk and the profit from the position. This implies that the opportunity locus must be linear.

By itself, the ray offers no advice on the actual position the corporation should take. This decision rests upon a number of factors, including the preference for risk relative to profit, the size and volatility of earnings, and the volume of *FX* exposure. In Figure 4.2, an entry function is introduced as one possible mechanism for deciding the risk–return position. When profit opportunities are limited, as in the case of the ray OR_1, the intersection of the entry ray with the opportunity locus occurs at a low level of both expected profit and expected risk. If profit opportunities are good, as in the case of the ray OR_2, the intersection occurs at a higher level of expected profit and expected risk. The shape of the function is designed so that risk does not increase proportionately with profit: As conditions become favorable, the entry function determines that most of the bounty is taken out in the form of higher levels of expected profit rather than in greater risk. This function consequently limits the ability of the program to take extreme positions in response to perceived opportunities for great profit.

The slope of the opportunity locus in Figure 4.2 is the best statistic for summarizing the worth of the currency management strategy. In the figure, the slope of the opportunity locus is defined as the standardized profit. Technically, the standardized profit is equal to the level of profit divided by the standard deviation of profit. Since the opportunity locus is linear, the standardized profit is independent of the scale of the position. For an economic interpretation of the standardized profit variable, one needs to remember that approximately 95 percent of the observations drawn from a normal distribution lie within plus or minus two standard deviations of the mean. Thus, if the standardized profit is 2, then 95 percent of the observations will lie between zero and 4; if the standardized profit is 3, then 95 percent of the observations will lie between 1 and 5, and so on.

The standardized profit variable provides the essential link between profit and risk in the management strategy. The variable is defined as

$$k = \frac{\pi}{\sigma(\pi)} \tag{4}$$

where π represents profit and $\sigma(\pi)$ represents the standard deviation of profit. The standardized profit is given to the corporation by the conditions in the marketplace, but the scale of the operation can be varied in a number of ways. For example, suppose that k is again equal to 2 and the objective is to make $1 million from the management program over the quarter. What is the range of possible outcomes? Substituting into equation (4), we have

$$\sigma(\pi) = \frac{\$1m}{2} = \$500,000 \tag{5}$$

Using the two standard deviation rule, we can say that if the expected profit is $1 million, 95 percent of the outcomes will lie between zero and $2 million dollars. Since this opportunity does not require the placement of a great deal of capital – margins can be placed in interest-bearing assets – a standardized profit of 2 represents an extremely favorable risk–return tradeoff.

Is the actual return that good? At present, all of the evidence on the model is based upon in-sample simulation. Since the parameters of the forecasting equation were chosen to minimize the forecast error, in-sample tests are likely to overestimate the profitability of the strategy. However, in an earlier version of this approach, post-sample tests were run for a period of one year and the forecasting ability of the model was maintained (Bilson 1981). In all models of this type, the values of the parameters may change as the market assimilates the information contained in the model. It is consequently best to view the results as a description of how the strategy would have worked if applied in the past rather than as a promise of future performance.

Viewed in this light, there is no doubt that the model would have led to an extremely profitable active currency management strategy

Table 4.3. *Expected and actual standardized profit*

Date	SRE	SRA	CRE	CRA
11.77	1.77	2.33	0.00	0.00
12.77	1.13	0.27	1.77	2.33
1.78	2.18	0.24	2.90	2.51
2.78	1.59	0.11	5.08	2.74
3.78	3.12	1.72	6.67	2.85
4.78	1.81	0.75	9.79	4.58
5.78	1.76	0.58	11.60	5.33
6.78	2.98	3.64	13.36	5.92
7.78	4.49	6.66	16.34	9.56
8.78	2.01	3.38	20.84	16.23
9.78	1.59	1.57	22.86	19.62
10.78	2.13	2.37	24.45	21.19
11.78	2.15	1.62	26.58	23.57
12.78	1.83	2.72	28.74	25.19
1.79	1.85	3.37	30.57	27.92
2.79	2.94	4.42	32.43	31.29
3.79	4.03	4.52	35.57	35.72
4.79	3.57	3.39	39.41	40.24
5.79	1.76	2.54	42.98	43.64
6.79	2.22	2.37	44.75	46.18
7.79	1.94	2.73	46.97	48.55
8.79	2.90	5.04	48.92	51.28
9.79	2.93	2.64	51.82	56.32
10.79	3.13	2.57	54.76	58.97
11.79	3.34	3.42	57.89	61.54
12.79	1.69	1.55	61.24	64.97
1.80	1.73	2.06	62.94	66.52
2.80	4.72	4.00	64.67	68.59
3.80	1.17	0.90	69.40	72.60
4.80	2.07	0.49	70.57	73.51
5.80	3.62	4.01	72.64	74.00
6.80	2.06	2.24	76.27	78.02
7.80	3.84	3.43	78.33	80.26
8.80	2.57	2.02	82.17	83.69
9.80	3.63	3.78	84.75	85.72
10.80	6.28	7.28	88.34	89.50
11.80	3.86	4.17	94.66	96.79
12.80	2.58	2.67	98.52	100.97
1.81	2.92	1.13	101.11	103.64

Note: SRE, expected profit/standard deviation; SRA, actual profit/standard deviation; CRE (CRA), cumulation of SRE (SRA).

over the sample period. In Table 4.3, the SRE series is the standard-ized expected profit and the SRA series is the standardized actual profit. The mean of both series is approximately 2.6. To return to the previous example, if the expected profit is set equal to $1 million and the SRE is 2.6, then 95 percent of the outcomes should lie within the range from $230,769 to $1,769,230. In other words, the proba-bility of actually making a loss with this level of standardized profit is very small. In fact, over the sample of thirty-nine observations, no losses were realized from the strategy.

The model also accurately forecasts the variation in actual profit. Most important, during those periods when expected profit was high, that is, greater than 4, actual profit also turned out to be greater than 4 in each instance. In fact, the model appears to underpredict large profits, thus imparting a conservative bias to the strategy. Overall, the correlation between expected and actual stand-ardized profit is .8, which suggests that the model is successful in identifying periods when an open position is profitable.

So far, the discussion has centered upon the profit–risk tradeoff from a single entry into the market. It is important, however, to take account of the fact that the strategy is a continuing one and that over time, the profit forecast errors will tend to cancel. By construc-tion, the standard deviation of a single observation is unity. If the distribution of the forecast errors is normal, the standard deviation of the average of four independent drawings – four quarterly observations – is .25, and the standard deviation of the average of eight independent drawings is .13. Since the expected profit is simply the average of the expected profits from the individual drawings, it is clear that the profit–risk tradeoff becomes more favorable over time. This feature of the results is illustrated in the last two columns of Table 4.3 in which the cumulative expected and actual profit series are described. By the end of the sample period, the cumulative series were over 100 standard deviations from zero!

This type of predictable, low-risk profit is not typically associated with the management of foreign exchange exposure. The key to the success of the model is not in the superiority of its forecasting equations, since these equations are far more simple than most of the alternatives used in the forecasting industry at the present time. Instead, the success is due to the use of diversification to reduce risk. There are two important types of diversification present in the model. First, by creating composite forecasts, the model creates a portfolio of information from which a consensus view of the forward rate bias is derived. By taking account of the interaction between forecasts, extreme positions in any currency are avoided. Second, by creating the open positions as part of an overall portfolio strategy, the model allows for both cross-currency and cross-maturity hedging. Since the forecast errors are often highly correlated, small market biases may be profitably exploited.

There are two reasons why the picture painted in Table 4.3 may be too optimistic. First, as was mentioned, all of the tests are in-sample and there is no guarantee that the performance will continue to hold up in the future. The second reason is the neglect of transactions costs. Under normal circumstances, transactions costs are not an important consideration in the formulation of a hedging strategy. However, once cross-maturity spreads are considered, the correlation between the forecast errors is so high that the model is induced to take large offsetting positions in the different maturities of the same currencies. This feature of the model will be illustrated next, and a solution to the problem will be described in section 7.

To illustrate the workings of the model, we consider the *Predex Forecast* issued at the end of April 1981. The first step in the construction of the portfolio is to estimate the implied bias in the forward rate by currency and maturity. For purposes of comparison, we also include the Predex estimate of the bias. The statistics, all of which are expressed in the dimension of percent per annum, are presented in Table 4.4.

The composite forecast model predicts a 2 to 3 percent downward bias for the three European currencies, a slightly larger downward bias for the yen, and a small upward bias for the Canadian dollar. The composite forecast model typically predicts a smaller bias with similar forecasts for related currencies and maturities. In contrast, the Predex forecasts are far larger in absolute value, and they do not exhibit the same pattern of cross-rate consistency. For example, in the six-month market, the French franc is expected to depreciate by 12 percent (on an annual basis) against the dollar, and the Deutsche mark is expected to appreciate by 20 percent. Given that the European Monetary System was not expected to break up over the quarter, it is difficult to reconcile these forecasts. The Predex forecasts are also highly variable over the maturity dimension: In the case of the Japanese yen, for example, the spot rate is expected to depreciate by 17 percent and the 9-month forward rate is expected to depreciate by 61 percent over the same quarter. These forecasts are not consistent with the observed volatility of international interest rate differential.

Having obtained the forecasts of the bias, the next step is to construct the portfolio. In the "real world," the portfolio cannot be

Table 4.4. *Illustrative position for April 1981*

Currency	Forecast of bias		Position ($ Mil.)	Exp. profit ($ '000)	Act. Profit ($ '000)
	Predex	Model			
C$-3	1.80	0.90	158.65	357.45	−5,782.44
C$-6	4.63	0.40	−261.68	−259.85	10,885.19
C$-12	−2.84	0.36	98.85	90.16	−4,279.32
Net			−4.18	187.76	823.43
FF-3	−6.28	−2.52	−66.16	416.63	10,746.96
FF-6	−11.97	−2.49	91.92	−571.57	−15,974.44
FF-12	−37.47	−3.30	−35.06	289.04	6,671.67
Net			−9.03	134.10	1,444.19
DM-3	22.10	−1.98	161.99	−802.51	−26,034.70
DM-6	20.77	−3.72	−201.99	1,880.78	31,482.04
DM-12	7.48	−3.30	42.72	−372.82	−6,495.08
Net			2.72	705.18	−1,047.74
BP-3	46.97	−2.21	−58.35	322.70	10,550.31
BP-6	48.51	−2.65	82.14	−545.27	−14,583.93
BP-12	88.40	−3.18	−25.38	201.94	4,484.36
Net			−1.59	−20.63	450.74
JY-3	−17.16	−5.82	−59.58	866.24	8,542.81
JY-6	−32.82	−6.06	75.16	−1,139.35	−9,936.51
JY-12	−61.64	−6.52	−16.36	266.68	2,034.62
Net			−0.78	−6.43	640.94
Total			−12.86	1,000.00	2,311.54

Notes: These statistics describe a hypothetical strategy taken at the end of April 1981 and realized at the end of July 1981. The bias is the difference between the forward rate and the forecast of the future spot rate, expressed in annual percentage terms. The position is the amount bought or sold in the forward market in April. This position is based upon the forecast of the bias from the portfolio model. The expected profit for the entire position is set equal to $1 million. Columns may not add exactly due to rounding errors.

created without a specification of the corporation's preferences but, for illustrative purposes, we assume here the simple objective of making $1 million over the quarter. Since the standardized expected profit is 1.89, the 50 percent confidence limits for this strategy are between 470,619 and 1,529,380; the 95 percent confidence limits are between −58,761 and 2,058,761. Hence, although we cannot be certain of making a profit on the transaction, the range of possible outcomes does appear to be favorable.

The position described in Table 4.4 has a number of interesting characteristics. The most notable feature of the model's diversification strategy is the large "butterfly" spreads in every currency. A butterfly spread is a short-long-short or a long-short-long spread across the maturity spectrum. In the Deutsche mark case, for example, the model suggests buying $161 million worth of marks in the 3-month market, selling $202 million in the 6-month market, and buying $42 million worth in the 12-month market, leading to a net open position of only $2.71 million. The propensity for these large butterfly spreads is clearly a problem with the model, since the transactions costs required to take the position are probably greater than the expected profit. We will return to this problem later.

In this particular instance, the actual profit on the position, $2.33 million, lies outside the 95 percent confidence limits. Two events may be behind this result. First, the unanticipated election of François Mitterrand to the presidency of the French Republic led to a sharp depreciation of the French franc and the Deutsche mark. Second, the continuation of high interest rates in the United States was associated with an appreciation of the dollar against all of the major currencies. It does not appear to be unreasonable, under these circumstances, to argue that the events that occurred in this particular quarter are unusual.

5.   The performance of Predex

In the composite forecast model, the spot rate was shown to be the most heavily weighted forecast of the future spot rate. In general, the weights on the Predex forecast were small, but the Predex weights were significant in three of the five currencies. Given that the commercial forecast must be paid for, the corporation must decide whether its contribution to the composite forecast is worth the price. This issue is discussed in this section.

The basic question is the following: For a given level of risk, is the increase in expected profit greater than the purchase price of the service? To answer the question, the model is reestimated with the weights on the Predex forecast set equal to zero. The standardized profit variables are then recalculated and compared with the results from the complete model. The results of these calculations are summarized thus:

	With Predex	Without Predex
Average SRE	2.66	2.50
Average SRA	2.69	2.40

The actual expected profit arising from the purchase of the service depends, of course, on the dimension of the *FX* exposure. If the dimension is expressed in terms of risk, assume that the standard deviation of the total profit from the active management strategy is set equal to $10,000 per quarter – a modest scale for most commercial operators in the currency game. Using the average expected profit, the expected profit with Predex for this level of risk is $26,600, and the expected profit without Predex is $25,000. Hence, the value of the service is $1,600 per quarter. If the quarterly risk level is increased to $100,000 per quarter, the value of the service is increased to $16,000 per quarter. It is likely, therefore, that it will be worthwhile to use the Predex forecast if the scale of the foreign exchange operation is of a reasonable size.

This general procedure may be extended to more than one service. Starting from a position with all services, the portfolio is reestimated with each service omitted in turn. If a particular service is found to have an expected profit that is less than its cost, then that service is eliminated from the composite forecast and the procedure begins again. In this way, a subset of services may be selected for the final composite forecast.

This evaluation procedure differs from the usual "horse race" approach in a number of ways. First, notice that it is still likely to be worthwhile to purchase the Predex forecast even though it receives a relatively small weight in the composite forecast. The objective of the evaluation is not to find the best service; it is to find the best portfolio of services. Second, note that it is not possible to evaluate any service independently. A service may be a valuable addition to one portfolio, and an unnecessary addition to another. For both of these reasons, the traditional methods of evaluation are of limited practical use.

6.   Transactions costs

It is obvious that the illustrative position outlined in Table 4.4 is impractical in a number of respects. In order to make $1 million over the quarter, one would have to take an absolute open position of $1,435 million which, with a 5 percent margin requirement, would require approximately $70 million worth of margins and would incur transactions costs of around $700,000. Apart from the fact that a position of this size would influence the market prices and hence remove the perceived profit opportunity, it is simply not worthwhile to tie up this volume of funds in order to earn a posttransaction cost

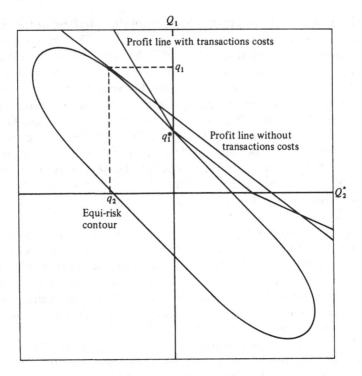

Figure 4.3.   Accounting for transactions cost. In the absence of transactions costs, the profit line is linear. If the equi-risk contour is elongated, the optimal position often results in large spread positions. When transactions costs are considered, the profit line is made up of three linear segments. Accounting for transactions costs often eliminates the spread positions.

profit of $300,000. If the program is to be made practical, it must first be modified to take account of transactions costs.

The problem faced by the program is illustrated in Figure 4.3. In the maturity space, the equi-risk contours are extremely elongated because of the very high correlation between the forecast errors. (For example, the correlation coefficient between the forecast errors for the three- and six-month maturities of the Canadian dollar is .982) In this situation, a slight tilt in the profit function induces large offsetting positions in the two maturities.

When transactions costs are considered, the profit function becomes

$$\Pi = \pi_1 Q_1 + \pi_2 Q_2 - t |Q_1| - t |Q_2| \tag{6}$$

where $|Q_1|$ denotes the absolute value of Q_1 and t denotes the

Table 4.5. *Illustrative position with transactions costs*

Currency	Estimated bias	Position ($ m)	Expected profit	Actual profit
C$-3	0.90	−.018	−0.04	89.32
C$-6	0.40	−11.792	−11.79	490.25
C$-12	0.36	−0.086	−0.07	3.72
Net		−11.896	−11.90	583.29
FF-3	−2.52	−25.958	163.53	4,216.23
FF-6	−2.49	24.232	−150.84	−4,210.91
FF-12	−3.30	−8.282	68.32	1,575.85
Net		−10.008	81.01	1,581.17
DM-3	−1.98	188.063	−930.91	−30,221.72
DM-6	−3.72	−256.788	2,386.81	40,020.41
DM-12	−3.30	67.174	−554.18	−10,212.12
Net		−1.551	901.72	−413.44
BP-3	−2.21	−2.739	15.13	495.21
BP-6	−2.65	0.498	−3.29	−88.41
BP-12	−3.18	1.819	−14.46	−321.37
Net		−0.422	−2.62	85.43
JY-3	−5.82	−17.949	261.15	2,573.43
JY-6	−6.06	10.524	−159.43	−1,391.27
JY-12	−6.52	4.451	−72.55	−553.48
Net		−2.974	29.17	628.67
Total		−26.851	1,000.00	2,465.12

Note: In computing this position, transactions costs of .0005 per dollar purchased or sold are assumed.

transactions costs per dollar purchased or sold. A reasonable estimate of t is around .0005. If the profit line is derived from equation (6), it can be shown to have three linear segments, as illustrated in Figure 4.3.

In Figure 4.3, the equi-risk contour is elongated to reflect the positive serial correlation in the forecast errors for the two maturities. The profit line that ignores transactions costs leads to a classic spread position in which purchases of Q_1 are partially offset by sales of Q_2. When transactions costs are included in the profit line, the spread position is eliminated and an outright open position in Q_1, q_1^* represents the new optimal position.

In Table 4.5, the portfolio for April 1981 is computed under the assumption that transactions costs are .0005 per dollar of foreign currency bought or sold. This estimate is roughly consistent with observed bid–ask spreads on the interbank market and with the commission fees charged on the International Money Market in Chicago. The most important characteristic of the revised position is the large reduction in the scale of the positions taken. Although butterfly spreads are still taken in the French franc and the Deutsche mark, the spreads taken in the British pound and the Japanese yen are now short-long-long and an outright short position is taken in the Canadian dollar.

The inclusion of transactions costs reduced the expected profit per unit of risk. In this particular example, the SRE declines from 1.89 to 1.1. With an SRE of 1.1, and an expected profit of $1 million, the 95 percent confidence limits for this position lie between a loss of $1.2 million and a profit of $3.2 million. The actual realized profit, $2.4 million, lies within these confidence limits. It is interesting to note that the actual profits from the revised position exceed those from the earlier position. In addition, the transactions costs have been reduced from $700,000 to $300,000.

7.   Constrained operations

Although some variant of the unconstrained model might be useful for a pure speculative portfolio, most corporations are not interested in foreign exchange speculation as an independent activity. Typically, foreign operations yield revenue and cost flows denominated in the foreign currency and a decision must be made to hedge or not hedge the net exposure. More generally, some fraction of the net exposure will be hedged. In this section, we consider how the hedge ratios for a number of currencies and maturities can be determined simultaneously.

To illustrate how this is done, we return to Figure 4.1, which presented the equi-risk contour and the profit line for a two-currency case. In the earlier analysis, we demonstrated that the optimal position was at the tangency of the profit line and the risk contour, leading to purchases q_1 of Q_1 and q_2 of Q_2. Now consider the case in which the corporation has a long position in the first currency and a short position in the second currency. In terms of Figure 4.4, the company expects to receive OA units of Q_1 and it expects to have to pay OB units of currency 2.

The exposure management strategy is now subjected to the following limitations:

A. Sales of Q_1 must lie within the range from zero (no hedge) to OA (complete hedge).

B. Purchases of Q_2 must lie within the range from zero (no hedge) to OB (complete hedge).

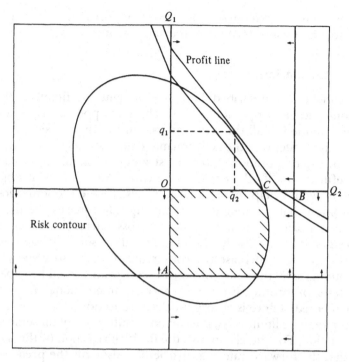

Figure 4.4. Constrained operations. The corporation has a long position of OA in Q_1 and a short position of OB in Q_2. The currency manager is not permitted to either reverse or extend these natural positions. In addition, the level of risk represented by the risk contour is not to be exceeded. The most profitable position satisfying these contraints is represented by point C.

C. The solution must not exceed the risk limit inherent in the equi-risk contour.

These limitations force the solution to lie within the shaded area in Figure 4.4. The profit line is contracted toward the origin until it reaches point C in Figure 4.4. At this position, about 80 percent of the short position in the second currency is hedged whereas the hedge ratio for the first currency is zero. This is the most profitable position that is consistent with the operational constraints.

As with the unconstrained case, the general principles behind the constrained hedge model apply to any number of currencies and maturities. In addition, the types of constraints may be considerably relaxed. It may be possible, for example, to hedge the natural position in any maturity, or it may be possible to hedge a position in one currency with a forward contract in another. Finally, the risk contour may be extended when profit opportunities appear to be favorable and contracted when they appear unfavorable.

8.   Conclusion

The conclusions described here are a blend of financial theory, econometrics, and operations research. The approach is capable of being extended in all three directions. On the finance side, it would be useful to integrate the active management strategy with the other parts of the corporation's financial strategy. In addition, it may also be useful to modify the objective function. An asymmetric objective function would help to avoid large losses. In the econometrics, the assumption that the weights in the composite forecast are the same for all maturities but independent across currencies needs to be relaxed, and it may also be useful to introduce some efficient market priors to further increase the conservatism of the strategy. On the operational side, the range of possible constraints could be expanded and tests of profitability within a constrained model need to be implemented. There is clearly much more to do.

Despite these limitations, the current results do contain some useful information. For the economist, the decisive rejection of the hypothesis that the forward rate is a sufficient statistic for the prediction of the future spot rate suggests that risk premia may be more important than expectations as the reason for forward premia or discounts on foreign currencies. For the international currency manager, the evaluation procedures outlined here are quite different from the conventional procedures, and the fact that the results from the evaluation differ so strongly from the conventional approach is food for thought. More important, perhaps, the portfolio approach integrates the evaluation with the cash management strategy. In other words, the portfolio approach not only tells the manager which services to use, but it also demonstrates how the services are to be employed. Finally, this analysis attempts to take account of the operational constraints that are often imposed on the structure of an international cash management strategy.

All of this leads back to the question raised in the first section: Is it worthwhile to adopt an active strategy? The answer to this question is probably positive, particularly for large multinational corporations. However, the adoption of an active strategy does require a substantial initial investment in forecasting services, equipment, and staff. Given the substantial gains and losses that may result from unanticipated changes in exchange rates, this investment would certainly yield a substantial reduction in risk and probably also an increase in return.

Appendix A

In this appendix, some of the details of the econometric procedures are described. The main problems to be dealt with are heteroskedasticity, autocorrelation (AR), and contemporaneous correlation in the residuals.

As far as the heteroskedasticity is concerned, it is more reasonable to presume that the variance of the forecast error is proportional to the square of the exchange rate rather than constant through time. To correct for this problem, all equations were divided through by the level of the spot rate.

The residuals in the forecasting equation are autocorrelated because of the overlapping forecast problem. (The program uses monthly data with a three-month forecasting horizon.) If the overlapping forecasts are the only source of autocorrelation, the first-order autocorrelation should be approximately .67 and the second-order autocorrelation should be approximately .33. All other autocorrelations should be zero. In order to avoid the problems associated with the estimation of a second-order moving average process in a system of equations, the autocorrelation is approximated by an autoregressive process of order 1. For an AR1 parameter of .6, the first three autocorrelations are .6, .24, and .09. The AR1 consequently appears to be a reasonable characterization of the autocorrelation in the residuals.

The estimated AR parameters were constrained to be the same for each maturity. The resulting estimates and associated statistics are as follows:

Currency	AR1	DW-3	DW-6	DW-12
C$	.35 (6.7)	1.18	1.28	1.42
FF	.55 (11.8)	1.90	2.16	2.29
DM	.57 (13.3)	1.84	1.96	2.16
BP	.64 (12.0)	1.33	1.37	1.45
JY	.50 (9.2)	1.06	1.01	1.06

In these statistics, the Durbin-Watson (DW) statistics are given for all maturities. The AR1 transformation appears to be successful in removing the autocorrelation from the European currencies, but not from the Canadian or Japanese currencies. In part, this may be due to the fact that the DW statistics are calculated from the untransformed residuals, not the residuals from the seemingly unrelated regression transformation.

The AR1 parameters were jointly estimated with the composite forecast weights using the nonlinear systems' estimation procedure in the TSP econometric package.[4] The contemporaneous correlation in the residuals was accounted for by the use of Zellner's seemingly unrelated regression procedure.

The most important aspect of the autocorrelation issue is not that the composite forecast weights are biased when autocorrelation is present but that the covariance matrix of the residuals is biased. In general, failure to take account of the autocorrelation will result in downward biased estimates of the variances and covariances. To provide a consistent estimate of the covariance matrix, the elements of the matrix were transformed by

$$\mathrm{Cov}(u_i, u_j) = \mathrm{Cov}(v_i, v_j)/(1 - r_i r_j)$$

where v_i and v_j are the residuals from the transformed regression, and r_i and r_j are the estimated AR1 parameters.

Appendix B

In this appendix, the portfolio selection principles are presented algebraically. Let $\mathbf{q}$ be a vector of positions in the forward market. Each element of $\mathbf{q}$, if positive, represents the purchase of a particular currency and a particular maturity. The number of elements in the vector corresponds to the number of possible currencies and maturities. Let $\mathbf{r}$ be the realized dollar profit vector. Each element of $\mathbf{r}$ corresponds to the realized dollar profit from the purchase (sale) of one unit of foreign currency for delivery at a particular maturity. The elements of $\mathbf{r}$ conform to the elements of $\mathbf{q}$ by currency and maturity. On the basis of the econometric results, $\mathbf{r}$ is assumed to be distributed $N(R, \Omega)$ where R is a vector of expected profits and Ω is the covariance matrix of the forecast errors.

Following basic financial theory, the portfolio manager is assumed to select the elements of $\mathbf{q}$ in order to minimize the variance of profits for a given expected level of profit. The problem can be stated as

$$\operatorname*{Min}_{\mathbf{q}} L = \mathbf{q}'\Omega\mathbf{q} + \lambda(\mathbf{q}'R - \pi^*), \tag{B1}$$

---

[4] Time Series Processor, version 3.5. Copyright 1980 by Bronwyn H. Hall and Robert E. Hall, Stanford, CA 94305.

where λ is a Lagrange multiplier and Π^* represents the target level of profit. The solution to this problem is given as

$$q = \Omega^{-1}R(R'\Omega^{-1}R)^{-1}\pi^* \tag{B2}$$

If this solution is substituted back into the definition of the variance of the portfolio, the equation for the opportunity locus is obtained.

$$\pi^* = K\,\sigma\,(\pi^*) \tag{B3}$$

In this equation, $\sigma(\Pi^*)$ is the standard deviation of profit and k is equal to $(R'\Omega^{-1}R)^{.5}$. (B3) demonstrates that the opportunity locus is a ray from the origin.

References

Bilson, John F. O. "The 'Speculative Efficiency' Hypothesis." *Journal of Business* 54:3 (July 1981): 435–51.

Goodman, Stephen H. "Foreign Exchange Rate Forecasting Techniques: Implications for Business and Policy." *Journal of Finance* 34:2 (May 1979): 415–27.

Goodman, Stephen H. "Who's Better than the Toss of a Coin?" *Euromoney* (September 1980): 80–4.

Levich, Richard M. "Analyzing the Accuracy of Foreign Exchange Advisory Services: Theory and Evidence," in Richard M. Levich and Clas Whilbourg (eds.), *Exchange Risk and Exposure*. Lexington, Mass.: Heath, 1980.

CHAPTER 5

Foreign currency accounting and its transition

YUJI IJIRI

1. Transition of foreign currency accounting

1.1. FASB Statement 8

Foreign currency accounting is one of the most controversial areas in accounting. After years of debate, the Financial Accounting Standards Board (FASB), a private rule-making body authorized to prescribe accounting standards in the United States, issued in October 1975 Statement 8 on foreign currency translation (FASB 1975). Immediately after its issuance, pressure mounted on the Board to rescind it. The Board resisted the pressure but finally in 1979 it agreed to review Statement 8 as a part of an overall postenactment review of all pronouncements.

In August 1980, the Board issued an exposure draft adopting an entirely different approach to foreign currency translation from the one prescribed in Statement 8 (FASB 1980). This resulted in more controversies. The Board decided to withdraw the exposure draft, a highly unusual event, and replace it with a new one, which was published in June 1981 (FASB 1981). In December 1981, the Board adopted Statement of Financial Accounting Standards No. 52 (Statement 52), *Foreign Currency Translation*. This new statement will take effect for years beginning on or after December 15, 1982, that is, from calendar year 1983 for many companies. Earlier application is allowed and encouraged; some companies adopted the standard for 1981 financial statements.

Why is there so much controversy about foreign currency accounting? Attempts to answer this question reveal some fundamental dilemmas in establishing the standards by which the performance of foreign operations is to be measured. This chapter is aimed at providing a perspective on foreign currency accounting by reviewing

The author is indebted to Richard J. Herring for his valuable comments and suggestions on an earlier draft of this chapter. Helpful comments by James L. Murdy are also gratefully acknowledged.

its theories and practices with the aid of a simple network model of
foreign currency transactions so that complex matters can be com-
prehended in the simplest manner.

1.2.   Four periods in history

To understand the significance of the change in practice to be
brought about by the new pronouncement and to evaluate its potential
economic consequences, a brief examination of the history of foreign
currency accounting is provided.

It is perhaps reasonable to divide the history of foreign currency
accounting in the United States into four periods. Their salient
features in practice may be summarized as follows.

1. Pre-1963: Predominance of the current–noncurrent method; de-
    ferral of and reserves for unrealized exchange gains and losses
    accepted. Accounting Principles Board's (APB) Opinion 6 marked
    the end of this period (American Institute of CPAs 1965).
2. 1963–75: Coexistence of the current–noncurrent method and the
    monetary–nonmonetary method; deferral of and reserves for un-
    realized exchange gains and losses accepted. FASB's Statement 8
    marked the end of this period.
3. 1975–82: Exclusive use of the temporal method, which is the
    monetary–nonmonetary method with a minor modification; defer-
    ral of and reserves for unrealized exchange gains and losses pro-
    hibited. FASB's Statement 52 marks the end of this period.
4. 1983–: A strict use of the current rate method coupled with a
    permanent deferment of translation gains and losses if they arise
    from the translation of the foreign entity's primary currency (called
    the "functional currency") into the reporting currency (the parent
    company's currency).

Briefly speaking, major controversies in foreign currency accounting are centered on two key issues:

Which exchange rate, historical or current, should be used in
    translating assets and liabilities of a foreign enterprise?
How should unrealized exchange gains and losses be recognized in
    income – immediately when a rate change occurs or deferred
    until the settlement?

Here, historical rate means the exchange rate that prevailed when
the asset or liability in question was originally acquired. Current rate
means the exchange rate that prevailed at the close of the accounting
period for which financial statements are prepared. The rate may
not be current by the time financial statements are published. Thus,
"closing rate" is a more accurate term, but the term "current

rate" has been widely used in the literature as well as in official pronouncements and will be used here also.

The current–noncurrent method applies the current rate to all current assets and current liabilities (i.e., those assets and liabilities expected to be converted into cash or settled in cash within one year) and the historical rate to all other assets and liabilities. This method has been supported by official pronouncements dating back to the 1930s (American Institute of CPAs 1931, 1934, 1939, 1953).

The monetary–nonmonetary method applies the current rate to monetary items (assets and liabilities denominated in fixed amounts of foreign currency) and the historical rate to all other items (nonmonetary items). Originally advanced by Hepworth (1956), its use gained acceptance among so many companies that the APB declared it as acceptable in a section of APB Opinion 6, which stated: "The Board is of the opinion that translation of long-term receivables and long-term liabilities at current exchange rates is appropriate in many circumstances." No specifications were provided, however, as to when such translations would be considered appropriate. Hence, the practice resulted in diverse uses of the current–noncurrent and the monetary–nonmonetary methods.

The temporal method is the same as the monetary–nonmonetary method except that nonmonetary items stated at current price in the foreign market are translated using the current exchange rate just like monetary items. The temporal method was originally advocated by Lorensen (1972) and adopted in FASB Statement 8.

The current rate method applies the current rate to all assets and liabilities regardless of whether they are current or noncurrent, monetary or nonmonetary. Many European countries have been using the current rate method. An approach similar to the one adopted in Statement 52 (i.e., the use of the current rate combined with a deferral of some exchange gains and losses) has been advocated by Parkinson (1972).

Exchange rate fluctuations create exchange gains and losses. Suppose that a U.S. company exports merchandise on November 30 for which the British customer agrees to pay 10 million pounds two months later. If the exchange rate is $2.10 to the pound on November 30, the receivable is valued at $21 million, setting aside the possible interest and collectibility issue. If the pound weakens to $1.80 by the time the receivables are paid and converted into dollars two months later, the company suffers a $3 million loss since 10 million pounds is worth only $18 million.

This $3 million loss is a realized loss since the deal has been closed and no more transactions are outstanding. No arguments have been raised against the view that such realized gains and losses should be taken into income. It is unrealized gains and losses that are at the focal point of controversy.

Suppose that as of December 31, while the receivable is still outstanding, the pound weakens from $2.10 to $2.00. Economically, the company has suffered a $1 million loss since the receivable is worth only $20 million. Yet the loss is "unrealized" since the transaction has not been completely settled yet. (Similarly, any gain and loss on a forward exchange contract are also unrealized until the contract is sold or closed, whether the contract is for hedging or for speculation, with a minor exception to be discussed later.)

Before FASB Statement 8 became effective in 1975, it was acceptable to defer such unrealized losses: Unrealized gains are normally deferred until realized for the sake of conservative accounting. It was also acceptable to make reserves for anticipated future losses. After Statement 8, all unrealized exchange gains and losses must be taken into income immediately upon the rate change, and no reserves are allowed for anticipated future losses (unless such losses meet the criteria stated in another FASB statement on contingencies).

Unlike earlier official pronouncements, Statement 8 distinguished, for the first time, between exchange gains and losses arising from a transaction such as already discussed and exchange gains and losses arising from a translation of foreign financial statements. If the sale of merchandise were carried out by a British subsidiary instead of the U.S. parent, an unrealized loss of $1 million would arise from the translation of the 10-million-pound receivable recorded on the books of the British subsidiary, hence, a translation loss instead of a transaction loss.

Although the distinction was made, the temporal method resulted in the identical treatment of a transaction and a translation. This is because under the temporal method, a foreign enterprise is viewed as a shell and all of its transactions were translated as if they were conducted by the parent company. This, however, is no longer true under the approach in Statement 52.

1.3.   Main features of Statement 52

The main features of Statement 52 may be summarized as follows:

1.   Use of current rate in translating all assets and liabilities.
2.   Exclusion of certain unrealized exchange gains and losses from income using a newly introduced notion of "functional currency" as a basis of determining which gains and losses are to be excluded from income.

Here, functional currency is defined as the primary currency of the economic environment in which enterprise generates and expends cash. Generally, the functional currency is the currency of the country in which the enterprise is located. However, there may be many circumstances where this is not true, as spelled out in Statement 52. For example, if foreign operations are a direct and integral component or extension of the parent company's operations, the parent's currency would be the functional currency.

This statement requires that the financial statements of a foreign enterprise first be given in the functional currency using the generally accepted accounting principles of the United States. Any exchange gains and losses from transactions other than in the functional currency are taken into income of that foreign enterprise. There is no difference between this and the current practice under Statement 8. The crucial difference arises from the translation of foreign statements stated in the functional currency into the reporting currency, that is, the U.S. dollars. Currently all gains and losses arising from this translation are immediately recognized in income. Statement 52, on the other hand, requires that all gains and losses arising from the translation of foreign financial statements expressed in the functional currency into the reporting currency be accumulated in a "translation adjustment" account as a direct adjustment to the shareholders' equity of the U.S. corporation.

Such an accumulated translation adjustment remains in the shareholders' equity account until there is a sale or a liquidation of the foreign enterprise. When such a sale or a liquidation occurs, the corresponding portion of accumulated translation adjustment is eliminated from this account and recognized in income as an addition (gain) or as a deduction (loss).

Hence, in the previous example of a sale of merchandise for 10 million pounds, if the sale is carried out by the U.S. parent, the exchange loss is immediately taken into income, whereas if it is carried out by the British subsidiary, the exchange loss is accumulated in the shareholders' equity of the consolidated entity until a sale or a liquidation of the subsidiary occurs.

Although exchange gains and losses from *transactions* in a foreign currency are recognized in income immediately, there are two exceptions to this, namely, gains and losses from intercompany foreign currency transactions that are of a long-term investment nature and from economic hedges of a net investment in a foreign entity. The former refers to intercompany foreign currency transactions between the parent and its subsidiary that are of a long-term financing or capital nature. The latter refers to foreign currency transactions that are intended to be and are effective as an economic hedge of a net investment in a foreign entity. Both exceptions are introduced for the sake of consistency with the treatment of translation adjustment so that if an exchange gain or loss goes to a translation adjustment account of shareholders' equity, a gain or loss from a related transaction (the parent side of the transaction or the hedging side of the transaction) will also go to the same account.

The introduction of the idea of functional currency and related deferment of recognition of exchange gains and losses created a whole new approach to the basic mechanism in foreign currency translation. Formerly, consolidated financial statements reflected the operations of the consolidated entity viewed uniformly from the standpoint of the U.S. parent. This is no longer true under the new Statement. However, the financial relationships among elements of a balance sheet of a foreign entity are preserved in the translation process since the entire statement is restated under one rate (the current rate), instead of applying different rates depending upon the nature of individual asset or liability.

2.   A network of foreign currency transactions

2.1.   Interest rate parity

Before various alternative methods in foreign currency accounting are examined, it will be useful to develop a basic network of foreign currency transactions that contains necessary 'ingredients for the discussion.

At a minimum, four types of cash concepts are needed. Let us denote by m' and M' a foreign currency and a domestic currency, respectively, at the beginning of a period and by m and M the same foreign and domestic currencies, respectively, at the end of the period. These symbols may be thought of as representing the indicated currency in a general sense or the amount of the currency held by an enterprise. In the latter case the unit of measurement will always be the unit of that currency; that is, m' and m are in marks if the foreign currency is German marks and M' and M are in dollars if the domestic currency is U.S. dollars. Exchange rates at beginning, r', and at end, r, are always expressed in price of a unit of foreign currency stated in domestic currency. Thus, foreign currency may be converted into its equivalent in domestic currency via $M' = r'm'$ and $M = rm$.

Depending upon the specific situation, r' may be referred to as

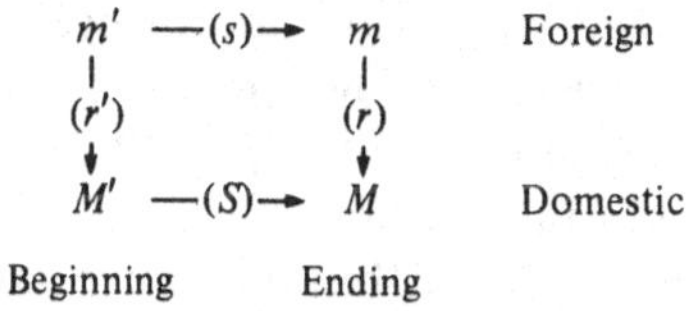

$$m' \;—(s)\!\rightarrow\; m \qquad \text{Foreign}$$
$$\big|\qquad\qquad\big|$$
$$(r') \qquad\qquad (r)$$
$$\downarrow\qquad\qquad\downarrow$$
$$M' \;—(S)\!\rightarrow\; M \qquad \text{Domestic}$$

Beginning   Ending

Figure 5.1.   Foreign and domestic currencies

current exchange rate and r, the future exchange rate or r, the current exchange rate and r', the past exchange rate. The same shift in time may be observed in m', m, M', and M, so as to look at these concepts and measures both from the standpoint of the beginning of the period and that of the end of the period.

Next, let s be 1 plus the interest rate prevailing in the foreign country and S be 1 plus the interest rate prevailing in the domestic country. To distinguish these from the interest rates, they will be referred to as *interest factors*. Then, foreign and domestic currencies may be expressed as a function of the same currency one period earlier, namely, $m = sm'$ and $M = SM'$, assuming there are no other transactions during the period.

Figure 5.1 depicts the relationship among the four currencies. In Figure 5.1, an arrow indicates the direction toward which the exchange rate or the interest factor is multiplied. Going the other way, the rate or the factor acts as a divisor. Normally, there is a spread between selling and buying rates as well as between borrowing and lending interest factors. However, for the sake of simplicity, such a spread is considered to be negligible.

The open interest parity relationship (sometimes referred to as the international Fisher Effect; see Aliber and Stickney 1975), states that investors operate in such a way that foreign investment, $M' \rightarrow m' \rightarrow m \rightarrow M$, will yield the same expected M as domestic investment. Hence, $M'S = M = M'(1/r')sr$. Therefore

$$r/r' = S/s \tag{1}$$

2.2.   Purchasing power parity

Another exchange rate relationship, purchasing power parity, was originally introduced by Cassel in 1916. It calls for an introduction of nonmonetary items into the picture. To simplify, let us assume that there is one commodity that is commonly available both in foreign and domestic markets and that there are no other commodities existing in either market. The price of the commodity is p' at the beginning and p at the end of a period in foreign market, expressed in units of foreign currency. The price of the same commodity is P' at beginning and P at end of the period in domestic market, expressed in units of domestic currency.

Alternatively, it may be assumed that a bundle of commodities commonly exists in foreign and domestic markets and that they are always traded at the given commodity mix. Then, these prices indicate the price of a unit of a commodity basket. (When the mix is altered between foreign and domestic markets, a complex issue of international price indexing arises, but the issue is set aside here to focus on the basic elements in foreign currency transactions.)

Let n' and n be the physical units of the commodity in the foreign market at the beginning and end of a period, respectively, and N' and N be the same commodity in the domestic market at the beginning and end of the period, respectively.

In addition, it is necessary to define a factor analogous to the interest factors for the commodity to link n' to n and N' to N. Let us define h as the "holding" factor for the foreign commodity and H as the holding factor for the domestic commodity. Here, the holding factor may be less than 1, equal to 1, or greater than 1, depending upon whether the holding cost is positive, zero, or negative. The factor's being less than 1 means shrinkage of the commodity over time, whereas its being greater than 1 indicates natural or contractual growth of the commodity over time. Any holding cost or holding revenue is assumed to be stated as a percentage of the physical units of the commodity (negative for holding cost), and the holding factor is 1 plus such a rate.

Figure 5.2 depicts flows of money and commodity in foreign and domestic markets and across the international boundary. The purchasing power parity relationship may then be expressed as the equality of the yields of domestic and foreign commodity investments. Namely, domestic investment $M' \rightarrow N' \rightarrow N \rightarrow M$ yields the same M as in foreign investment $M' \rightarrow m' \rightarrow n' \rightarrow n \rightarrow m \rightarrow M$. Hence, $M'(1/P')HP = M = M'(1/r)(1/p')hpr$. For simplicity, if we assume that $h = H = 1$, then letting $f = p/p'$ and $F = P/P'$ be foreign and domestic inflation rates, respectively, we have,

$$r/r' = F/f \tag{2}$$

which expresses the purchasing power parity relationship. (This equation expresses the "absolute" purchasing power parity as against the "relative" purchasing parity; the latter results in an equality between the ratio of changes in the exchange rates and the ratio of

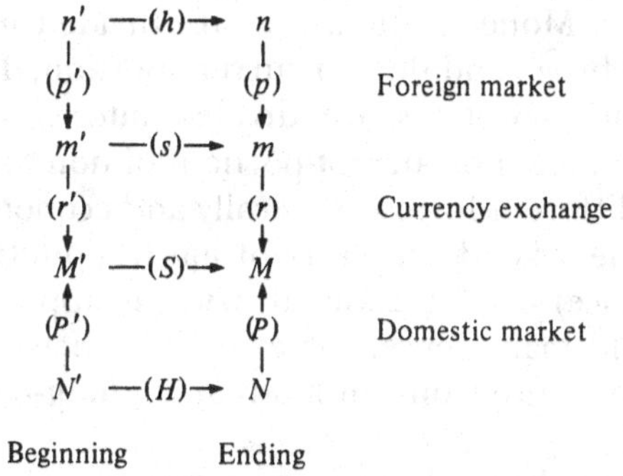

$$
\begin{array}{ccc}
n' & \!\!-(h)\!\!\rightarrow\!\! & n \\
| & & | \\
(p') & & (p) \qquad \text{Foreign market} \\
\uparrow & & \uparrow \\
m' & \!\!-(s)\!\!\rightarrow\!\! & m \\
| & & | \\
(r') & & (r) \qquad \text{Currency exchange} \\
\uparrow & & \uparrow \\
M' & \!\!-(S)\!\!\rightarrow\!\! & M \\
\uparrow & & \uparrow \\
(P') & & (P) \qquad \text{Domestic market} \\
| & & | \\
N' & \!\!-(H)\!\!\rightarrow\!\! & N
\end{array}
$$

Beginning   Ending

Figure 5.2.   Money and commodity flows

changes in the inflation rates.) Like equation (1), equation (2) is an expression of an equilibrium condition. The purchasing power parity relationship has been frequently confirmed empirically (see e.g., Balassa 1964, Aliber and Stickney 1975). However, there are studies that cast doubt on its validity over the short run and especially for the markets in the 1970s (see Frenkel 1981a, b).

It is highly unlikely that all of these mechanisms will work efficiently so that the equilibrium relationships hold instantaneously. Part of the difficulties in foreign currency accounting comes from the fact that these factors and rates are frequently inconsistent, but accountants must choose one of them as a standard basis for translation. For an extension of this analysis to international commodity flows, see the Appendix.

3.   A comparison of alternatives

3.1.   Current–noncurrent versus monetary–nonmonetary

Keeping in mind the transition of foreign currency accounting discussed in section 1 and the network of foreign currency transactions in section 2, let us now examine alternatives in foreign currency accounting. (See also the FASB Discussion Memorandum [1974], which summarizes some of the key issues in comparing alternatives in foreign currency accounting.)

First, let us compare the current–noncurrent method and the monetary–nonmonetary method. For this comparison, additional notations are necessary. Let c be net current items (current assets less current liabilities) and l be net noncurrent, or long-term, items (long-term assets less long-term liabilities). Both are expressed in units of foreign currency. Monetary items, m, are divided into the current portion, denoted by m_c, and the noncurrent portion, denoted by m_l. Likewise, nonmonetary items are divided into n_c and n_l. Although in reality current and noncurrent portions of nonmonetary items take considerably different forms, physically and economically, it is assumed here, for the sake of simplicity of illustration, that the same price p (current price) or p' (historical price) is applicable to both portions. This would make sense, for example, when a single commodity has a short-term use (consumption) and a long-term use (seeds for future crops).

Table 5.1 shows the difference between the two methods. The current–noncurrent method applies the current rate r to m_c and $n_c p'$ and the historical rate r' to m_l and $n_l p'$, whereas the monetary–nonmonetary method applies the current rate r to m_c and m_l and the historical rate r' to $n_c p'$ and $n_l p'$. Here, p' is used to indicate that nonmonetary assets and liabilities are valued at the historical cost, the price at the beginning of a period at which the items were assumed to have been acquired. Although in some cases (as in an application of the lower-of-cost-or-market method) some nonmonetary items may be stated in the current price, such cases are exceptions rather than the principle. Hence it is assumed that all nonmonetary items are stated at the historical cost. More details on this will be discussed in the next section when the monetary–nonmonetary method is compared with the temporal method.

It is easy to understand what the translated figure means for current, monetary items, $m_c r$. It represents the amount in domestic currency that may be obtained now by disposing of the items or that may be required to replace the items now, if transactions cost can be set aside.

Virtually all monetary items are adjusted for interest. Thus, if there were a premium or discount in the acquisition cost, it is amortized over the remaining life of the items so that the book value can reflect realization of interest throughout the life. Of course, the market value of the monetary items may differ from the book value due to fluctuations in the interest rate and the collectibility of receivables, but the discrepancy tends to be minor in view of the fact that it is a short-term, current item.

It is also easy to understand what the translated figure means for noncurrent, nonmonetary items, $n_l p' r'$. It represents the amount in the domestic currency that would have been required if the items had been acquired in the domestic currency at the time they were actually acquired in the foreign currency. They are valued at the

Table 5.1. *Current–noncurrent versus monetary–
nonmonetary method*

	Monetary items r	Nonmonetary items r'
Current items r	m_c	$n_c p'$
Noncurrent items r'	m_l	$n_l p'$

historical price p', that is, the foreign price at which the item was actually acquired and then translated at the exchange rate available at that time. Of course, depreciation may have changed the book value of the item from the actual acquisition cost, and the discrepancy may be accounted for as a reduction in the physical quantity n measured in units of service potential, just as depletion of oil and other natural resources is treated.

Controversies frequently occur with regard to the remaining two categories in Table 5.1. First, let us take current, nonmonetary items. Those who favor the monetary–nonmonetary method argue that $n_c p' r$ does not make sense since we are multiplying apples and oranges, that is, translating the historical price p' at the current exchange rate r. This price–rate mismatch has been one of the points of argument in foreign currency accounting.

Supporters of the current–noncurrent method argue that since current, nonmonetary items are relatively close to a point of realization where they are converted into monetary items, the discrepancy in rates r and r' is likely to be small and tolerable, except for LIFO (last in, first out) inventories for which the historical rate may be the exchange rate that was in effect decades ago.

More importantly, however, they question the logic of applying the current rate to noncurrent, monetary items, $m_l r$, the practice followed under the monetary–nonmonetary method. Long-term receivables and long-term debt may take years or decades before they mature. Why should income of a period be affected by frequent fluctuations of the exchange rates when the closing rate may have no relationship with what the rate ultimately might be at maturity? Why not fix the rate at the historical rate once and for all until maturity in a manner analogous to the historical cost principle that governs the price at which goods or services are valued?

Furthermore, these supporters point out a mismatch in a different sense. Quite often, foreign properties are acquired under a financing by foreign long-term debt, that is, $n_l = -m_l > 0$, focusing on this transaction only. Then, there is no net exposure to exchange rate fluctuation economically since assets and liabilities cancel out ($m_l + n_l = 0$), and this is the result obtained under the current–noncurrent method. Yet under the monetary–nonmonetary method, the liability side $i(m_l < 0)$ is exposed but not the asset side ($n_l > 0$) when in fact the two are an integral part of a foreign financing investment activity.

Although these arguments have merit, it seems difficult to overcome the argument for the price–rate consistency and the resulting simplicity in interpretation under the monetary–nonmonetary method. Furthermore, the monetary–nonmonetary method is given additional theoretical support by the purchasing power parity theory.

Those who support the purchasing power parity theory argue that $p'r'$ is also likely to reflect the "real" amount in the domestic currency that would have to be paid to acquire the item now in the domestic currency. If the purchasing power parity is observed accurately, then, as discussed in the previous section, $r/r' = F/f = F/(p/p')$. Hence, $p'r' = pr/F$, namely, the amount that must be paid now in the domestic currency, pr, adjusted for the domestic inflation factor F.

In particular, if the domestic inflation is negligible, that is, F is close to 1, $p'r' = pr$, which says that the translated amount using the historical rate reflects the current market value of goods in the foreign market translated by the current rate. This has been in fact approximately true in the case of hyperinflationary countries vis-à-vis the United States. Devaluation loss on inventories is normally recovered quickly a few months later by means of higher selling price of inventories.

Therefore, under the monetary–nonmonetary method, the translated amount maintains parity with the real cost of the item in the domestic market, and the principle of historical cost can be maintained in both markets. This balance will be disturbed if the current rate r is applied to the historical foreign price p'. More on this point later when the current rate method is examined.

3.2.   Monetary–nonmonetary versus temporal

The preceding analysis assumes that all nonmonetary items are carried at historical cost. This assumption was introduced to avoid an unnecessary complication that can occur when additional fine points are introduced at too early a stage.

Now it is time to be more precise. Note that the price–rate consistency attributed to the monetary–nonmonetary method is not exactly the consequence of the monetary–nonmonetary classification. Rather, the classification tied to the price–rate consistency is to divide items into current-price items and historical-price items, depending upon whether the item is priced under the current price or under the historical price in the foreign books of accounts. Then, the price–rate consistency is achieved by translating current-price items by the current rate and historical-price items by the historical rate.

This is the temporal method, aimed at achieving temporal consistency between the foreign price and the exchange rate. This consistency was also attributed to the monetary–nonmonetary method because monetary items are current-price items and most nonmonetary items are historical-price items, with the exception of current-price, nonmonetary items arising from an application of the lower-of-cost-or-market method or other minor exceptions to the prevailing historical cost principle.

The purchasing power parity relationship can still be applied to the temporal method since all historical-price items are nonmonetary, for which the purchasing power parity argument is applicable, and all current-price items do not require any restatement.

In fact, it is hard to support the translation of a current-price nonmonetary item using historical rate simply because it is nonmonetary. Therefore, the temporal method is an improvement over the monetary–nonmonetary method from a theoretical standpoint.

3.3. Temporal versus current rate

The difference between the temporal method and the current rate method is that historical-price items are translated at the historical rate $(p'r')$ under the temporal method whereas they, as well as current-price items, are translated at the current rate $(p'r)$ under the current rate method, which translates everything at the current rate.

Naturally, the supporters of the temporal method criticize the price–rate mismatch in the current rate method. What is a counter-argument by the supporters of the current rate method?

Supporters of the current rate method criticize those who view foreign operations strictly from the domestic standpoint as if the foreign entity were a shell, which is the basic premise underlying the emphasis on the price–rate consistency. They argue that foreign operations should be evaluated relative to their respective foreign environments in which the operations take place and not relative to the domestic environment. Functional currency is a way of establishing a standard of measurement in that foreign environment. Translation that occurs from the functional currency to the reporting currency is merely an incidental process for the sake of consolidation. Hence, the translated financial statements should not disturb the relationship among the figures in the foreign financial statements, and the only way of achieving this is to translate by a single rate. They then argue that the only rate meaningful for this single-rate method is the current (more precisely, closing) rate because all assets and liabilities are reported to reflect the status at the close of the period.

Although this argument is quite convincing in some respects, it has some serious weaknesses in its logic.

For most corporations operating in foreign countries, the ultimate objective of foreign investment is in recovery of investment in the domestic currency. If this is true, it seems that evaluation of foreign operations from the multi-environment viewpoint would not be useful except for local purposes. For example, a man climbing up a mast of the sinking Titanic may be commended if he climbs ten feet. But if the ship sinks thirty feet in the meantime, did he really gain ten feet or lose twenty feet? The loss of twenty feet seems to be the vital information for the investment-financing decision with respect to this foreign enterprise.

Second, what makes the matter worse is that the end result of translation is combined with statements of all other entities under a consolidated enterprise and reported in a single set of consolidated financial statements. A method meaningful for preparing stand-alone statements may not make sense when the statements are to be consolidated with other statements that may be prepared under entirely different methods. It is analogous to adding the distances climbed by men on different ships without adjusting for the changes in the ships' waterlines. In this regard, the domestic-environment view appears to be superior since it offers a unifying basis of consolidation. Under this view, regardless of how many different foreign environments the enterprise operations take place in, they are all viewed uniformly from the domestic standpoint.

The third problem with this multi-environment view is that even if its objective is accepted, that is, to view a multinational corporation from the multi-environment standpoint, the use of a single reporting currency defeats its entire objective. If the statements are reported in U.S. dollars, there is no way of avoiding the fact that financial figures on the statements are viewed from the U.S. standpoint.

This is because, when the reporting currency weakens, the financial statements of a multinational corporation look better (improved earnings and/or shareholders' equity) since its foreign investments are more valuable vis-à-vis the reporting currency. The converse is true when the reporting currency strengthens. It is normal for financial statements reported in one currency to show an entirely different trend compared with those reported in another currency.

A simple example here might be useful. Suppose an enterprise holds one unit of FC (foreign currency) and one unit of DC (domestic currency) from the beginning of a period to its end. At the beginning the exchange rate was 1FC = 1DC and at the end it is 2FC = 1DC. Did the enterprise gain or lose as a result of the rate change?

From the domestic standpoint, the enterprise lost 0.5DC since 1FC, which was worth 1DC at the beginning, is worth only 0.5DC at the end. But from the foreign standpoint, the enterprise gained 1FC, since 1DC, which was worth 1FC, is now worth 2FC. Which view is correct? In particular, how much did the enterprise gain or lose if it is truly a global company that does not distinguish between foreign and domestic countries. (For example, it has a 50% investment in country D and a 50% investment in country F at the beginning.)

To answer the question, a composite currency, such as the European Currency Unit (see a discussion in Rueschhoff 1976) must be brought in. But then, a difficult aggregation issue arises: Under what weights should different currencies be aggregated? A composite currency suitable for one corporation may not be suitable for another. And if a choice of composite currencies is allowed, intercorporate comparisons of financial data become very difficult.

The simplicity of the domestic-environment view seems to outweigh any benefit that may be achieved by introducing the multi-environment view. Although a full-scale implementation of the global view might be theoretically superior to the domestic view, it should be carried out only after careful studies on its impact on various parts of corporate financial reports.

4.   Interaction with inflation accounting

4.1.   Restate–translate versus translate–restate

The single most important problem that the new approach in Statement 52 presents is the urgent need to consolidate issues in foreign currency accounting and price-level adjustment.

Although the current rate method in itself contains temporal inconsistency between price and exchange rate, this inconsistency can be eliminated if the translation is combined with general price-level adjustment. This idea was first introduced on a limited basis in the second exposure draft of the FASB (1981). However, the idea was rejected in Statement 52.

The exposure draft required a price-level adjustment, using the local inflation rate, before translating into the reporting currency, if the cumulative inflation rate of the country during the most recent three-year period is approximately 100 percent or more. Statement 52 eliminated this provision and simply required use of the reporting currency as the functional currency for an enterprise in such a country.

Suppose a plot of land was acquired for 10FC ten years ago when 1FC = 1DC. If the inflation rate during the ten-year period is 1,900 percent in the foreign country and 100 percent in the domestic country, 10FC paid ten years ago is worth 200FC now in the foreign country, whereas 10DC (= 10FC) paid ten years ago is worth 20DC now in the domestic country. If the purchasing power parity theory is actually observed, the current exchange rate will be 10FC = 1DC. Under the exposure draft, the cost of land is first adjusted to 200FC using the foreign inflation rate and then translated as 20DC using the current exchange rate. Under Statement 52, the DC is used as the functional currency, which means that 10FC is immediately translated as 10DC upon acquisition of the land and stays at that amount. No further adjustments are made since price-level adjustment is not allowed in U.S. financial statements, although a supplemental disclosure is required on some price-level-adjusted financial data.

If nonmonetary items are price-level adjusted, their translated price is changed from $p'r$ to $p'fr = p'(p/p')r = pr$, under the assumption of a single commodity (or a single mix of commodities). Because of multiple commodities with varying mixes, $p'f$ is not exactly equal to the current cost p. This is the aggregation issue that lies at the heart of the age-old debate between constant dollar accounting using general price-level adjustment and current cost accounting using specific price adjustment.

Although the choice between general price-level adjustment and specific price adjustment is an extremely important issue in accounting, it has been debated elsewhere independent of foreign exchange accounting, and the issues will not be repeated here other than to point out one conceptual note. That is, inflation is not merely fluctuations in individual commodity prices, which can occur without inflation. Inflation is an erosion of the purchasing power of money.

Hence, it is most logical to use general price-level adjustment to adjust for the effect of inflation, though specific price adjustment may be introduced for some reasons other than inflation.

If the price–rate consistency in the current rate method can be attained only by coupling the translation process with a price-level adjustment, the domestic statements as well as foreign statements must all be adjusted for price-level changes in order to make consolidated statements meaningful. When this is done, then and only then can the entire set of financial statements acquire consistent meaning, showing the amounts of investment measured in the dollar equivalent of the purchasing power of current foreign currencies that were sacrificed in acquiring goods and services.

Currently, price-level-adjusted data are presented only partially and as supplemental information. A full-scale implementation of the price-level adjustment on a worldwide basis would not only make financial statements consistent under the current rate method, but would also be likely to stabilize exchange gains and losses reported in financial statements. This is because a significant part of the problems in the recognition of exchange gains and losses stems from the differential inflation rates among different countries that are often reflected in the exchange rate.

In the past, two basically different approaches have been proposed for the interaction of foreign currency translation and price-level restatement. One is the restate–translate method under which items in foreign statements are first restated using the inflation rate observed in the foreign country, and the restated amounts are then translated using the current exchange rate. The preceding discussion follows this method.

Using the notations introduced earlier, this means that a nonmonetary item n in a foreign country will be restated from the historical cost np' to the price-level adjusted historical cost using the foreign inflation rate $f = p/p'$, obtaining $np'f = np$, and then translated to npr using the current exchange rate r. Under the assumption of a single commodity or a constant commodity mix, the result of restate–translate, npr, shows the current amount of the domestic currency needed to acquire the nonmonetary item in the foreign country.

The other approach, called the translate–restate method (see, e.g., Zenoff and Zwick 1969), means that a nonmonetary item n stated in historical cost np' is first translated into the domestic currency using the historical exchange rate r' to $np'r'$ and then restated using the domestic inflation rate $F = P/P'$, obtaining $np'r'F = nr'p'(P/P')$. Conceptually, the result of translate–restate shows the purchasing power in the domestic market that was sacrificed in order to obtain the foreign goods or services.

Although each method has its own logical support, it is clear that the adoption of the current rate method paved a way for the restate–translate method.

4.2.   *The capital charge*

It has been pointed out (Ijiri 1976) that price-level-adjusted figures may be viewed in two different ways, one being the dual of the other. One is to consider them to have been prepared under the same accounting principles as figures in conventional statements but only expressed in a different unit of measurement, namely, in terms of the current purchasing power rather than in the nominal unit of money.

A dual viewpoint is to consider price-level-adjusted figures to have been prepared under the same nominal unit of money as in conventional statements but prepared under accounting principles different from conventional ones. The difference comes in the realization principle.

Price-level adjustment may be viewed as a way of relaxing the realization principle, which prohibits recognition of unrealized change in values of nonmonetary items so as to allow recognition of unrealized gains and losses of such items at a uniform rate specified by the rate of inflation. Thus, a plot of land costing $1 million ten years ago is price-level adjusted to, say, $2 million, not because it is now expressed in a different kind of dollars, but because appreciation in the land price is recognized to the extent of general price-level increase, which in this case amounted to $1 million.

This view seems to support the current rate and the restate–translate methods, since viewed from this angle it seems to make sense to adjust the land price in a foreign country because of inflation in that country, not because of inflation in the domestic country.

An important part of the dual interpretation is not only to recognize appreciation in nonmonetary items based on general price-level increase but also to recognize appreciation in owners' equity that must be preserved in order to maintain the purchasing power of the owners' investment. An enterprise having m and n from the beginning to the end of a period with no changes in them gains from appreciation of nonmonetary items at the rate of inflation, $np'(f - 1) = np - np'$, recognized under this dual interpretation. But at the same time there is a "capital charge" to maintain the purchasing power of the owners' investment at the beginning of the period, w'; namely, $w'(f - 1) = (m + np')(f - 1)$. The difference between the two is the net effect of adjustment on income in this stationary example, which amounts to a gain of $np'(f - 1)$ less a loss of $(m + np')(f - 1)$ or $-m (f - 1)$. Under the primal interpretation, this is called a price-level gain (or loss, if negative) on monetary items, whereas under the dual interpretation the nonmonetary items and the capital charge on owners' equity caused the price-level gain.

4.3. Exchange gains and price-level gains

When foreign statements are price-level adjusted, their translated statements produce both price-level gains (or losses) and exchange gains (or losses). The two types of gains are related in a way that is commonly observed in analysis of variance between actual cost and standard cost.

Assuming no transactions during the period, the net worth w of a foreign enterprise changes from its beginning state $w' = m + np'$ to $w = m + np'f = m + np$ at the end of the period after price-level adjustment. Their translated version is

$$w'r' = mr' + np'r' \tag{3}$$

at beginning and

$$wr = mr + npr \tag{4}$$

at end. Comparing the two, it may be noted that $mr - mr'$ is all exchange gain since monetary items are unchanged in the foreign statements. On the other hand, $npr - np'r'$ is a joint effect of the price-level change and the exchange rate change.

On the foreign statements, the price-level gain is shown as $np'f - np' = np - np'$; hence, the translated amount of price-level gain is $np'(f - 1)r' = npr' - np'r'$ using the exchange rate at beginning. (Using the current rate is another possible approach.) This leaves $npr - npr'$ as exchange gain, that is, the rate differential multiplied by the ending amount of nonmonetary items expressed in foreign currency.

Exchange gain of monetary items $mr - mr'$ and of nonmonetary items $npr - npr'$, combined with price-level gain of nonmonetary items $npr' - np'r'$, completely accounts for the change in the translated amount of the net worth of the foreign enterprise from $mr' + np'r'$ to $mr + npr$, as shown in Table 5.2.

However, in price-level-adjusted statements, the increment of net

Table 5.2. *Reconciliation of exchange gain and price-level gain*

	Exchange gain	Price-level gain	Total
Monetary	$mr - mr'$		$mr - mr'$
Nonmonetary	$npr - npr'$	$np'(f - 1)r'$	$npr - np'r'$
Net worth	$wr - wr'$	$np'(f - 1)r'$	$wr - w'r'$
Capital charge		$-w'(f - 1)r'$	$-w'fr' + w'r'$
Net income	$wr - wr'$	$-m(f - 1)r'$	$wr - w'fr'$

worth is not all recognized as income but only the residual after a capital charge, the amount to be charged additionally in order to maintain the purchasing power of the owners' equity. The capital charge is computed in a manner analogous to nonmonetary items except that the sign must be reversed. Hence, the price-level component of the capital charge is $-w'(f - 1)r'$.

There has been a proposal (see Shwayder 1972) to restate the shareholders' equity account of a foreign subsidiary not by the foreign inflation rate, but by the domestic inflation rate, which would result in a capital charge of $-w'(F - 1)r'$. It is also useful for the purpose of evaluation to analyze the change in net worth of a subsidiary, taking into account the differences between the domestic and foreign inflation rates as discussed in Wyman (1976) for the translate–restate approach.

Basically, however, under the restate–translate approach adopted in the exposure draft for hyperinflationary countries, restated figures are inflation free as far as the foreign market is concerned. Since the underlying philosophy of Statement 52 is to respect the integrity of the foreign environment as the primary place where operations take place, mixing the domestic inflation rate in the analysis may go counter to this underlying view. Thus, if and when a price-level adjustment becomes a required process for U.S. financial statements, it will be the restate–translate approach, using the foreign inflation rates, that must be used in order to maintain the consistency between the adjustment and the translation.

4.4. Open interest rate parity and discounting

Before leaving the topic of interaction with inflation accounting, an issue related to this topic may be briefly mentioned.

Purchasing power parity has been introduced in accounting and its implications for accounting methods have been discussed quite widely. However, it is interesting to note that very little has been done in foreign currency accounting on the implications of the open interest parity relationship to accounting. To some extent, however, price-level adjustment and interest rate adjustment (discounting receivables and payables) present issues that are largely symmetrical – at least conceptually.

For example, instead of the restate–translate versus translate–restate issue, there is an issue of discount–translate versus translate–discount. To implement the interaction of discounting and translation, a future exchange rate at maturity is needed, since a foreign receivable is first translated in domestic currency using an exchange rate that is expected to be available upon maturity and then discounted using domestic interest rate.

Viewing Figure 5.1 from the standpoint of the beginning of the period, treating the end of the period as a future point in time, the discount–translate method means that a receivable or payable m is first discounted by the foreign interest factor s to arrive at m/s, which is then translated to domestic currency as $(m/s)r'$. The translate–discount method produces instead mr/S, using the future exchange rate and the domestic interest factor.

Pros and cons of these alternatives need to be explored in more detail in relation to the underlying accounting principles on discounting and amortization of premiums and discounts.

5.   Disposition of exchange gains and losses

5.1.   Income volatility under Statement 8

So far the discussions have been limited to the effect of a translation method on the balance sheet. As stated earlier, the other side of the issue in foreign currency accounting is how to dispose of exchange gains and losses.

Corporations complaining about Statement 8 frequently pointed out the volatile impact it had on income and the defensive hedging and other means they had to take to protect the integrity of reported income. Studies conducted to find out the economic consequences of Statement 8 (see, e.g., Peat, Marwick, Mitchell & Co. 1977, and Shank, Dillard, and Murdock 1979) consistently showed increasing hedging activities and various changes in the methods of foreign financing in order to reduce the volatile impact of Statement 8.

The primary reason for the income volatility is the requirement in Statement 8 that all exchange gains and losses be taken into income immediately in the period of the rate change and that no reserves be provided for anticipated losses (unless such losses meet the criteria in another FASB statement on contingencies). This eliminated a route for smoothing the impact of exchange rate fluctuation by deferring gains and losses or by setting reserves.

A secondary reason is that the use of the temporal method increased the net amount of exposure for many corporations, especially those with a large amount of foreign debt. Corporations using the current–noncurrent method prior to Statement 8 had a relatively small fraction, corresponding to the net working capital, of total assets exposed to the rate change as far as accounting exposure is concerned. This situation was drastically changed for many corporations after Statement 8 was introduced. If the corporation had a large amount of foreign debt with a relatively small amount of monetary assets, a switch to the temporal method could result in exposure of more than 50 percent of the total assets.

These two reasons, in conjunction with the volatile exchange markets in recent years, created significant fluctuations in reported income. Therefore, even when economic risk of operating in a foreign country is unchanged, "accounting risk" as measured by the volatility of the net income figure is worsened for many corporations as a result of Statement 8.

Although it is questionable whether such an accounting risk is a meaningful way to evaluate a corporation (see Shapiro 1977 on the definition and measurement of foreign exchange risks), the concern by corporations over the risk forced them to take hedging and other actions that they would not take under a different accounting method.

5.2.   Income smoothing

A key question that may have to be raised here with respect to the disposition of exchange gains and losses is whether income smoothing (by reserves for or deferment of exchange gains and losses) should be viewed as acceptable or even necessary for proper financial reporting.

An anti-smoothing view states that it is possible to take an accurate picture of an enterprise at the end of a period and, by comparing it with a picture taken at the beginning, it is possible to determine accurately the performance of an enterprise in a given period. Thus, the emphasis is on an accurate determination of the short-run income. Every factor that existed at the time such an assessment was made, whether it was ordinary or extraordinary, permanent or temporary, should be taken into account in the determination of income.

A pro-smoothing view starts with a fundamental premise that income of an entity can be determined only in the long run and that periodic income can be determined only by a collection of artificial rules. Therefore, under this view, emphasis is on the long-run profitability. Periodic income is viewed as important not in itself but in its ability to reflect the long-run profitability of the enterprise. Thus, it is considered misleading and undesirable to incorporate factors that make income figures so volatile that their long-run trend is clouded.

Use of current rate suffers in this regard since it is subject to temporary fluctuations. Although volatility exists with historical rate, it should be remembered that historical rate is not a single rate but rather a collection of rates at different points in time at which various assets and liabilities were acquired; hence, their impact on income is gradual.

Unlike news media and other means of disseminating financial information that can provide information on a weekly or even daily basis, financial statements suffer from their basic timing limitations; that is, they are published only once a year (annaul reports) or four times a year (quarterly reports) and at best a month or two after the close of the period. If they were published daily, like stock prices, the use of the current rate might be ideal since the task of sorting out the permanent and temporary factors could be passed on to the readers. Unfortunately, this is not the case in financial statements.

It is analogous to reporting stock prices only four times a year. Given this limitation, would it still be better to report the price at the close of each quarter because it is the most recent price available at that time, or would it be better to report, say, quarterly averages of daily prices because they are more likely to reflect the long-run trend of the stock price than four prices picked out of a fluctuating series? It is statistically obvious that a series of four prices a year can show quite a misleading trend whereas a series of quarterly changes has a much better chance of reflecting an underlying trend if there is any.

In addition to the misleading effect on trend, the use of current rate on all assets and liabilities in quarterly statements can also make foreign operations look riskier than they actually are because of volatile income figures when no reserves or deferments are allowed on exchange gains and losses.

5.3.   *Economic reality and accounting information*

All of these issues on income smoothing and related accounting "manipulations" may appear to be nonsense. After all, accounting information is useful only to the extent that it reflects the economic reality of the enterprise. Theoretically, managers should pursue their business in such a way that the "true" income of the enterprise is maximized. Their decisions should not be affected by how the consequences of their decisions might be reflected in the accounting income.

However, in reality few people can neglect the accounting consequences of their decisions. Only two kinds of managers can neglect accounting consequences completely: those who are extremely naive about the business world and those who are in a highly secure position (say, a son of the founder) in a highly secure enterprise (e.g., a monopolistic or a governmental enterprise).

Ordinary managers cannot neglect accounting information, which is only a surrogate for the economic reality, because no one can comprehend the economic reality with certainty. The greater the uncertainty, the more reliance people place on tangible surrogates. Those with more information and with more time and intelligence to absorb and analyze the information will be able to see through the accounting information and be less influenced by the manipulations of the accounting numbers that may have taken place. But most people must make decisions with only a limited amount of information, time, and intelligence. Oftentimes, they have no choice but to take whatever surrogates are available at their face value. That is when surrogates have a critical impact on decisions. Earnings per share, return on investment, or debt–equity ratio in an enterprise evaluation; degrees, certificates, or grade point average in a personnel evaluation – these are all examples of surrogates that can impact decisions.

The ultimate case of surrogates affecting decisions is when the interested parties agree to create a certain legal consequence based on the outcome that a surrogate has, for example:

1. An employee profit-sharing plan (incentive compensation plan) in which bonuses are determined by the accounting income.
2. A partnership agreement under which the distribution of proceeds is determined by the accounting income.
3. Income taxes, import duties, value-added taxes, and others that are levied at least in part based on accounting numbers.
4. Cost-plus contracts, mergers, and acquisitions, and other contracts in which, due to a high degree of uncertainty, a fixed-price contract is not possible and the parties decide to use accounting data to be generated in the future as a basis for determining the price.
5. Loan covenants that are based on accounting numbers such as net working capital, debt–equity ratio, and times interest earned.

In each of these situations, accounting information is not a surrogate for an economic reality; it *is* the economic reality in the sense that actual cash flows are legally determined by the information.

Considering these serious impacts on decisions (and hence on cash flows to and from the enterprise) that accounting numbers may have, it can be understood why foreign currency accounting is such a serious issue among multinational corporations. The severity of immediate recognition of all exchange gains and losses under Statement 8 may then be fully recognized. And the managers' desire to smooth income so as to minimize accounting risk arising out of foreign exchange activities may also be evaluated in the proper perspective.

The point elaborated in the foregoing discussion is critical not only in understanding foreign currency accounting of an enterprise, but also in understanding foreign exchange activities of the enterprise. This is precisely why an accounting article such as this appears in a volume on managing foreign exchange risk.

5.4. A possible solution

Although translation adjustment introduced in Statement 52 as a part of owners' equity has the effect of shielding a significant portion of exchange gains and losses from affecting current income immediately, it results in shielding some clearly permanent displacement of the exchange rate between functional and reporting currencies, along with its temporary fluctuations.

If the position taken by Statement 8, that is, immediate recognition in income of all exchange gains and losses, represents one extreme, the position taken by Statement 52 seems to represent another extreme, under which exchange gains and losses, at least a significant portion of them, are virtually permanently (until liquidation of the subsidiary) shielded from income determination.

One may wonder, however, whether there is not a theoretically meaningful way of disposing of exchange gains and losses between immediate recognition and permanent deferment.

Take long-term debt denominated in foreign currency, for example, and compare it with depreciation accounting on long-term assets. As soon as a long-term asset is installed, its resale value may be decreased substantially. However, the lower-of-cost-or-market method is not practiced in the case of a long-term asset, because under the assumption of going concern the asset is not expected to be sold in the near future but is expected to be put in service for a long period of time. Depreciation accounting thus neglects market value and concentrates on fair allocation of the asset's cost over its useful life.

The same approach may be taken with regard to long-term debt. Its dollar value may fluctuate due to the exchange rate fluctuation, as well as the fluctuation in the foreign bond market. But under the going-concern assumption, the debt is not supposed to be liquidated in the current market, but is to stay outstanding until the end of its term. In this case, the current exchange rate is used only as the best indicator of the exchange rate that will prevail when the debt is liquidated. If so, it would be most appropriate to amortize the gain or loss over the life of the debt. The amortized amount may be treated as a deduction from or addition to interest expense, which is certainly justifiable from a theoretical standpoint.

Undoubtedly, this is a domestic-environment view; the foreign debt of the subsidiary is viewed solely from the domestic standpoint. But the problems associated with the multi-environment view have already been pointed out. The simplicity of the domestic-environment view that underlies the temporal method is highly attractive. When the temporal method is coupled with the amortization of exchange gains and losses on long-term monetary assets and liabilities, the volatile impact on income from exchange rate fluctuation can be substantially mitigated. A major portion of complaints about Statement 8 could have been resolved without introducing the complex machinery of functional currency. (See the dissenting opinions in Statement 52.)

6.   Concluding remarks

Many controversies in foreign currency accounting bear striking resemblance to the dilemma observed in the aggregation theory.

The framework presented in Figure 5.1 may be compared with the one in the aggregation theory (see the framework of aggregation in Ijiri 1971) in the following manner. Instead of having foreign and domestic markets, there are micro- and macrophenomena. Instead of the beginning and end of a period, there are independent and dependent variables.

Thus, for example, m', which is now interpreted as a micro independent variable, may be first converted into a micro dependent variable m via $m = m's$ utilizing the functional relationship s observed in the microphenomena, and then the resulting m may be "aggregated" using an aggregation function r on the dependent variable, obtaining msr. On the other hand, the same micro independent variable m may be first aggregated to a macro independent variable M via an aggregation function r' on the independent variable, and then their relation to the macro dependent variable may be determined by using the functional relationship S observed in the macrophenomena, obtaining $mr'S$.

The two outcomes, msr and $mr'S$, are not normally equal and this is the source of dilemma in the aggregation theory. Numerous articles have been written on such issues as how to select aggregation functions r and r' so that the microfunction s can be aggregated consistently with the macrofunction S, which is exactly the issue posed by the open interest rate parity relationship.

The dilemma in the aggregation theory essentially stems from *overidentification*; that is, there exists more than one legitimate way of determining a given variable M (i.e., msr and $mr'S$), yielding conflicting results. Yet in many cases it seems impossible to say one is right and the other is wrong.

The same is true with foreign currency accounting. It suffers from the same luxury of overidentification as plagued the aggregation theory.

The important point to be emphasized here is that a single method must somehow be selected and adhered to. Otherwise a vast number of legal relationships built upon accounting figures will be left unresolved.

The Financial Accounting Standards Board has made this important choice after years of studies. With so many alternatives on so many issues in foreign currency accounting, it is highly unlikely that what is prescribed in Statement 52 can satisfy anyone in every detail. Everyone is likely to have complaints on at least some aspects of the draft.

In particular, if the Board is going to allow (permanent) deferment of exchange gains and losses anyway, one may wonder whether the temporal method coupled with amortization of exchange gains and losses on long-term monetary items over their lives is not a simpler solution to the problems created by Statement 8.

The idea of functional currency has a theoretical justification in the assumption of multiple environments but will certainly make foreign currency accounting enormously complex. Given a rather considerable degree of latitude allowed the corporation in selecting the functional currency for each subsidiary, comparability among multinational corporations is likely to suffer even among those operating in a relatively similar mix of foreign environments.

However, the advantage of having a unified method for the sake of avoiding indefinite arguments seems to outweigh improvements that might be possible if the debates are to be continued.

The current rate method, combined with translation adjustments as pronounced in Statement 52, can do at least a satisfactory job in resolving many problems created by Statement 8, has theoretical justifications of its own, and most important, opens a new avenue for price-level adjustment in the sense that the proposed approach is complete only when it is combined with price-level adjustment. The last is perhaps the most important task that must be completed.

Appendix: Money and commodity flows

A.1.   Real interest rate parity

This appendix extends the networks in Figures 5.1 and .5.2 to show that they are in fact only a part of the overall network of money and commodity flows in the three-dimensional space whose coordinates are characterized by foreign/domestic, money/commodity, and beginning/ending.

Let us first reverse the role of money and commodity depicted in Figure 5.2 and create another diagram, shown in Figure 5.A.1. In this diagram, the international boundary is crossed by shipment of the commodity rather than remittance of money. Hence, instead of exchange rates r' and r, we have transportation factors t' and t, the factors at the beginning and end of a period, respectively.

Here, the transportation factor incorporates the cost of shipping the commodity from the foreign market to the domestic market. The cost is expressed in terms of physical units of commodity that must be given up to cover the transportation cost; thus, the transportation factor is normally a fraction representing 1 minus the transportation cost.

Although the exchange rates are not exactly reversible because of the discrepancy between the buying and selling rate, the discrepancy is relatively small and in this model the rates are treated as reversible. The transportation factor is in reality definitely irreversible, since the transportation cost must be paid in going one way or the other. However, for the sake of pursuing the symmetry between Figures 5.2 and 5.A.1, let us assume for now that the transportation factor is reversible. That is, if one unit of commodity shipped from the foreign market reaches the domestic market in t units, the latter shipped back to the foreign market reaches there in the original one unit. Though unrealistic, the assumption helps highlight the revers-

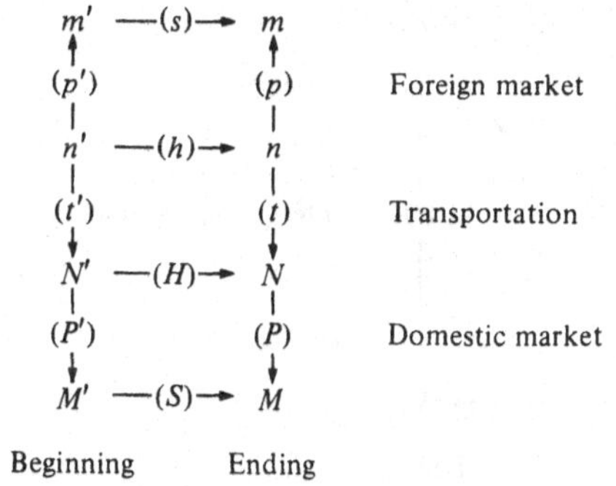

$$
\begin{array}{ccl}
m' \;—(s)\!\rightarrow\; m & \\
\uparrow \qquad\qquad \uparrow & \\
(p') \qquad\quad (p) & \text{Foreign market} \\
\mid \qquad\qquad \mid & \\
n' \;—(h)\!\rightarrow\; n & \\
\mid \qquad\qquad \mid & \\
(t') \qquad\quad (t) & \text{Transportation} \\
\downarrow \qquad\qquad \downarrow & \\
N' \;—(H)\!\rightarrow\; N & \\
\mid \qquad\qquad \mid & \\
(P') \qquad\quad (P) & \text{Domestic market} \\
\downarrow \qquad\qquad \downarrow & \\
M' \;—(S)\!\rightarrow\; M &
\end{array}
$$

Beginning   Ending

Figure 5A.1.   Commodity and money flows

ible and irreversible roles of money and commodity in international markets.

Suppose that the holding factors h and H are both equal to 1. Now, an enterprise holding N' units of commodity in the domestic market considers two alternatives, namely, invest in domestic money or invest in foreign money, both of which appear to be better than just holding the commodity. The first investment means a path $N' \rightarrow M' \rightarrow M \rightarrow N$ and the second means a path $N' \rightarrow n' \rightarrow m' \rightarrow m \rightarrow n \rightarrow N$. Suppose that the outcomes of the two are equal due to arbitrage. This means that $N'P'S/P = N'(1/t')p's(1/p)t$. Using the inflation factors $F = P/P'$ and $f = p/p'$, we have $N'S/F = N'(s/f)t/t'$. If we define G and g to be real interest factor, namely $G = S/F$ and $g = s/f$, then we have

$$t/t' = G/g \qquad\qquad\qquad\qquad (A.1)$$

Compared with equations (1) and (2), which represent the interest rate parity and purchasing power parity theories of exchange rate determination, equation (A.1) may be said to represent the real interest rate parity theory elaborated in Frankel [1979]. Here, however, what is related to the relative real interest is not the relative exchange rate of currencies but rather the relative transportation factor, such as the relative charter rates of tankers. The equation highlights the fact that what underlies the real interest rate parity concept is a notion of the rate of exchange of commodities across the international boundary. (See Giddy [1976] for other theories on exchange rate determination.)

It may also be noted here that Figure 5.A.1 depicts the pressure on the exchange rate provided by the international shipment of gold

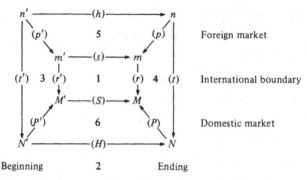

Figure 5A.2.   All possible paths of money and commodity

Table 5.A.1. *Arbitrage possibilities*

	Path of arbitrage	Consequence
International money market	$(M' \to m' \to m \to M \to M')$	$r/r' = S/s$
International commodity market	$(N' \to n' \to n \to N \to N')$	$t/t' = H/h$
International commodity shipment, current	$(M' \to m' \to n' \to N' \to M')$	$r'/t' = P'/p'$
International commodity shipment, future	$(M \to m \to n \to N \to M)$	$r/t = P/p$
Foreign market	$(m' \to n' \to n \to m \to m')$	$p/p' = s/h$
Domestic market	$(M' \to N' \to N \to M \to M')$	$P/P' = S/H$

(treated as commodity in the diagram) when the international gold standard was in effect.

A.2.   *Money and commodity flows: a summary*

Figure 5.A.2 combines Figures 5.2 and 5.A.1 to show all possible paths that connect money and commodity in foreign and domestic markets at two points in time. Looking at the diagram as a cube, each of its six faces represents an arbitrage or an equilibrium possibility. The six possibilities and their effects on various factors in the market are stated in Table 5.A.1. The consequences stated in the table assume that the rates and factors are reversible. Since normally they are not reversible, rates or factors are determined only within a certain range rather than as a single value that the indicated equation implies.

It is highly unlikely that all of these arbitrage or equilibrium possibilities work efficiently so as to have instantaneous and consistent adjustments of the exchange rate, transportation factor, interest factor, and holding factor, for current and future and for foreign and domestic markets. Part of the difficulties in foreign currency accounting comes from the fact that these factors and rates are frequently inconsistent, but accountants must choose one of them as a standard basis for translation.

References

Aliber, Robert Z., and Stickney, Clyde P. "Accounting Measures of Foreign Exchange Exposure: The Long and Short of It." *Accounting Review 50*, 1 (January 1975), 44–57.

American Institute of CPAs. *Foreign Exchange Losses.* American Institute of CPAs, December 1931. (Bulletin of the AICPA No. 92)

American Institute of CPAs. *Memorandum on Accounting for Foreign Exchange Gains.* American Institute of CPAs, January 1934. (Bulletin of the AICPA No. 117)

American Institute of CPAs, Committee on Accounting Procedure. *Foreign Operations and Foreign Exchange.* American Institute of CPAs, 1939. (Accounting Research Bulletin No. 4)

American Institute of CPAs, Committee on Accounting Procedure. *Foreign Operations and Foreign Exchange.* American Institute of CPAs, 1953. (Accounting Research Bulletin No. 43, Chapter 12)

American Institute of CPAs, Accounting Principles Board. *Status of Accounting Research Bulletins.* American Institute of CPAs, 1965. (APB Opinion No. 6)

Balassa, Bela. "The Purchasing Power Parity Doctrine: A Reappraisal." *Journal of Political Economy 72* (December 1964), 584–96.

Cassel, Gustav. "The Present Situation of the Foreign Exchanges." *Economic Journal 31* (1916), 62–5, 319–23.

Financial Accounting Standards Board. *An Analysis of Issues Related to Accounting for Foreign Currency Translation.* Financial Accounting Standards Board, February 1974. (FASB Discussion Memorandum)

Financial Accounting Standards Board. *Accounting for the Translation of Foreign Currency Transactions and Foreign Currency Financial Statements.* Financial Accounting Standards Board, October 1975. (Statement of Financial Accounting Standards No. 8)

Financial Accounting Standards Board. *Foreign Currency Translation.* Financial Accounting Standards Board, August 1980 and June 1981. (Exposure Drafts)

Financial Accounting Standards Board. *Foreign Currency Translation.* Financial Accounting Standards Board, December 1981. (Statement of Financial Accounting Standards No. 52)

Frankel, Jeffrey A. "On the Mark: A Theory of Floating Exchange Rates Based on Real Interest Differentials." *American Economic Review 69*, 4 (September 1979), 610–22.

Frenkel, Jacob A. "The Collapse of Purchasing Power Parities During the 1970's." *European Economic Review 16* 1 (May 1981a), 145–65.

Frenkel, Jacob A. "Flexible Exchange Rates, Prices and the Role of 'News': Lessons from the 1970's." *Journal of Political Economy 89*, 4 (August 1981b), 665–705.

Giddy, Ian H. "An Integrated Theory of Exchange Rate Equilibrium." *Journal of Financial and Quantitative Analysis 11* (December 1976), 883–92.

Hepworth, Samuel. *Reporting Foreign Operations.* Ann Arbor: University of Michigan Press, 1956.

Ijiri, Yuji. "Fundamental Queries in Aggregation Theory." *Journal of the American Statistical Association 66*, 336 (December 1971), 766–82.

Ijiri, Yuji. "The Price Level Adjustment and Its Dual Interpretation." *Accounting Review 51*, 2 (April 1976), 227–43.

Lorensen, Leonard. *Reporting Foreign Operations of U.S. Companies in U.S. Dollars*. American Institute of CPAs, 1972. (Accounting Research Study No. 12)

Parkinson, R. MacDonald. *Translation of Foreign Currencies*. Toronto: Canadian Institute of Chartered Accountants, 1972.

Peat, Marwick, Mitchell & Co. *A Survey of the Economic Impacts of FASB Statement No. 8*. New York: Peat, Marwick, Mitchell & Co., December 1977.

Rueschhoff, Norlin G. *International Accounting and Financial Reporting*. New York: Praeger, 1976.

Shank, John K., Dillard, Jesse F., and Murdock, Richard J. *Assessing the Economic Impact of FASB No. 8*. New York: Financial Executives Research Foundation, 1979.

Shapiro, Alan C. "Defining Exchange Risk." *Journal of Business 50* (January 1977), 37–9.

Shwayder, Keith R. "Accounting for Exchange Rate Fluctuations." *Accounting Review 47*, 4 (October 1972), 747–60.

Wyman, Harold E. "Analysis of Gains or Losses from Foreign Monetary Items: An Application of Purchasing Power Parity Concepts." *Accounting Review 51*, 3 (July 1976), 545–57.

Zenoff, David B., and Zwick, Jack. *International Financial Management*. Englewood Cliffs, N.J.: Prentice-Hall, 1969.

Perspective: Some informal remarks on debt management and liquidity

EUGENE H. ROTBERG

I will begin by making some general comments about the experience of the World Bank with respect to some of our policies concerning foreign exchange risk and liquidity management. I must say, however, that I am not at all sure that our experience is relevant to others' experience or to the decisions that everyone has to make, or, indeed, even to the points made in the previous chapters. Nonetheless, the World Bank does operate in the marketplace, both in dollars and other currencies, and perhaps the way we make financial decisions may provide some useful insights.

First, some facts: The World Bank has $30 billion equivalent in outstanding debt, of which only $9 billion is denominated in U.S. dollars. The balance is primarily in Deutsche marks, Japanese yen, Swiss francs, and Dutch guilders, with smaller amounts denominated in twelve other currencies.

The risks and costs of assuming foreign exchange risks are borne by the developing countries to whom the Bank lends. Thus, if the

Bank borrows a currency that appreciates, that cost, including the foreign exchange risk, is borne, on a pooled basis, by all of our borrowers – to whom the Bank lends the currencies it borrows. The Bank currently borrows at fixed interest rates for five to fifteen years in six to eight different currencies. Since it must repay the currencies it borrows, it passes on that currency risk to its borrowers. There is no Predex survey that predicts what the Deutsche mark will be vis-à-vis the dollar fifteen years from today. There is no forward market to hedge risks for fifteen years. Thus, a World Bank borrowing in Deutsche marks is disbursed over many years to borrowers who must repay those Deutsche marks but whose foreign exchange reserves are normally constituted in dollars. The nature of the problem is immediately obvious.

How we decide what currency to borrow is a threshold question. Let us assume for a moment that we have a choice of borrowing perhaps 200 million Swiss francs for fifteen years at a cost of 8 percent. Alternatively, we can borrow the equivalent amount, $100 million, for the same period at a cost of 17 percent. Let us assume that in our infinite wisdom we are certain that the Swiss franc will revalue against the U.S. dollar by 50 percent – that is, from 2 SF = $1 to 1.5 SF = $1 – and will remain at the level throughout the life of the loan; the books of our borrowers will therefore show a rather substantial loss or reduction of reserves in U.S. dollar terms.

Our guidelines are rather straightforward. We should ignore the implications of accounting convention that require showing the potential foreign exchange loss in deciding what to borrow. The fact is, that unless the Swiss franc, in the example, revalues from two to one to .61 SF = $1, it pays, in financial terms, to borrow Swiss francs. The only issue is whether you believe that the interest rate differential – 8 percent versus 17 percent or 9 percent a year, compounded over fifteen years – will or will not be offset by the revaluation of the Swiss franc. That is the critical issue, even for a dollar-based institution. Borrowing dollars is too easy a decision. No one, unfortunately, will levy criticism for the opportunity loss from not having borrowed Swiss francs.

Several years ago, when the Deutsche mark was 1.70 and the Swiss franc was 1.55 and the yen was 170 to the dollar, we took a position that these currencies would devalue against the U.S. dollar. We concluded that, given the prevailing exchange rates and a 7 percent interest rate *differential* from U.S. dollars, there would be a significant inflow into U.S. dollars and out of the Swiss franc. We believed that it was quite irrelevant that Switzerland, at the time, had a 1 percent inflation rate and the U.S. inflation rate was 11 percent. In short, we did not believe that the real return (nominal rates less inflation rates) predicted future exchange rates when the rate differentials and rate levels were that far apart. Foreign currency traders, in short, know and care little about purchasing power parity. Thus, we borrowed Swiss francs, Deutsche marks, and yen and lent them in the expectation that it would be in the best interest of our borrowers. In the last four-and-a-half years, the exchange rate gain from having borrowed $15 billion equivalent of Swiss francs, Deutsche marks, and yen was $1.5 billion. The nominal cost (the interest rate) of those borrowings was 7.2 percent. Both of these "risks" were passed on to our borrowers as an alternative to borrowing dollars, which, had we borrowed them on the same dates and maturity, would have cost 10.95 percent in nominal terms.

I must confess, however, we did not expect those currencies to devalue as much as they did against the dollar in the last four-and-a-half years; certainly not. We simply did not expect them to continue to *appreciate* by the interest rate differential. In fact, what occurred, strange world, was a double-kicker: both a low nominal interest rate and a devaluing currency. Currently, the Bank continues to borrow Swiss francs, Deutsche marks, and yen, given current interest rate differentials between those currencies and the U.S. dollar.

As many know, we have recently tapped the Swiss franc and Deutsche mark not only by borrowing those currencies in capital markets, but also by assuming through forward contracts the streams of payments of others in those currencies – who are uncomfortable with the currency risks attendant to those liabilities. We simply contract to assume the Deutsche mark or Swiss franc obligation – the stream of another's future liabilities – in return for their contracting to meet our liabilities in dollars. In short, we look to the future. We ask ourselves whether we prefer Deutsche marks at 10.25 percent or dollars at 17 percent and will take the former from a corporation that wishes to book a profit or cut the loss from its previous borrowing in Deutsche marks.

We also look to trade-related swaps. Is there steel manufactured in Germany or are there ships built in Japan whose export depends on buyers' being willing to assume yen or Deutsche mark obligations for many years? These buyers, because of the absence of long-term foreign exchange forward contracts, have little way to protect themselves, except through costly six-month forward contracts, against appreciating yen or Deutsche marks. We are prepared to tap into the world's trading markets by offering a forward contract whereby we take yen, Swiss franc, and Deutsche mark liabilities contracted in international trade and, in return, offer our dollar obligations.

One might ask why there is not a foreign exchange market for eight or ten years. There is none simply because banks would be too exposed. They cannot prudently maintain that kind of open foreign exchange position. A commercial bank finds it quite difficult to hedge long-term foreign exchange liabilities. The management of the World Bank calculates the break-even points, that is, the interest rate differential in U.S. dollars versus the potential foreign exchange risk. The ultimate taker of risk is a developing country; management's job is to make decisions that will prove to be in the best interests of our borrowers.

Some might ask whether there is a better way than to burden developing countries with Swiss francs, Deutsche marks, and yen. The answer is simply that we think it is better and wiser in financial terms to borrow Swiss francs at 8 percent than dollars at 17 percent. You may say, however, that dollars cost 17 percent, and that cost, expressed in dollar terms, is known and certain. The *effective* cost in dollar terms of the Swiss franc is unknown. In *neither* case is the opportunity cost known. It is, we think, unacceptable to simply borrow dollars and ignore the implications of not borrowing Swiss francs. Better to borrow the Swiss franc or yen or Deutsche mark *if* one believes it will not revalue by the interest rate differential over the life of the borrowing than to pretend there is no choice. In short, make a conscious, rational decision that you think will be to the financial benefit, in real terms, of the ultimate risk taker.

I would now like to call attention to some of our policies concerning liquidity management.

At the end of the fiscal year, June 30, 1981, the assets of the World Bank, expressed in United States dollars, amounted to $58 billion, of which $8.5 billion was invested as relatively short-term liquid assets in obligations of governments, banks, and financial institutions of its member countries. Most of our liquidity was in U.S. dollars ($6 billion) with substantial holdings in Deutsche marks, pounds sterling, Japanese yen, and French francs. These liquid resources are designed to provide the World Bank with flexibility on the timing of its borrowing operations; when bond markets deteriorate, we will draw down our liquidity until markets stabilize. However, because the liquidity is derived from borrowing funds before those resources are needed in the Bank's operations, it is necessary to actively manage the portfolio in order to minimize the cost of carrying these "advance" borrowings.

The Bank places its liquidity in negotiable instruments, primarily government or government-guaranteed bonds and bank obligations such as certificates of deposit or eligible bankers' acceptances. No instrument can have a maturity in excess of five years and three months. The portfolio is actively managed. Trading volume can reach hundreds of billions of dollars equivalent a year. My comments here are designed to set forth some of the management principles and basic premises that guide the decision making in the investment of our short-term liquid resources.

Everything we own is available for sale, all the time.

The portfolio is managed with a view toward obtaining the highest potential future total return.

The staff should pay no attention to the cost of a security after it is purchased in determining whether or not to sell it. Cost is a past event; it tells us nothing about whether we should hold a security or sell it.

There is no such thing as a "hold" recommendation. If we own it, we would buy it now if we did not already own it. If we believe its future potential is mediocre, we should sell it.

We attempt to pay no attention to the accounting consequences of our sales; indeed, we should not normally know whether we have a gain or loss when we sell from our portfolio. We should ask ourselves one question: Is the potential future rate of return greater if we hold to some specific date in the future or is it better that we sell the security and use the proceeds for an alternative, potentially better investment?

Permit me to use examples. If we purchase a security at a 10 percent yield and it rises to a yield of 15 percent and the staff concludes that yields will rise further – perhaps to 15.5 percent – that security should be sold immediately, irrespective of the fact that it was purchased at a yield of 10 percent, if there are, alternatively, other investments of the proceeds with a lesser potential for loss over the same time frame. The mistake has already been made in connection with the initial purchase. All we are doing by selling is admitting to our error and reporting the loss on our books. Few corporations do not have substantial losses that, though not shown on their books, have nonetheless occurred in respect to their financial transactions. It is irrelevant that their income statements may not reflect the fact that they bought bonds at par when everyone knows that the market is at 60 or 70. An error in market judgment has been made irrespective of what a company is required to show to shareholders or bondholders. A sale merely publicizes the mistake.

Another example may be illustrative. If a security is trading to yield 12 percent and another of identical quality and maturity is trading to yield 12.25 percent, we should sell the former and purchase the latter, regardless of the consequences of such action on our accounting statements, that is, whether we have a gain or loss – if we believe that the aberration in yields is, in fact, an aberration and is not likely to get worse. If we expect it to get worse, we should wait.

We should move the portfolio from an average life of four years to an average life of two weeks if we believe that there is a high probability that interest rates are likely to rise, and we should do the reverse if we think that rates are likely to decline, subject to liquidity constraints in the secondary market.

We should measure ourselves against perfection. Obviously, we also measure ourselves against some traditional indexes. We measure ourselves against what could have happened if we had invested only in one-day money. We measure what would have happened had we bought a portfolio equally balanced between one-day, three-month, one-year, two-year, and five-year securities. We measure ourselves against our performance had we randomly selected from within the maturity range from one day to five years. We measure ourselves against what would have happened if we had done nothing. Finally, we measure ourselves as I have indicated, in hindsight, against perfection. What would have happened if for each week for fifty-two weeks we shifted the portfolio from long to short perfectly to maximize the total financial return each week of the year. We also seek to determine whether our performance is due to daily day-to-day trading or to more long-term evaluations of interest rates.

We seek to predict interest rates for five different time periods and for six different instruments ranging from one day to five years at probabilities of 1 in 2, 1 in 4, and 1 in 10. We seek to hold that security that has the greatest probability in giving us the highest rate of return with the least amount of risk. Conversely, we sell those securities that have the lowest potential return and highest risk. Risk is defined as uncertainty – in probability terms.

The point of assessing and quantifying probabilities is simply to honestly reflect our own anxieties about particular securities over particular time periods in the future. We hope to measure whether or not, in the past, we have assessed our own uncertainty when we ascribe probabilities to future interest rates. For example, if a colleague predicts that there is a three-in-four chance that a three-month U.S. Treasury Bill one month from today will trade between 11 percent and 11.5 percent, we should go back and ask, with respect to predictors of interest rates, whether in fact in three chances out of four their short-term, that is, one month, predictions of short-term paper were or were not borne out by subsequent events. That helps make decisions. I would not seek to extract a prediction of interest rates that is more precise or more exact than what the staff feels. The point is to measure and reliably quantify unsuredness and uncertainty. If the staff believes there is one chance in two (i.e., fifty-fifty) that the market for three-month Treasury Bills will be between 9 percent and 18 percent one year from today, that is a perfectly acceptable recommendation, because they are saying they are unsure, and that is what I want to know. In order to be "right" half of the time, in this example, rates should fall below 9 percent or rise above 18 percent. Then we know the staff can accurately and quantitatively reflect their own uncertainty.

The point of interest rate forecasts is to enable us to make investment decisions on whether we should hold short or long instruments. In making these predictions, we review the major outputs of econometric models that describe the status and the projected status of the U.S. economy. We talk to many banks to assess loan demand. We talk to perhaps half-a-dozen economists a week. We review scores of economic write-ups and publications each week. We monitor the position of Wall Street. We discuss the general technical condition of the market with a dozen major dealers in New York. We have open lines to about twenty firms throughout the country. We have daily telephone communications with the largest banks and dealers active in each European market. We develop in-house forecasting models using financial variables such as money supply, federal funds, foreign exchange, and "real economy" variables (e.g., business loans, housing starts, retail sales, and CPI). In short, we try to bracket interest rates and do so for a variety of maturities and instruments and at varying probabilities. Then we make investment decisions with respect to how we want our liquidity invested.

Financial rates of return (not "accounting" or book yields) are calculated for the portfolio as a whole as well as for specific sectors such as treasury bills, certificates of deposit, government notes, and Eurobonds. Often we will shift from domestic CDs and to Euro

CDs depending on spread differentials, or from short-term to long-term instruments quite quickly. Or we will shift from one instrument to another because of market pressure or market aberrations that make virtually identical securities more (or less) valuable than they should be on the basis of historical relationships.

I would like to make one final point, perhaps the most critical. The staff is trained to admit to error and admit to making mistakes. No one "overrules" anyone else. We measure ourselves in terms of opportunities lost, not what our books show. If we buy a security at par and it trades at 105, and we sell it and it later trades at 110, we made a mistake. We should have waited. We record what we said should have been done, what we in fact did, and what would have happened if we had made optimal decisions – in hindsight. There is a certain subtle correlation between being comfortable with admitting to fallibility and error and being able to say what one thinks. And being able to say what one thinks correlates better with being right than does studied vagueness or fear of making a prediction or decision.

Perspective: Managing foreign exchange exposure

HARRY TAYLOR

My assignment is to offer a perspective from my vantage point as a lender, investor, and financial adviser. Let me admit that in my own bank I am part of what Professor Bilson described as the corporate constraint imposed from above. Given the complexities that are involved in this situation, I am tempted to fall back on the cogent advice of Gertrude Stein, who once said on the exchange of currency: "Money is always there, but the pockets change. It is not in the same pockets after a change and that is all there is to say about money." The members of the Financial Accounting Standards Board would do well to emulate her ability to arrive quickly at the heart of the matter. In their defense, I doubt whether Miss Stein had ever been advised of the collapse of Bretton Woods. If she had, it is hard to imagine what she might have said upon learning that sterling could actually float, and dirtily to boot.

I plan to do two things: first, to offer some comments on the specific subjects addressed by Professors Ijiri and Bilson and, second, to shift the focus to other matters that are equally fundamental to the subject at hand and to take some of these things away from the context of the World Bank and back into the commercial arena. I refer to global cash management, leading and lagging, and various financial strategies that can do as much to minimize risks as straight operations in the foreign exchange markets. We clearly cannot eliminate risk, but we can manage it. The first principle in managing risk, in my book, is to minimize it, provided the cost of doing so, in terms of opportunities lost, is acceptable.

Let me begin then with a personal perspective on the two preceding chapters. Simply stated, the ability to manage international risk has been rendered far more difficult by the existence of floating rates. Looking back, Bretton Woods provided a stable framework for an extraordinary period of global economic growth and international order. As an aside, let me also say that I personally do not believe that return to the gold standard, in any narrow sense of that word, has the same potential for stability that the Bretton Woods system had, or at least, not the same potential at an acceptable social and political cost. Unfortunately, the arrangements that followed Bretton Woods afford no such stabilities and hence the inability to continue with the current and noncurrent approach to which Professor Ijiri alluded.

In the absence of a viable alternative, such as the harmonization of economic policy, which we hear a lot of discussion upon but do not see very much action about, there will always be the need for a procedure to account for, in some way, exchange rate volatility. Yet, the search for an effective procedure has not been successful.

Although FASB 8 attempts to quantify the impact of exchange rate volatility, it also gives rise to some unusual situations and often results in swings in reported earnings that have little or nothing to do with a company's basic profitability or the astuteness of management. In fact, it is not unreasonable to argue that FASB 8 could do just the opposite, masking both the deterioration of basic profitability and the incompetency of management. Conversely, good management can be made to look bad, at least when judged against the stop-action snapshots that FASB asks we distribute at the end of each quarter to our respective audiences. Surely this type of outcome does little to reflect accurately the altered international environment.

Take, for example, the case of two major oil companies, Exxon and Royal Dutch Shell. The former, because it keeps its accounts in dollars, was able to report a large advance in earnings for the second quarter of 1981, whereas the latter, which keeps its accounts in sterling and Dutch guilders, reported an equally sizeable loss. Yet both companies sell the same products in essentially the same market and are buying their oil in the same currency, the dollar. This example, far from being isolated, points to the basic failure of FASB 8 – its failure to communicate effectively. The fact is that accountants are in the business of communications, whether they like it or not, and they do not always rise to the occasion. Instead, they often confuse rather than illuminate.

Here I remember what Professor Ijiri stressed: "Reported income is economic reality." I would agree if he changed the verb "is" to "should be." Reported income should be economic reality. FASB 8 was never really a problem for people who took the trouble to understand it, and that should certainly include any bankers worth their salt. But FASB 8 does present a problem in the way that a company is presented in the media, and where else but in the media are our broad perceptions born? In today's world, whether we like it or not, we live or die at the hand of the investigative reporter and the TV correspondent.

The new standard, FASB 52 or the son of FASB 8, as it has been called, would help to eliminate some of the big swings in reported earnings, and thus one might welcome it. By and large, FASB 52, by moving foreign exchange translation losses out of the income statement and onto the reserve component of the equity and the balance sheet, would be better than its predecessor, but it does hold up the possibility of being too kind to management. For one, it would make it easier for management to live with its mistakes over a longer period of time. If you had a bad investment in a country subject to high inflation and a depreciating currency, and if your investment is not profitable, then you have the worst of all worlds, because you normally expect to have an above-average cash flow from an investment in a depreciated currency environment which serves to offset the depreciation in your underlying fixed assets. Shades of Argentina, for those who have operations there.

So where I come out is that problems will remain. Son of FASB 8 will be wiser than its father, but we must face up to the fact that it will not solve all our problems, potential or real.

Those comments lead me from Professor Ijiri to Professor Bilson. For no matter how we ultimately account for exchange rate volatility, the question remains: How does a corporation deal with foreign exchange volatility? A good way, as Professor Bilson suggests, is to correctly forecast exchange rates and then adopt an active strategy so as to benefit from those forecasts. Of course, there is one potential drawback in this. If everyone were to both adopt an active strategy and then follow the same forecast, the result would be no market at all. Of course, such lemminglike behavior appears farfetched, and it is certainly not in the tea leaves at this moment.

That aside, let me agree strongly with Professor Bilson's suggestion that the important thing about using a forecasting service is not to be correct as to a precise rate, but to be correct as to which side of the market to be on. He gave an example of a three-month forward rate of Deutsche marks being 50 percent and the forecasting service predicting a value of forty-five cents for the spot rate in three months. If the price then goes down to thirty-five cents, so much the better; but as long as appreciation as suggested by the forecast is more than what the forward market has assessed, the company comes up ahead through following such a strategy.

Then there is the matter of methodology in forecasting trends, and it is here that I disagree with some of Professor Bilson's observations. For example, he says that it is not unreasonable to argue that such events as the election of Mitterrand are, and I quote, "unusual." But the sheer fact of life in today's world is that the unusual has become the norm, which points to the shortcomings of any forecast that is not, in part, judgmental. Professor Bilson also states that if current U.S. money supply statistics are, and here again I quote "bad" – whatever "bad" is – the dollar will depreciate against all the European currencies. But the fact is that the markets have become irrational. Now, when market participants read of an increase in the U.S. money supply, they anticipate that the Federal Reserve will reply by pushing interest rates higher, thereby strengthening the dollar. The same occurs when inflation is reduced, and here the results are not only illogical, but contradictory, as well, depending upon which side of the ocean you live on. When the Labor Department announced that the CPI had risen by 1.2 percent in September 1981, European exchange dealers expected the result to be downward pressure on the dollar. But in New York, dealers said that the higher-than-expected inflation rate would push the dollar higher because higher inflation would pull interest rates up. So where do we go from there?

All of this gives validity to that standard definition of a foreign exchange dealer: someone who knows the price of everything and the value of nothing. In short, there is now an illogicality about how markets respond to statistics, an illogicality that simply cannot be traced, in my book, through technical means, or not at the present state of the art.

Now let me get into the second part of my discussion in which I offer some comments on actions other than exchange rate forecasting that can help in minimizing risk. As I see it, there are other areas of the active end before you necessarily get involved in Professor Bilson's world. They might have fewer risks attached to them. For one, corporations can manage their cash flows more effectively worldwide. Although the term "cash management" has been around for some time, I can testify from my own experience at Manufacturers Hanover that real interest in cash management services is still only beginning to develop in an earnest and sophisticated way. The objectives and techniques involved may seem simple and old hat, but, in fact, they are not. Even major multinationals are only now beginning to centralize, in some cases, their cash management functions, which I should hasten to add need not be accompanied by a centralization of other functions or an erosion of autonomy among subsidiaries, as some fear. Many are only beginning to take actions that to some people may seem obvious, such as the avoidance of duplication in intracompany payments. One subsidiary may have receivables covered in Deutsche marks whereas another has liabilities to cover in Deutsche marks. From the corporate point of view, both could offset each other and, through internal arrangements, can be protected without incurring a forward market expense. This can be very substantial over a large multinational group operating a whole range of currencies.

To get to this point, a company needs information and it needs systems that enable it to act quickly on that information. One point is worth making in this regard: If a bank is going to do a good job in assisting corporations in this area, it has to have dedicated people and it has to have a low level of turnover among those people, because they literally have to get to know a company in all its international aspects even better than the people on the inside. In addition to those human resources, the bank also must have a very high level of computer sophistication, both in software and hardware.

Now let me turn to some other actions that can help to minimize risks. One thing you can do, of course, is to borrow in a currency other than your own functional currency, and Mr. Rotberg has shown in his perspective how the World Bank approaches that. You can borrow in this currency without hedging or with partial hedging or with hedging for a different tenure of the loan, to which Professor Bilson alluded. In short, you can follow an active strategy in relation to the currency you are borrowing. You have to realize that if you do hedge fully, inevitably you will come back to the cost of your functional currency, because the forward market premium or discount will, by and large, take the effective rate for the currency you borrow back to the level of interest rates in your functional currency, whatever that is. If you are prepared to take the view that exchange rates are not going to be a problem for you or that the deterioration of exchange rates will be more than offset by the gains you achieve through interest costs, as Mr. Rotberg describes, then this is an active strategy that takes you equally as much into the area of potential additional gains as does the sort of active strategy that Professor Bilson discussed in relation to his portfolio of exchange risks and exchange positions. And in the process, it meets your financing needs as well.

It is also possible to link the local borrowing strategy with an active strategy of leading and lagging on payables and receivables. By doing so, you can possibly even get yourself into a position where you have a natural hedge that guards against the additional exchange risk of borrowing in another currency. This again, in my submission, is an active strategy. In addition to this, for the longer-term exposure management there is the possibility of doing what Mr. Rotberg describes in the swap market, and this is basically a private forward deal for a longer period of time than the normal futures market permits.

I do not mean to say that I am against Mr. Rotberg's doing his own deals, and plenty of them. But I also do not mean to say that the other side of the market always has to be the World Bank. The other side of the market can equally be an industrial company in a different country or an industrial company in the United States itself that has a different pattern of overseas investments. One can give a lot of examples, but I can think of a U.S. company that had an exposure through holding maturing stocks of Scotch whiskey in the United Kingdom that it wanted to cover, which was done very effectively through a currency swap. I can think of a central bank with an exposure in Canadian dollars that it wanted to cover, and we found a Canadian bank that wanted to borrow U.S. dollars. Effectively, we transformed that central bank's obligation into U.S. dollars, which is where its export earnings came from and where it held its reserves.

Here again, when you move into this area, it is still necessary to address the exposure during the life of the deal on an active basis, because by going this route, you are in a position where, if currency swings or turns go in your favor on a swap or in a parallel loan or on a back-to-back, whatever you want to call it, you can either undo it or do another. This locks in the benefits so you do not lose them down the road.

In the days when there were exchange controls in the United Kingdom, a significant part of our business in London was enabling U.K. pension funds to invest in U. S. securities, which we did through parallel loans. Most of these deals were undone, to the benefit of both sides, when the pound sterling got up into the 2.30 − 2.40 category.

Finally, we might also achieve protection by taking advantage of interest rate futures markets as they become more developed and more applicable to more currencies. Clearly at the moment these markets are not at that stage of development, other than the case of the dollar.

So, to my mind, the distinction between active and passive is more complex than Professor Bilson might suggest. Moreover, to say that to be active in the foreign exchange market is necessarily the best route to go has not, in my book, been proven. Each strategy for a company should take into account the totality of that company's affairs and its ongoing needs, not only its immediate needs. In short, a strategy should be kept specific.

In closing, let me remind you of the meeting between Isadora Duncan, who was a beautiful lady and a very famous dancer in the early part of this century, and George Bernard Shaw. Isadora said to Shaw: "We should have a child with my looks and your brains," to which Shaw replied, "But what, madam, if it had my looks and your brains?" The type of union and the quality of the product that Isadora had in mind is what we are searching for in this complex area of foreign exchange. We can only search for it if, by monitoring the outcome through an active strategy we can control the result, which, as Shaw rightly pointed out, is not always easy in this uncertain world.

Index